PRAISE FO

MW00564321

We may feel more divided than ever, but this volume gives perspective to the multitude of times in human history when deep divisions have characterized our world and shows how nonviolence was used to bridge those divides. If you are looking to turn your students on to the study of nonviolence, this is the book for you. The incisive case studies included reveal the truly global nature of nonviolent social change. This is an accessible study that considers many angles from which to explore the who, what, when, and why of nonviolence.

Lynne M. Woehrle, Associate Professor of Sociology, University of Wisconsin-Milwaukee, and Director of the Master of Sustainable Peacebuilding Program

War No More is a well-researched examination book on nonviolent approach to conflicts. Michael K. Duffey has painstakingly examined the philosophies and actions taken by groups all over the world to bring a peaceful resolution to conflict. This is a must-read book for all who live peace.

Arun Gandhi, grandson of Mahatma Gandhi, and founder of the Mohandas K. Gandhi Institute for Peace in the United States

In his most timely *War No More: An Introduction to Nonviolent Struggles for Justice*, Duffey joins his unwavering dedication as an educator and lifelong commitment to nonviolent activism as an instrument in peacemaking and building a nonviolent culture, particularly in the United States.

Judith Mayotte, author of *Disposable People? The Plight of Refugees*

This book takes the reader on a thematic journey through a variety of successful nonviolent struggles in the hope of inspiring new ones. It is an important addition to the growing literature in the field.

Irfan Omar, Professor of World Religions, Islam, and theologies of nonviolence in the Department of Theology, Marquette University

Duffey's work challenges the inevitability of violence as he examines war's devastation. Duffey explores successful nonviolent movements across the globe while specifically addressing the role of nonviolent activism against the violence of the United States's foreign and domestic interventions. This approach challenges students and instructors to re-examine existing assumptions about violence and considers the power and pragmatism of nonviolence, including on a personal level. Duffey's work is essential reading for those considering the possibilities of peace in a twenty-first-century world.

Thomas Durkin, Lecturer in Interdisciplinary Peace Studies and Research & Grant Coordinator, Marquette University Center for Peacemaking

Duffey's primer on nonviolence could hardly be timelier. It is thoughtful, readable, and eminently practical. Highly recommended.

Andrew J. Bacevich, Professor Emeritus of International Relations and History, Boston University, and President of the Quincy Institute for Responsible Statecraft

War No More

War No More

An Introduction to Nonviolent Struggles for Justice

Michael K. Duffey

Marquette University

ROWMAN & LITTLEFIELD
Lanham • Boulder • New York • London

Credits and acknowledgments for material borrowed from other sources, and reproduced with permission, appear on the appropriate pages within the text.

Published by Rowman & Littlefield
An imprint of The Rowman & Littlefield Publishing Group, Inc.
4501 Forbes Boulevard, Suite 200, Lanham, Maryland 20706
www.rowman.com

86–90 Paul Street, London EC2A 4NE, United Kingdom

British Library Cataloguing in Publication Information Available

Library of Congress Cataloging-in-Publication Data

Names: Duffey, Michael K., 1948- author.
Title: War no more : an introduction to nonviolent struggles for justice / Michael K. Duffey.
Description: Lanham, Maryland : Rowman & Littlefield, 2021. | Includes bibliographical references and index. | Summary: "This introduction to nonviolent movements analyzes fourteen classic and contemporary cases to show how nonviolent strategies can work where violent warfare has failed. Drawing on practitioner knowledge and diverse philosophical and religious texts, Michael K. Duffey offers a multifaceted argument for embracing nonviolent resolutions to conflict"— Provided by publisher.
Identifiers: LCCN 2021011854 (print) | LCCN 2021011855 (ebook) | ISBN 9781538158579 (cloth) | ISBN 9781538158586 (paperback) | ISBN 9781538158593 (epub)
Subjects: LCSH: Nonviolence—Case studies. | Nonviolence—Philosophy. | Nonviolence—History.
Classification: LCC HM1281 .D84 2021 (print) | LCC HM1281 (ebook) | DDC 303.6/1—dc23
LC record available at https://lccn.loc.gov/2021011854
LC ebook record available at https://lccn.loc.gov/2021011855

∞™ The paper used in this publication meets the minimum requirements of American National Standard for Information Sciences—Permanence of Paper for Printed Library Materials, ANSI/NISO Z39.48–1992.

This book is for Mary Beth. She made many helpful corrections and suggested changes in style and nuance. Mary Beth is certainly a practitioner of nonviolence. Thanks for putting up with all the time I spent in front of a computer screen.

I know that our four children will create a more just and peaceful world.

Contents

Foreword

The title of Dr. Michael Duffey's excellent book, *War No More*, says it all. For those for whom the title evokes the response—"No more war—of course, isn't it about time—but **how**"? You will find a very convincing compendium of peacemaking practices that have faced down towering violence time and time again and that—sing alleluia—at last provide humanity an alternative to war. For those on the other hand who greet the title with the response—"Oh not again, another dreamy idealist who thinks humanity can do away with violence and war. What happens when you are confronted with a criminal person or country that wants to do you and your loved ones harm? Do you just let them?" You will find that the author answers your concerns. He provides you many examples of how to answer the question—"what would you do, if . . ." and they demonstrate bravery and dedication beyond belief.

Gandhi has given us an entirely different insight into power. Hannah Arendt, the great political philosopher says it is a revolution for politics equivalent to the Copernican revolution in the study of the heavens. When Gandhi asked, "how does a British occupying force of 100,000 succeed in keeping a country of (at that time) 300 million, in bondage?" His answer: "We let them." Gandhi said, "Power rises. We at the bottom have the power. It is not held by those at the top to trickle down to us at the bottom through their minions. The Brits have power because we give it to them. If we stop cooperating with them they will have no power." Gandhi went on to demonstrate the truth of his insights into power. Power understood as domination, violence, from the top-down oppression, tottered and fell as the Indians took back their power. The author then depicts our wars, especially the last five wars of choice: Korea, Vietnam, twice in Iraq, and Afghanistan. That review forces the reader to say—"what empty, inane, destructive actions those were." Not only were they slaughterhouses of destruction, but they also accomplished nothing. The contrast between what Gandhi accomplished and these recent wars is stark. He sent an imperial power packing through active nonviolence and almost no loss of life. We, who think violence, the weapons of war, give power, end up empty, with horrendous loss of life and destruction.

Those first chapters set the stage for us to learn more about this alternative power—the power of satyagraha or creative, nonviolent action. The case studies are legion and eye-opening. Even if you are familiar with many of these stories you will find additional insights into what makes them so effective. Read on and enjoy. Ring the church bells. We have an alternative to war. *War No More*, indeed.

Dr. Terrence Rynne
Scottsdale, Arizona

Preface

Two experiences shaped my vision. I was a college student at the height of the Vietnam War, lost friends there, and was appalled at what our government was doing. I joined the Peace Corps and went to Nepal, one of the poorest countries in the world. Later I traveled to Central America often, was shocked by the poverty, and learned about the effects of U.S. involvement in Central America, poverty, and violence. It was clear that the aspiration for a "global village" was a world of exploitation.

Meeting people with positive visions of nonviolent change has been a joy. Meeting Arun Gandhi, Mubarek Awad, John Lewis, and Mairead Corrigan, winner of the Nobel Peace Prize, has been inspiring. Nelly Trocmé Hewett, the daughter of André and Magda Trocmé has shared her experiences growing up in occupied France while her community saved Jews. I hope readers will be inspired by the story of the rescue of Jews by Christians in southern France. I am grateful to Terrence Rynne, an American Gandhi scholar and member of an advisory group working in Rome to guide the Catholic Church to recover the nonviolent teachings of Jesus. All these people and a host of others are doing such important work. Hopefully readers will come to appreciate the power of nonviolence to create a more just and peaceful world.

Michael K. Duffey
January 2021

Introduction

This book introduces nonviolent struggles for justice and how they have succeeded. Twentieth- and twenty-first-century movements overcame dictatorships, corrupt governments, and occupations. Eighteen of these movements are examined here. This book addresses the guiding principles, strategies, and tactics that accounted for their successes. Practitioners of nonviolent activism learned the importance of respecting opponents rather than attacking them and working for social healing. These cases provide a blueprint for present and future nonviolence struggles.

What is nonviolence? Nonviolence is not harming persons and communities. Harm includes emotional harm. Degrading or threatening a spouse, condemning others as evil, and creating paralyzing fear in another are also violent acts. Given the harm being done to the environment, nonviolence means healing the harm being done to the natural world.

But speech that condemns is not necessarily violent when it challenges consciences to act justly. Martin Luther King, Jr. spoke forcefully in the struggle for racial equality; he called on hating the evil but loving the evildoer.

Chapter 1 describes the carnage of the horrific wars from 1914 to the present that have taken at least 150 million lives, some estimates much higher.[1] This chapter examines the two world wars and the five American "wars of choice": the Korean War, the Vietnam War, the Gulf War, and the "wars on terror" since 9/11 in Afghanistan and Iraq. In every war, civilians have perished in rising numbers. The death toll of combatants and civilians in the world wars was staggering. Since the Korean War, civilian deaths have surpassed combatant deaths. Conflicts not examined here also targeted civilians; in the Balkan and Rwanda genocides, the preponderance of those killed were civilians. But there is a diminishing sensitivity to statistics, in which numbers cannot capture the horrors. It may be useful to consider the plight of survivors, for whom the struggle for survival does not end when the shooting stops.

Chapter 2 introduces Gandhi, the father of modern nonviolence. He organized campaigns for the rights of Indians in South Africa, and then several campaigns in India, culminating in the struggle for India's independence from Great Britain. Understanding Gandhi's greatness requires appreciating the spiritual principles by which he lived. He coined the word *Satyagraha* to mean the vigorous pursuit of truth through the struggle for justice. He taught that *Satyagrahis* must practice *ahimsa*, non-harm. They must learn to accept *tapasya*, self-suffering. The fruit of this way of life is *moksha*, liberation. Four Gandhian campaigns in India are described.

A skeptic's question is whether Gandhian nonviolence could have prevented the evils of the Third Reich and Imperial Japan? An answer must begin regarding Germany with the failure of German citizens to oppose the rise of Hitler. But communities in German-occupied Denmark and Southern France used nonviolent means to thwart the Nazi's "final solution," the extermination of the Jewish people.

Chapter 3 examines the successful nonviolent strategies and tactics in the Philippines, Poland, East Germany, Serbia, Liberia, and Tunisia. In each case, dictatorships were overthrown without bloodshed. Each of these movements introduced new tactics into nonviolent struggle.

Chapter 4 focuses on the U.S. Civil Rights movements of the 1960s, the campaigns associated with Martin Luther King, Jr., and the Student Nonviolent Coordinating Committee (SNCC). This chapter also examines the contributions of Malcolm X and the Black Panthers. The stories of the 1960s struggle then move to the early twenty-first century with the birth of the Black Lives Matter movement responding to police violence against blacks. The frequent lack of accountability is another dimension of U.S. systemic racism yet to be dismantled.

Chapter 5 explores three other nonviolent movements. The first is La Causa, the campaign of migrant farm workers for a union to bargain for fair wages and safe working conditions. The second nonviolent struggle is that of Native Americans to protect their lands and way of life. The third movement was the successful movement in South Africa to dismantle apartheid, miraculously achieved without bloodshed.

Chapters 6 and 7 focus on the chronic violence of the United States and the prospects for change. The United States is an empire, and like empires, it employs violence to achieve its ends. At home, American life is awash in violence. The years of COVID-19 were a mirror of the animosity that threatens compassion and the common good.

Chapter 7 explores the process of creating effective nonviolent action. The first challenge for creating a nonviolent nation is convincing Americans that nonviolent change is possible. This chapter describes concrete steps for struggling against endless war-making and the arms trade, as well as eliminating racism, gun violence, and environmental destruction.

Chapter 8 has two objectives. The first asks, what are the teaching on nonviolence in world religions? Briefly examined are Hinduism, Buddhism, Judaism, Christianity, Islam, Sikhism, and the indigenous spirituality embodied in the Osage people of North America. The second objective focuses on personal growth. The virtues of empathy, justice, and mercy, as well as the abilities to apologize, forgive, reconcile, and resist retaliation, are essential human qualities and hallmarks of the practice of nonviolence. Through these qualities, we can be the change we want to see, as Gandhi advised.

The Afterword first considers how we often think about war. Wars are sometimes celebrated even when they produced disastrous results. After the Civil War monuments were erected in the South praising its noble cause and courageous leaders and soldiers, despite the destruction, animosity, and cruelty toward freed slaves the war produced. Similarly, Ireland's "Easter Rising" against Britain in 1916 did not contribute to freedom and democracy in Ireland, but eight more decades of violence. Hopefully, the evidence in this book will persuade readers that nonviolent responses to conflict are possible and necessary.

Some readers may be skeptical of the power of nonviolence to resolve conflict. Violence functions as historical markers, while successful nonviolence is less known and celebrated; it is simply less dramatic. But war-making brings endless sorrow into the world, as lives are cut short or people live out their days in suffering. Albert Einstein, an ardent pacifist, believed that nonviolence was still in its infancy but could mark a turning point in human relations. Describing the evolving power of nonviolence is the primary goal of this book.

Appendix 1 briefly considers why two nonviolent movements failed, the Arab Spring in Egypt, and the many decades of violent conflict between Israelis and Palestinians. Appendix 2 is a thought experiment: could the end of slavery in the United States have been accomplished without the Civil War? Could the strategies and tactics that succeeded elsewhere have resolved the North-South conflict?

Concerning terminology, the book speaks of "justice" more frequently than "peace." "Peace" has many connotations. An unfortunate meaning is not upsetting the system. King was accused of "disturbing the peace," which meant not stirring up resistance to segregation; he called that "peace" the peace of the dead. Or peace may be conceived as an other-worldly reality. But "justice" is a struggle in the present to secure the dignity of human beings. There are four facets of justice. Commutative justice is honoring agreements, treaties, and contracts. Criminal justice obliges society to punish people for breaking the law. But punishment cannot be vengeance. Social justice is the requirement to provide access to people of all colors to life's necessities: food, housing, health care, education, all that is required for community participation and personal fulfillment. Restorative (or "reparative") justice requires that victims be made whole again by returning, in some fashion what has been stolen from them. Racial injustice has plagued the United States from well before its beginning. Ensuring equal justice for people of every color has not happened in the United States. Three of the chapters address the systemic nature of racism still needing to be overcome.

Chapter 1

A Hundred Years of Horrific War-Making

Consider this. An estimated eight million people died in natural disasters in the twentieth century. More than one hundred million died in wars and genocides. The violence human beings have inflicted on one another was more than twelve times greater than nature's "violence." In the future, damage to the environment—man-made as well—will cause the death of millions more, as well as the destruction of the ecosystems on which all life depends. War is organized killing on a large scale. In the twentieth and twenty-first centuries that has meant war well beyond localized violence. On land, from the air, possibly from space, sea, and under the seas weapons are launched—conventional, atomic, chemical, and biological. There is no end to new generations of weapons and the resulting carnage.

At the turn of the twentieth century, the American industrialist Andrew Carnegie crusaded for the abolition of war. In 1903, he endowed the "Palace of Peace" at The Hague in the Netherlands, as the home of the International Court of Arbitration.[1] In 1907, Carnegie funded the "National Arbitration and Peace Congress" in New York City, where 1,200 delegates gathered "advocating for the abolition of war as a means of settling national disputes." Carnegie described the congress's purpose:

> We are met [*sic*] to urge the speedy removal of the foulest stain that remains to disgrace humanity since slavery was abolished—the killing of man by man in battle as a mode of settling international disputes.

The great hope was for an international authority to arbitrate disputes between nations. The Congress delegates hoped that through these means wars would become obsolete.

In the West, moral judgments about war-making are found in the Just War Tradition. The tradition is comprised of several criteria to restrain war. The first

5

section of this chapter briefly describes the eight Just War criteria; six of them ask *when* war is morally justified and two of them dictate *how* war must be conducted to be morally just. Section Two considers seven wars through the moral prism of the JWT. The increasing direct attack on civilians in wartime has become the most egregious violation of just war-making. So great is the inhumane treatment of those on "the other side," that nomenclature has arisen to describe it as "crimes of war" and "crimes against humanity." Section Three delves more deeply into the consequences of war on the lives of survivors. Section Four considers the moral obligation to resist wars judged to be unjust, in obedience to one's conscience.

THE JUST WAR TRADITION

Marcus Tullius Cicero (106 BCE–43 BCE) was a Roman philosopher and statesman. He grew increasingly critical of Rome as its republican character had deteriorated into a violent empire. He wrote: "In times of war, the law falls silent." For Cicero's criticism, Marc Antony had him assassinated. Cicero identified "two ways of settling a dispute: first, by discussion; second, by physical force" and argued that "since the former is characteristic of man [and] the latter of the brute, we must resort to force only in cases we may not avail ourselves of discussion" (Miller 1913, 1.11.33–1.13.41). Peace is war's only legitimate purpose, he wrote. An aggressor must be subjected to limited punishment so "to be brought to repent of his wrong-doing, in order that he may not repeat the offense and that others may be deterred from doing wrong. . . . Consideration must be shown to those who lay down their arms and throw themselves upon the mercy of our generals." Cicero insisted that "there be limits to retribution and to punishment."

By the fifth century CE, the Roman Empire was in disarray. Christian authorities assumed the Empire's governance. St. Augustine's addressed the question of how war ought to be conducted if it was to be moral. "Be a peace-maker even in waging war so that by your conquest you may lead those you subdue to the enjoyment of peace" (Duffey 1995, p. 19). St. Augustine knew what the Roman Legions might do and condemned "the cruelty of revenge" and the "lust for domination" (Duffey 1995, p. 21).

Jus ad bellum criteria

Over the centuries, theologians and jurists articulated other important relevant considerations. Today, eight criteria comprise the JWT. Six criteria consider the conditions that must exist to warrant war (the *jus ad bellum* criteria). Two criteria concern the restraints required in the conduct of war (the *jus in bello* criteria). Recently, an additional criterion has been proposed that obligates victors to tend to the healing and reconstruction of the defeated society (a *jus post bello* criterion). The Just War criteria set a high bar for restraint. What is evident is that modern war-making falls far short.

1. The only **just cause** for initiating military action is in the defense of innocent people who are presently being harmed by invasion, oppression, or occupation. It is not legitimate to punish an adversary for past injustices. It is not legitimate to attack preemptively to prevent what might occur in the future (what *might* occur in the future is only speculative). Making war for "regime change" is prohibited. Likewise, to undertake war to protect or promote a value (e.g., capitalism, communism, democracy, "a way of life") is prohibited. Ideological purposes are dangerous, for it is often unclear when their goals have been met.[2]
2. **Right intention** means probing the motivation for war-making. Wars may have a hidden purpose, such as acquiring resources, punishing adversaries, and reducing the power of another nation to maintain a "balance of power"?
3. **Legitimate authority** means that only the highest authority is empowered to initiate war. In the time of kingdoms, only kings were permitted to initiate war; wars initiated by lesser rulers might well multiply war-making. In democracies such as the United States, authorization to initiate war is a shared prerogative between executive and legislative branches. With the rise of an international authority in the United Nations, the hope has been to place the authority to initiate war in the UN Security Council. Of course, the UN authority does not ensure that military actions will be fewer or less deadly.
4. Initiating war is permitted only as a **last resort** when other means of achieving justice have been exhausted. This requirement underscores the essential role of diplomacy. Diplomats are skilled in means of resolving conflicts. Ethicist Michael Walzer insists that going to war ought not to be an easy place to arrive. "To get there," he writes, "one must indeed try everything (which are a lot of things) and not just one thing. . . . [Diplomats] learn by doing over and over again. . . . What exactly did they try when they were trying everything?" (Walzer 2001, 318).
5. **Strategic proportionality** means assessing whether the good that military action will achieve will outweigh the harm it will inflict. Judgment of proportionality must be as honest as possible, not inflating the good or ignoring the harm. To inflate the "good" that will come from a military victory is the sure sign of "war fever."
6. **Likelihood of success** may seem like an obvious expectation and that without such an expectation no one would initiate military action. But

war-making may be foolhardy, with too little thought given to the possibility of failure—at the expense of overwhelming suffering. Wars are not permitted to preserve the "national honor" of a weak nation; they are unlikely to win. It would be better for them to suffer occupation.

Jus in bello criteria

7. **Civilian immunity** prohibits directly attacking noncombatants, that is, civilians. This moral criterion has been corrupted in at least three ways. First, harm to civilians is often described as "collateral damage" that is unintended. But civilian casualties are not a surprise but can be anticipated. Second, it may be claimed that all civilians are contributing to the war effort and not exempt from attack. Are those who produce food and other necessities for both soldiers and civilians in some sense soldiers? Workers in munition plants may be, but children, the ill, the elderly, caregivers, hospital workers, and so on surely are not. Third, an egregious immoral development is intentionally attacking civilians as a military strategy to undercut a societies' morale.[3]

8. **Tactical proportionality** requires that enemy forces be subjected to attack only to the degree necessary to defeat them. Captured or surrendered forces are prisoners of war with rights intended to ensure their humane treatment. As will be noted below, that criterion has been violated most of the time in the U.S. wars of choice.

WORLD WARS I (1914–1919) AND II (1939–1945)

On August 1, 1914, Germany declared war on Russia and two days later on France. The well-oiled German military machine roared through Belgium into France. Alliances between the powers were tripwires for engulfing all of Europe in war, with France, Belgium, Britain, and later the United States facing Germany and the Austria–Hungary Empire, Bulgaria, and the Ottoman Empire. The German military high command had long planned a two-front war, first crushing France quickly and then moving East to defeat an ill-prepared Russian army.

Germany justified its aggression on grounds of self-defense, claiming that it was a victim of "encirclement" by hostile nations. It also claimed the right to assert European dominance. However, Germany was the aggressor nation, initiating an offensive war violating the first criterion of justifiable war.

A genuine "last resort" requires concerted diplomatic efforts to avoid war. But European nations focused instead on creating mutual defense pacts. Historian Gordon Martel concludes that the worldview shared by the great powers made preventing the war unlikely, fueled as it was by politicians' and generals' hubris:

> Each of the great powers decided in 1914 that they had vital interests at stake—interests for which it was worth risking defeat, dismemberment, impoverishment, and social revolution. Had they anticipated the extent of the carnage, the duration of the war, the political and social chaos it caused they might have made different decisions. But it is doubtful. By and large, the men who made the decisions, drawn mainly from the traditional ruling classes of Europe, believed it was better to die honorably than to survive in disgrace (Martel 1987, p. 72).

Fueled by new military capability, nationalism, and alliances, the "Great War" took more lives than in any war in human history, to date. Where had such popular support for war come from? Shirley Williams lamented the terrible irony of the war:

> The idealism and high-mindedness that led our boys and men in their hundreds of thousands to volunteer to fight, and often to die. The obscenity of the square miles of mud, barbed wire, broken trees, and shattered bodies into which they were flung, battalion after battalion . . . [eclipsed] the causes for which the war was fought on both sides (Brittain 1933, 9).[4]

Battalion after battalion, soldiers were cut into pieces by howitzers, machine-gunned from the air, suffocated by mustard gas, died of wounds, and from pneumonia in muddy trenches. In *Testament of Youth* Vera Brittain wrote of the losses of her fiancé, her brother, and many friends on the battlefields of France (Brittain 1933).[5] The war ended with a staggering loss of life, an estimated eighteen million. More than a third of the casualties were civilians who died from starvation, disease, and exposure.

The Armistice Germany signed in 1919 imposed huge reparations on the impoverished German people. Hitler gained power and throughout the 1930s Germany rearmed. The most dangerous development in Germany was the rise of the ideology of Aryan supremacy. The goal of the Third Reich was the "purification" of the races throughout Europe. The "inferior" people to be exterminated included the Jews, the Slavs the Roma, homosexuals, and the disabled. Nazi Aryan ideology produced the greatest crime ever committed, the murder of six million Jews and countless other human beings.

Diplomatic efforts to prevent German aggression proved futile. In 1938, Britain secured a non-aggression pact with Hitler in which he agreed to go no further than annexing part of the Czechoslovakian territory. But the German Army occupied all of Czechoslovakia, then Poland, and in 1940, France. In 1940, the German blitzkrieg bombed London, other British cities, and military installations, killing an estimated 45,000 civilians. In retaliation, the

Allies dropped incendiary bombs on thirty-seven German cities, burning several to the ground. The total number of German civilian deaths is not known but is estimated to have been as high as 400,000, with 800,000 wounded. The United States bombed Tokyo and Osaka in 1944 and 1945, the deadliest raids so far in the war; in only a few nights killing an estimated 100,000 civilians. The war against Japan ended when the United States dropped atomic bombs on Hiroshima and Nagasaki, killing almost 200,000 civilians and radiating thousands of survivors.

The war between the Axis powers (Germany, Italy, and Japan) and the Allies (Britain, France, Belgium, Russia, China, and later the United States) raged for six years. The death toll in World War II is estimated at between fifty and eighty million. The war has sometimes been called the "Good War," because of the sacrifices of so many to stop brutal imperialism threatening the world, with Nazification of the West and Japanese control of the East. From the perspective of the *jus ad bellum* criteria, the Allies were justified in their military cause. But the war had crossed a point of no return when on both sides civilian populations were intentionally bombed as a military strategy. Gordon Zahn summarizes the moral judgment of the war by a German writer of the next generation:

> In 1961 a young German writer drew a troubling parallel between the Nazi atrocity of Auschwitz and the American atrocity of Hiroshima. He found a common factor: the horrendous capacity for justifying the mass destruction of living human beings. Any mind capable of formulating such justification, [the German writer] said, had to be corrupt. He added that "This corruption is general." (Zahn 1979, p. 257)

The end of World War II brought a split between Eastern and Western Europe. In Russia and its 14 satellite nations, Marxist-Leninist ideology ruled governments and their economies. The West defended democracy and capitalism. Both sides possessed nuclear weapons, and an arms race ensued increasing the possibility of a nuclear war. Both the East and the West realized that nuclear war would mean mutual suicide. So, in addition to their nuclear arms race, the United States and Soviet Union defended and promoted their ideologies in "surrogate wars" in small countries of capitalism or communism. But calling the civil wars in El Salvador, Guatemala, and Honduras "low intensity wars" is a grave euphemism given the torture, death, and displacement of millions of civilians caught in crossfires between brutal government forces and small guerilla armies. Especially in Latin America, the United States protected pro-U.S. business regimes against guerilla movements that would have nationalized key resources.

The U.S. wars in Korea (1950–1953) and Vietnam (1963–1975) were ideological wars to "defend against communism" and "establish democracy."

The U.S.' war in North Korea ended with no peace treaty, the country remaining divided into North and South Korea. One U.S. veteran lamented, "We died for a tie." The war is sometimes referred to as the "forgotten war" among the Americas. But it would not be forgotten by the loved ones of hundreds of thousands of Korean casualties and 33,000 Americans.

A decade later, the United States began military action in Vietnam to prevent a "domino effect." The U.S. leaders claimed that the victory of communism in Vietnam would quickly lead to communist victories across southeast Asia. In 1964, Congress authorized President Lyndon Johnson to send troops to Vietnam. Only two senators opposed the resolution. One of them, Senator Wayne Morse, said: "We cannot win a war in Asia. We cannot win in Vietnam" (*Congressional Record* August 20, 1964). Morse warned that we would be sacrificing American lives for a doomed cause.

The war has been sold to the American people on the grounds that "godless communism" must be defeated. The realities of overwhelming harm being afflicted by the United States was dismissed by uncritical claims of the "good" being achieved. The U.S. Air Force attacked hospitals in Hanoi, the capital of North Vietnam, destroyed the dikes essential for producing rice, used Agent Orange that caused long-term health damages for Vietnamese and U.S. soldiers alike, and napalm bombs producing severe human flesh burns on Vietnamese peasants. North Vietnamese army supply lines in Cambodia were also attacked. Frustrated by the inability to defeat the North Vietnamese, some U.S. military planners even considered dropping "tactical" nuclear bombs on North Vietnam. Soldiers and airmen saw the results. Many were demoralized and depressed as the war continued without purpose. They were in an environment they could not understand, seeking enemies they could not recognize, and living in fear for their lives. Carl Marlantes describes the resulting brutal behavior:

> The true situation was Marines killing NVA without quarter, wherever we could find them, with me doing no more or less than any of the others. . . . We all shot anybody we saw, never offering a chance for surrender. (Marlantes 2010, pp. 101–102)

An Army officer allegedly told a war correspondent "We had to destroy the village to save it."[6] Rage produced massacres. There was no provision for the humane treatment of prisoners of war.

The combined Korean and Vietnamese casualties were between three and four million, an estimated 90 percent of whom were civilians. The U.S. military policy was not to count the enemy dead. Instead, officers in the field were pressured to report inflated numbers of enemy casualties, lies that eventually caused Americans to turn against the war. The United States withdrew hastily when the Army of North Vietnam overwhelmed Saigon, after twelve years of war. Fifty-nine thousand U.S. soldiers died and over a million Vietnamese. General Maxwell Taylor, Chairman of the Joint Chiefs of Staff (1962–1964) and ambassador to Vietnam (1964–1965), in an interview in 1979 identified what he saw as the fatal weaknesses of the U.S. venture into Vietnam:

> We didn't know ourselves. We didn't know our South Vietnamese allies and we knew even less about North Vietnam. Who was Ho Chi Minh? Nobody really knew. So until we know the enemy, and know our allies and know ourselves, we'd better keep out of this dirty business. It's very dangerous. (*Washington Post* April 21, 1987)

The Gulf War (1991)

Chapter 3 describes the nonviolent overthrows of the communist governments of Poland and East Germany in 1989, that contributed to the collapse of the Soviet Union in 1991. Now no credible adversaries threatened the United States. The arms race was over, and a peace dividend seemed possible. However, that same year the United States waged a brief but devastating war on Iraq to oust its dictator Saddam Hussein after Iraq invaded and annexed its neighbor, the Kingdom of Kuwait. Since the United States was in no way threatened, why did it choose to intervene? Why had President George H. W. Bush suddenly chosen to vilify Saddam Hussein as "the world's worst dictator"? Was the hidden purpose to protect the availability of oil from the Middle East? What became abundantly clear was that the administration intended to punish Hussein rather than to negotiate with him. Full surrender was demanded, as were large reparations to Kuwait. Hussein was called a war criminal. Bush actually referred to the Just War criterion of "just cause" and identified several just causes for U.S. military action: restoring of Kuwait's sovereignty, protecting Saudi Arabia (which did not need protection!), restoring Middle East stability, protecting U.S. vital interests, and establishing a "new world order"—none of these causes were clear or justifiable. What was Bush really after, what was the real intention of an invasion of this oil-rich region when the United States needed a reliable supply? If the goal of the United States was the withdrawal of Iraqi forces from Kuwait, there were diplomatic means to accomplish that. But the *jus ad bellum* was cast aside, as would be the *jus in bello* criteria.

In two weeks of January 1991, the U.S. Air Force dropped more bombs on Iraq than it had in the entire Vietnam War. "Operation Desert Storm" destroyed most of Iraq's 450,000-man army; those who survived the bombardment and attempted to surrender were buried in the desert sands. The bombing of civilians in Baghdad and Basra was relentless. When their electric power grids were destroyed, U.S. air war planners defended the bombing, claiming that 25 percent of the grid was left operational for the sake of civilians. But Baghdad has a population of nine million, roughly the size of New York City. It could not survive on one-fourth of its electric power necessary for water purification, hospital operations, refrigeration, and much more. In addition, the bombing of bridges, rail lines, and roadways into the cities quickly led to shortages of food and other essentials. The air strike that hit a bomb shelter in Baghdad took over 400 lives.

The war lasted six weeks. General Norman Schwarzkopf finally ordered a halt to the bombing, saying that the United States should not appear to be brutal in the eyes of the world. The horror visited on Iraqi cities was more aptly "Operation Civilian Slaughter." Saddam Hussein survived the war and boasted he had stared down the United States. As if the pain inflicted on Iraqis was insufficient, President Bush reimposed economic sanctions, despite having discounted that option before the war as an ineffective means of toppling Hussein. The death toll was staggering, including several hundred thousand Iraqi children dying of malnutrition and communicable diseases when the United States imposed sanctions that followed the merciless war. The number is disputed; thus, no number is listed here. All would agree that it was in the hundreds of thousands.

The Wars on Terror: Afghanistan (2001–2021) and Iraq (2003–2011)

The United States invaded Afghanistan a month after 9/11 to find and destroy the al Qaeda leadership. The U.S. forces, first toppling the Taliban, fundamentalists who ruled Afghanistan, oppressing "lax" Muslims and banning women from playing public roles in Afghani society. Lt. Col. Nathan Sassaman told a *New York Times* reporter that "with a healthy dose of fear and violence, and a lot of money for projects, I think we can convince [Afghanis] that we are here to help them" (Sassaman 2006). A few years later Sassaman publicly called the war a mistake, for which he was harshly criticized by the Pentagon. Peter Marsden contrasted the goals of the anti-terrorist occupation of the country with the desperate needs of Afghanis, asking where the country might be now if the international community had considered the needs of the people rather than make war on a small number of terrorists.

In *Accountability for Killing: Moral Responsibility for Collateral Damage in America's Post-9/11 Wars*, Neta Crawford studied U.S. Air Force policies for the killing of civilians in the Afghan and Iraq wars. She began with the story of a raid on the night of May 4, 2009. Taliban forces were believed to be occupying two adjacent Afghan villages. U.S. bombers dropped five 500-hundred-pound bombs and two 2,000-pound bombs on them. The estimates of fatalities varied; the Afghan government and human rights groups claimed that approximately 140 civilians were killed and twenty-five were wounded. The Department of Defense claimed that the number was much lower. The unintentional or incidental killing or maiming of civilians is considered lawful if it is "not excessive in light of the military advantage anticipated from the attack" (Crawford 2013, p. 7).[7] The Pentagon recognized that such collateral damage may undermine U.S. missions, and after the bombing raid in 2009, it concluded that the raid that night was troublesome, and especially the dropping of 2,000-pound bombs.[8] Meanwhile, the Taliban moved elsewhere.

This chapter has stressed the growing number of civilian deaths, unintentional and intentional, that has risen dramatically in the past 100 years, violating the *jus in bello* criterion of noncombatant immunity. Crawford explored whether the claim that the deaths of civilians since the 1960s referred to as "collateral damage" by the military, are morally justifiable. Her research led to the conclusion that the death and maiming of civilians are often foreseen and foreseeable and must be avoided. It cannot be claimed as accidental. She writes:

> Collateral damage is a foreseeable, and as we have seen, often preventable consequence of choices made in both the war zone and far from the battlefield and sometimes well before a war has begun (Crawford 2013, p. 466).

Crawford makes several important observations about the protection of civilians. First, she responds to the objection that avoiding civilians can make U.S. forces more vulnerable. Yes, they may be vulnerable, but civilians are more vulnerable (Crawford 2013, p. 216). Second, moral responsibility for the protection of civilians resides throughout the chain of command from soldiers to commanders, Pentagon officials, the President, Congress, and U.S. citizens. Third, crimes against civilians are often blamed on "bad apples" in the military. But the conduct of individuals is also formed by the institutional military environment. Third, Congressional and citizen oversight, she points out, need the research arms of the General Accounting Office, the Congressional Research Service, and the Office of Management and Budget if Congress and the public are to assess and control military operations. Crawford emphasizes what is most important, the protection of human life.

> If the United States were to explicitly value human life as an end in itself, and not primarily to victory, and stop practices that the civilians in these war zones consider brutal and cynical . . . then the United States would arguably be more successful at "winning hearts and minds." But, even if protecting civilians did not ease the path to victory, it is a value and set of practices worth promoting, in and of itself (Crawford 2013, p. 473).

Finally, citizen dialogue is necessary regarding acceptable collateral damage and the protection of civilians. She urges the need for a "robust democracy" in which citizens are part of the dialogue (Crawford 2013, p. 457). In chapter 7, a suggestion is offered for raising the consciousness of U.S. citizens about the suffering civilians in their country's foreign wars. The term "collateral damage" has been criticized as abstract and a euphemism. "Damage" connotes fallen walls and roofs, shattered glass, and destroyed possessions. It is not used to mean death. In addition, a misleading description of the air war is the reference of weapons as capable of "surgical strikes." Their accuracy and thus protection of civilians have not proven to be true.

After events such as what happened in May 2009, the Taliban disappeared in mountainous regions, year after year regaining ground. After twenty years of the U.S. presence, terrorist cells still operated freely throughout the country. The U.S. government grew weary and wanted to leave, opening negotiations with the Taliban in 2019 that continued into 2020, despite the Taliban's continuing terrorism violating the terms of U.S. withdrawal.

In 2003, the United States invaded Iraq for a second time, charging Saddam Hussein with possessing weapons of mass destruction and harboring terrorists. Neither claim was true. The actual intent was to kill Hussein, which the 1991 invasion had failed to do. (In 2003, U.S. forces finally located Hussein in Tikrit and executed him.) The United States remained in Iraq until 2011, as the country continued to descend into chaos. Death tolls in Iraq and Afghanistan are unknown; thousands of civilians were killed, many by terrorist attacks in markets and cafes, at weddings, at Iraqi army recruiting stations. U.S. drones missing targets also claimed the lives of civilians. How much difference did it make to victims whether they are struck by terrorist bombs or U.S. missiles? The United States did establish at least one prison, the infamous Abu Ghraib prison in Baghdad where prisoners were tortured and sexually abused. Army Reservist Aidan Delgado, deployed to Iraq in 2003, was one whistleblower revealing the violation of a human right in the prison (Cohn and Gilberd 2009, p. 34).

An additional JWT criterion, "justice after war," (*jus post bello*) must also be a part of the moral evaluation of war. Was it prepared to rebuild Iraq and Afghanistan? Did the United States consider the animosity its actions would create? Hatred of the United States had burst into flame on 9/11, nurturing the rise of al Qaeda. Fixated as it was on eliminating al Qaeda in Afghanistan and on punishing Iraq, the United States failed to attend to the growth of a new terrorist organization in 2004, ISIS, which organizes an estimated 30,000 fighters, with the goal of conquering Iraq, then Syria, and establishing a caliphate across the Middle East. Its tactics include filming grisly executions for the West to see, and its notoriety attracted disaffected Muslim youths from the Middle East as well as the West. The primary strategy of Western nations as well as Iraq and Syria was to destroy ISIS by assassinating its leaders and driving out its forces. As of 2019, ISIS had been driven from territories it had controlled in Syria and Iraq. The battles against ISIS in its major cities had been devastating for civilians. Whether the decimation of ISIS would contain terrorism was unlikely; its suicide bombers and other forms of terrorism are difficult to prevent.

An international group of foreign policy experts advised approaching ISIS differently.[9] In their judgment, the West should not

1. identify citizen protests with terrorism, for most Middle East protest movements are nonviolent, aimed at replacing nondemocratic and corrupt regimes;
2. inflate ISIS's military capability;
3. characterize ISIS as "the worst terrorists ever" because it plays into its recruiting strategy, attracting recruits to ISIS's "glorious cause";
4. quickly resort to military options or employ drones (considered a cowardly form of warfare).

Instead, governments should

5. find points of contact that may dial down ISIS's aggression, and not ignore its political grievances.
6. pursue negotiations.[10]
7. recognize that terrorism thrives on the breakdown of social order. The overthrow of Hussein and the civil war in Iraq were opportunities for ISIS. Securing the political and economic needs of societies reduces popular unrest and the attraction of ISIS.

From 2001 to 2019, the United States spent over a trillion dollars on its wars on terrorism.

THE WAR AFTER THE WAR

The agony of war only deepens after the fighting stops and the smoke clears. Statistics do not convey the pain and loss suffered by survivors, usually worse off than they were before the war. Those in the West, not suffering the bombings, the raids, the assassinations, the interrogations, the torture, and the hunger and homelessness, cannot begin to understand war's horrible aftermath. Not since the U.S. Civil War 150 years ago have Americans experienced war at home. Americans who were on the ground in the world wars, Korea, Vietnam, Afghanistan, and Iraq know about war. But only 1 percent of Americans went to Afghanistan and Iraq. Back home, the public sees on television screens a few seconds of the effects of bombings and hears equally short news items about the horrors of suicide bombings, and desperate people fleeing for their lives. Foreign wars are just that—far away. How often are conflicts summarily dismissed, with such judgments as "they have been fighting for centuries" or "they are used to it"? Such opinions are usually expressed with absolutely no historical knowledge. "They" are forgotten.

War planners who appear so adept at strategizing how to win wars (but often underestimate the will of the opposition) do not address how to reconstruct a defeated nation. George Packer's study of the chief architects of the 2003 Iraq War describes the attitude of then Vice President Dick Cheney:

> Like the President [George W. Bush] Cheney maintained an almost mystical confidence in American military power and an utter incuriosity about the details of its human consequences. (Packer 2005, 148)[11]

Secretary of Defense Donald Rumsfeld, also a chief instigator of the war, made the statement that things were going so well in Iraq that tourism would soon resume. In fact, if Western tourists ventured into Iraq—and were not shot—here is what they could have expected to find:

- Civilians dying from their injuries because of no medical help; frantic parents trying to save the lives of their children, but hospitals damaged or destroyed, medicines unavailable; X-ray and kidney dialysis machines not working for lack of electricity.
- Broken pipes mixing potable water and sewage, with cholera and typhoid quickly breaking out.
- Food shortages quickly occur because transportation has been impossible as a result of the destruction of roads, bridges, and rail lines; In 1991, U.S. bombs destroyed or damaged thirty-three of Baghdad's thirty-six motor and rail bridges.
- No physical therapy is available, mental health help nonexistent.
- Toxins released into the atmosphere and deep carbon footprints from the gas emissions of military equipment.
- Legal systems no longer functioning, criminal activity spiking, and no police protection.
- Despite the claim that regime change would bring democracy to Iraq and Afghanistan, more corruption and chaos followed the war.
- Humanitarian workers are sometimes attacked, given the intense animosity toward foreigners.
- Mental health issues are common among U.S. veterans. A therapist noted that for many of them war is not over but intrudes in their lives "over and over again."[12] An army general lamented that "suicide is the toughest

enemy I have faced in my thirty-seven years in the army."[13] The same is true of many on the other side.

There are so many tragedies after the war. Millions of people are forced to flee war-torn regions. At no time in history have more people been displaced within their countries or forced to flee across borders. The UN Office of the High Commissioner on Refugees estimates that in 2019 there were at least 79.5 million refugees across the world, the largest number from Africa and failed Middle East states. Many will live in refugee camps for years, which are crowded places that are incubators of disease. Refugees who can enter other countries often face severe discrimination. This is especially true for Muslim refugees. At present, Islamophobia is rampant.

Cultures were severely damaged. In the 1991 Iraq War, the country's museum of priceless antiquities was ransacked. Viet Thanh Nguyen, a first-generation Vietnamese American, describes the results of the American war in Vietnam:

> My parents and everyone I know lost homes, wealth, relatives, country, and peace of mind. . . . our family story is a story of loss and death, for we are here [in the U.S.] because the United States fought a war that killed three million of our countrymen. Our Vietnam war never ended. (Nguyen 2015, pp. 390, 392)

Judith Mayotte puts a face on refugees. At the invitation of aid organizations, she worked with Sudanese, Cambodian, Eritrean, and Afghani refugees living either in other countries or displaced in their own war-torn countries. Aid workers, with insufficient resources, try to provide water, food, makeshift housing, and medical care for thousands of people living in camps. Camps are vectors for disease. Refugees may live in camps so long that babies born there might reach adulthood without knowing any other life.

How will refugees be able one day to reclaim what they have lost? Mayotte reminds readers that refugees are often well-educated, professionals, and business owners. Being refugees multiplies post-conflict suffering; most tragic is that they are unable "to move on with their lives." Some have "lost their inner spirit and the traditions that made them a people" (Mayotte 1992, p. 91). After her years getting to know refugees and hearing their stories, Mayotte writes:

> As I journeyed among the refugees and to the nations to which they will return, I became tangibly aware of the centuries it takes to build a culture and a nation, and the few years it takes to obliterate the land and the people who gave spirit and life to that culture and nation (Mayotte 1992, p. 304)

As Mayotte was writing, the Cold War ended. She was—and is—hopeful that the world community could make peace a priority in order to prevent the armed conflicts that drive people from their homes. Thirty years later the number of refugees across the world has tripled. Yet now there is another factor that has caused the number of worldwide refugees to rise dramatically, climate degradation. For example, the Sahara Desert continues to extend south, making more land untillable; starving populations must move. Resource wars often follow as they try to resettle on other people's land. Climate change exacerbates violence, whether armed violence or starvation. The poor starve because other humans are making war on the environment. A stable peace also depends on commitment to healing the environment.

Hamid Bozarslan warns of the dire situations in war-torn places in the Middle East, writing that "it could be that by 2020 there will be no Syrian society, no Iraqi society, and no Yemeni society either" (Hénin 2015, 139). How would Iraq be healed? The U.S. military is the first to admit that it does not have experience or expertise in postwar rebuilding. That is left to nongovernmental organizations and other nations more familiar with local culture and politics, and with fluency in local languages.[14] To their credit, U.S. servicemen sometimes offered humanitarian services of their own, such as rebuilding schools. But the cost of rebuilding Iraq's infrastructure after the 2003 war was estimated to be 120 billion dollars. Paul Bremer was tasked with the job and given a fourteen-billion-dollar budget. The U.S. Treasury Department sent several billion dollars in cash, much of which was stolen by Iraqi politicians. The principal method for assisting Iraq's reconstruction was funneling large amounts of cash to Iraqis claiming to need funding for projects. One American military officer reported that he walked around Baghdad with hundreds of thousands of dollars of cash in his pocket, doling it out to Iraqis for projects that he later learned were never even begun.[15] There was no accountability and much money disappeared. The rebuilding efforts were more than not disasters. James Risen writes:

> Between $12 and $14 billion, mostly in 100-dollar bills, was taken from East Rutherford [the depository of U.S. paper money] and flown to the war zone in Iraq in 2003 and 2004, with virtually no supervision or safeguards. Another $5.8 billion was taken from the New York Federal Reserve to Baghdad by electronic fund transfers. All told approximately $20 billion was sent to Iraq without any clear orders or direction on how the money was to be used. The controls on the money were so lax that few credible records exist of how much cash there was or where the cash went once it arrived in Baghdad. (Risen 2014, p. 5)

One of war's greatest tragedies is the lack of compassion for victims on the "other side." They are invisible, though for a few seconds, the faces of a few are flashed on U.S. nightly news. But they have names. A civil war has raged in Syria from 2012 to the present. Aid workers referred to Aleppo as a "slaughterhouse" and "hell hole." Five-year-old Amrann Daqnesh was fatally wounded after being rushed to seven hospitals, none of which was functioning. Two-year-old Alan Kurdi's body was washed up on the shore of western Turkey in 2015. His family had fled Syria and was attempting to cross the Mediterranean when their inflatable boat sank. His mother and two brothers also drowned. Alan's father was photographed holding his dead son on what an aid worker "called a children's graveyard." The photo of the child was heartbreaking. A photo of Samar Saddam shows her standing in front of what was once her home in Mosel, Iraq. It was destroyed in February 2017. Her family, is nowhere to be found. She is frantically trying to locate her brother who lived in another part of the city, but she cannot reach him. Aid workers report that thousands of Mosel civilians have been killed in the nine-month battle between ISIS and coalition forces.

Since 2014, Saudi Arabia has been bombing the Houthi people in northern Yemen because they are aligned with Iran. (The U.S. complicity is noted in chapter 6.) In April 2018, a missile fired by a Saudi bomber struck a bus carrying a school group. Thirty-four children were killed. Among them were Arryin Zakaria, ten years old, and Yousef Hussein Tayeb, fifteen years old. The complete list of names was published by "Voices of Creative Nonviolence," an American humanitarian and peace organization, that set up exhibits in several American cities of blue backpacks similar to the ones given to the youths by UNICEF. The United States had a role in these deaths since the Saudi jets were purchased from American corporations and were refueled by the U.S. Air Force aerial refueling aircraft.

Would knowing more about these people impact how Americans think about war? Would we see our common humanity? Chapter 7 suggests other possible means for more intimate contact with at least a few war victims, perhaps bringing them close enough to be "real people."

WHEN WARS ARE UNJUST

None of the U.S. wars of choice was morally justified. Who is obliged to apply the Just War criteria? Who bears responsibility for determining when a war is morally justified and how it must be conducted? Is it political leaders, military planners, military officers, or soldiers, sailors, and airmen? Is not the answer all of the above? This moral obligation might be termed "obedience to conscience in wartime." This obedience requires dissent among decision-makers and conscientious objection by those being conscripted and those already in uniform. Consider the opposition to the Iraq War (2003).

Government Officials and Military Leaders

Ann Wright and Susan Dixon assembled the statements by U.S. officials and high-ranking military officers (active and retired) who protested a war against Iraq (2003). Several government officials sent letters of resignation. Wright, who had served in the military for 26 years followed by diplomatic service for 15 years in the U.S. State Department, resigned in protest. In her letter of resignation, Wright noted that "most of the world considers our statements about Iraq as arrogant, untruthful, and masking a hidden agenda" (Wright and Dixon 2008, p. 34). She wrote that

> leaders of moderate Muslim/Arab countries warn us about the predictable outrage and anger of the youth of their countries if America enters an Arab country with the purpose of attacking Muslims/Arabs, not defending them. (Wright and Dixon 2008, pp. 34–35)

Elizabeth Wilmshurst, deputy legal advisor to the British Foreign Office, described the two possible conditions for use of military force: self-defense or authorization by the United Nations Security Council that expresses the world body's determination that aggression must be resisted. Neither of these conditions existed in the U.S.' (aided by Britain) invasion of Iraq (Wright and Dixon 2008, p. 47).

Clare Short, Britain's Secretary of State for International Development also resigned, protesting that Prime Minister Tony Blair was leading Britain to war under pretenses (Wright and Dixon 2008, pp. 48–50). She charged that the government's "failure to prepare for afterward, the chaos, the criminality, the looting, the continuing death, the unemployment, the lack of electricity and water, is a complete disaster" (Wright and Dixon 2008, p. 50).

Over 100 U.S. generals, admirals (active and retired), and diplomats accused the government of violating the Geneva Conventions in the Iraq War, conventions that require humane treatment of prisoners of war (Wright and Dixon 2008, pp. 120–129).

Soldiers

In the United States, members of the Peace Churches are excused from military service because of their belief that all killing is wrong (those churches include Quaker communities, Mennonites and Amish, and the Church of the Brethren).[16] This is not the place to describe in any detail the dissent to the seven wars examined here, except to note certain developments. In World War I, only a handful of Christians from other denominations, Catholic and mainline Protestants, refused to serve and received prison terms. Gordon Zahn, a U.S. sociologist and also a pacifist, researched the experiences of conscientious objectors during World War II (Zahn 1977). He reports that records reveal only seven Catholic war resisters in Germany, six of whom were executed (Zahn 1962). Surely others who were unknown must have existed. Zahn also researched the refusal of Franz Jäggerstätter, an Austrian peasant, to serve in the Army of the Third Reich. Jäggerstätter called the German war an unjust war. He was executed in Berlin three weeks before the Allies reached the city (Zahn 1971). Zahn found that in World War II almost

12,000 men in the United States were granted Conscientious objector status
(CO) and assigned to alternative service of "national importance" in 151
work camps (Zahn 1962, 37).[17]

The draft was reinstated during the Vietnam War. By the end of the Vietnam
War, nine million had served, nearly three million serving in Vietnam. Protest
against the war in Vietnam was extensive and the number of resisters was in
the hundreds of thousands. The number of those who sought CO status was
approximately 470,000; 170,000 were granted CO status and 300,000 applications were denied. An estimated 600,000 more evaded the draft; 200 were
prosecuted and more than 50,000 fled the country (Swarthmore College Peace
Collection 2007). Army doctor Howard Levy refused orders to deploy, asserting that the war was not in U.S. self-defense or authorized by the UN Security
Council, and was thus an illegal war (Cohn and Gilberd 2009, p. 18). After
the war, the U.S. Supreme Court ruled that eligibility to claim CO status must
be extended to non-religious applicants whose dissent is deeply morally held.

In the six-week-long Gulf War, no U.S. ground forces or draft were necessary since the air assault on Iraq required almost no military personnel. However, in the 2003 Iraq War, some soldiers refused orders to deploy or redeploy
to Iraq. Lt. Ehren Watada refused to deploy on the grounds that the Iraq War
was illegal. He wrote that orders "should be respected but never blindly followed" (Wright and Dixon 2008, p. 163). Watada continued:

> No one's conduct is justified by claiming that he or she is "following orders."
> Enlisting in the military does not mean relinquishing one's right to seek the
> truth—neither does it excuse one from rational thought nor the ability to distin-
> guish between right and wrong. (Wright and Dixon 2008, p. 164)

Watada was especially addressing just cause, truthful intentions, last resort,
and civilian immunity.

Camilo Mejiá refused redeployment because of what he had witnessed and
participated in an entire country reduced to ruin (Wright and Dixon 2008,
p. 142). He wrote: "I was afraid of losing my soul in the process of saving
my body" (Wright and Dixon 2008, p. 141). Pablo Paredes refused to deploy,
arguing that the Marines would be in the position of committing war crimes.
At his court-martial, he said: "I believe I have a higher duty to my conscience
and to the supreme law of the land. Both of these duties dictate that I must not
participate in any way, hands-on or indirect, in the current oppression that has
been unleashed on Iraq" (Cohn and Gilberd 2009, p. 15).

Applications for CO status are routinely denied to those already in the
service, as was the case for all of these applicants.[18] Seldom do military chaplains support active service members seeking conscientious objector status.
Chaplains often reason that people who oppose war should not have signed

up in the first place. This is flawed reasoning, for non-pacifists make moral judgments of the particular war they confront. For that, Watada, Mejiá, Paredes, and many others were court-martialed, imprisoned, received dishonorable discharges, and denied veterans benefits. Their consciences were formed by JWT. It is the moral obligation of individuals to act in accord with their consciences. Dissenting and refusing to serve in an unjust war should be the first criteria of the JWT.

Many of the most committed antiwar activists are veterans. In the midst of the Vietnam War, the Vietnam Veterans Against the War formed. They marched and held meetings to convince Americans that the war must end. Iraq Veterans Against the War also did the same.[19]

Citizens

When the JWT does not restrain violent responses to conflict, it loses its usefulness. The Catholic Church expressed its judgment about the future of the tradition after the Gulf War: "We can only conclude that modern war is always wrong" (*Civlitá Cattolica* 1991). The JWT has lost its moral relevance.

Examining alternatives to war is the primary purpose of this book. Gandhi pioneered ways to prevented what could have been a bloody war to end British rule of India. In the United States, black civil rights activists struggled nonviolently for racial justice. Blacks in South Africa overcame apartheid nonviolently. Such has also been the case in Eastern Europe, the Middle East, and Africa. But in both its domestic culture and its foreign involvement, the United States has been slow to learn and practice nonviolent approaches to critical issues domestic and foreign. Violence is its chronic response. The following chapters suggest how embracing nonviolence happens.

The Just War criteria set the bar very high, in fact, today unreachable. With the exception of resisting the aggression of the Third Reich, none of the wars briefly described here can claim moral or legal justification in struggles for justice. Skeptics contend that war-making is inevitable because of the fallen human condition. But Cicero observed that human beings' rational nature means they must not behave brutishly. Even when wars happen, leaders and soldiers—and citizens—must call for restraint. Neither Cicero nor St. Augustine in their wildest dreams could have imagined the shape of modern war.

FOR DISCUSSION

1. The recommendations of the International Crisis Group did not influence U.S. policies toward ISIS. Describe a U.S. anti-terrorism policy that might have been implemented reflecting an ICG recommendation.

2. Some claim that civilians in foreign wars the United States are fighting are actually supporting their countries' war efforts and should be treated as combatants. Where should the line be drawn between civilians and soldiers?

3. What safeguards would you suggest that should be in place to protect civilians in wartime?

4. How can negotiations with terrorist organizations be undertaken? What are the limits to working with them?

5. The JWT was intended to prevent war but has failed. Why? Would you add any additional criteria?

6. The Geneva Conventions require the humane treatment of surrendering enemy combatants who become prisoners of war. The United States claims that such treatment did not apply to those who are believed to have masterminded or participated in the 9/11 attacks. Why should or should not they be exempt from the protections required by the Geneva Conventions to provide humane treatment of prisoners of war?

7. How can people on the "other side" come to be recognized as people "just like us"?

8. What conditions are most likely to feed terrorism?

9. "One side's terrorists are the other side's freedom fighters." How does this saying apply to what you read and what advice does it offer?

Chapter 2

Mohandas Gandhi, the Father of Modern Nonviolence

Modern nonviolence began in South Africa where Mohandas Gandhi (1869–1948) led a movement to secure the rights of Indian workers there and then returned to India where he fostered the activism that led to its independence. Gandhi forged nonviolent means of securing justice without resorting to violence. His keen political instincts arose from his ever-deepening spiritual well. His life became increasingly transparent, his personal-spiritual life fusing with his public–political life.

EARLY LIFE AND SOUTH AFRICA

Gandhi was born in the state of Gujarat in western India into a merchant class family. His childhood was unremarkable. At the age of thirteen, he was married to Kasturbai, which was an arranged marriage. The marriage was at first stormy, for Gandhi was taught that husbands must rule their wives. Kasturbai would not obey, regardless of his attempts to force her. It would take him years to realize that male dominance over women was a form of violence.

Gandhi had grown up admiring all things British. When he was eighteen, his family arranged for him to study law in London. Now was his opportunity to become every bit the British gentleman. Gandhi was not a practicing Hindu, although his mother was very pious. Now away from Hindu culture, he took an interest in Hindu sacred texts, particularly the Bhagavad Gita. In addition, he read the New Testament and became an admirer of Jesus and his teachings.

When Gandhi returned to India from London, he found no employment and accepted an offer to serve as an attorney for a Muslim trading firm in Durban, South Africa. But soon after he arrived, an incident occurred that changed his life. Gandhi was on a night train in a first-class coach. A conductor ordered him to leave the "whites only" coach. When Gandhi refused, he was thrown off at the next station. Gandhi became painfully aware that education did not permit one to cross the color line. What had happened that night had steeled his determination to fight discrimination against Indians.

The white South African government passed legislation discriminating against indentured Indians who had come to South Africa to work in mines and fields. Indians had been promised that after five years they would be allowed to remain. But a prohibitively high annual tax of three pounds was assessed on Indians who wished to remain in South Africa. Other laws applicable only to Indians were passed, requiring that they had to carry passes at all times and prohibiting them from moving between states. The ultimate humiliation was the denial of the legitimacy of any but Christian marriages.

Gandhi organized a host of protests. He planned a civil disobedience campaign, the public burning of government passes (for which he was clubbed by a policeman when he refused to stop), a women's march across state borders, and strikes by coal miners and rail workers. Various forms of nonviolent resistance lasted for eight years, until the passage of the Indian Relief Act (1914) that repealed the tax, the pass laws, the prohibition of travel by Indians, and the marriage law. Reflective of Gandhi's respect for his political opponents throughout those years was a lifelong friendship he formed with Prime Minister Jan Smuts with whom he had long contended. In 1914, Gandhi, Kasturbai, and their four sons returned to India. The stage was set for the next thirty-four years of nonviolent activism to achieve India's independence.

GANDHI'S PRINCIPLES

Gandhi came to realize that his desire to experience the divine required an active commitment to the liberation of the poor and oppressed. Discipline was at the center of how he came to live. The *Bhagavad Gita*'s teachings on renunciation and control of the ego formed his convictions. Gandhi described the consequences of an unprincipled life and untamed ego:

> He who is ever brooding over results ever loses nerve in the performance of duty. He becomes impatient and then gives vent to anger and begins to do unworthy things; he jumps from action to action, never remaining faithful to any. He who broods over results is like a man given to the objects of senses; he is ever-distracted, he says good-bye to all scruples, everything is right in his estimation and he therefore resorts to means fair and foul to attain his end. (Fischer 1954, p. 18)

Gandhi linked inner and outer life through the term he coined, *satyagraha*. *Sat* is translated variously as God, truth, or changeless reality. *Agraha* means intense struggle. The practice of *satyagraha* requires two disciplines: *ahimsa* (non-harm, non-injury) and *tapasya* (self-sacrifice, self-suffering, the deepest form of love). Gandhi called *Satyagraha* and *ahimsa* two sides of the same coin. The fruit of *satyagraha*, *ahimsa*, and *tapasya* is *moksha*, the liberation of self and others from the prison of ego. Gandhi's religious inspiration was eclectic, drawing from Jesus' Sermon on the Mount and Tolstoy's pacificism, He said he appreciated the Qur'an, and called Buddha the greatest teacher of *ahimsa* (Rynne 2008, pp. 23–25, 28–29).[1]

These principles shaped Gandhi's extraordinary-ordinary life of action. "Extraordinary" because of the degree of his ego-mastery and "ordinary" in the sense that Gandhi led only a few political campaigns and resisted celebrity status. Gandhi was both an ascetic and an activist. He chose to remain a poor man, in solidarity with the millions of his fellow Indians. He never held political office. As his moral stature grew, he won the hearts of Indians. Gandhi was adamant that means and ends are organic; an unknown German philosopher wrote that means are ends in embryo.[2] Gandhi's life demonstrated that only good can overcome evil.

GANDHI'S NONVIOLENT CAMPAIGNS IN INDIA[3]

It may come as a surprise that Gandhi led only a few large-scale movements. While these were of great importance, his speaking and voluminous writing were also means by which he taught nonviolence and influenced his countrymen. Here are the four of his *satyagrahis'* campaigns.

1917 The Bihar State Campaign against Economic Exploitation

Shortly after his return to India, Gandhi was approached by a man from the state of Bihar in northeast India who implored him to come and help the impoverished farmers. Gandhi went to Bihar, where he saw tenant farmers suffering a cruel economic injustice at the hand of British plantation owners. As many as a million Bihari sharecroppers worked on these farms. They were required to grow indigo on 15 percent of their small plots of land and turn it over to their landlords as rent. But when synthetic dye replaced indigo, growing indigo was no longer profitable. Landowners raised sharecroppers' rents, which they could not pay. Gandhi gathered the farmers and encouraged them to agitate. He was ordered by authorities to leave the state, and when he refused, was arrested for inciting violence. He was tried and found guilty.

On the day of his sentencing, several hundred farmers gathered to demand his release. Fearing a riot, the police implored Gandhi to calm the crowd. He did, and his case was dismissed. Gandhi remained there for several months to ensure rent decreases and partial return of the higher rents already paid. Gandhi encouraged farmers to become self-sufficient; they organized and recruited local lawyers to help them resist any future injustices.

Gandhi called poverty the worst form of violence. He initiated what he called "village uplift," in which volunteers worked in villages offering education in hygiene, health, literacy, improvement in the status of women, and means of improving their economic situation. Regardless of whether political campaign goals were met, successful village uplift was a lasting victory, essential for future Indian self-rule.

1919 The British Rowlatt Acts Suppressing Indians' Civil Rights

Having supported the British in World War I, Indians believed that Britain would grant India independence after the War. Instead, the Imperial Legislative Council in New Delhi passed the Rowlatt Acts banning political rallies, prohibiting the distribution of political literature, and curtailing free speech. Gandhi denounced this denial of Indians' civil rights, organized protests, a three-day national strike, and distributed banned literature. But when sporadic violence broke out across the country Gandhi halted the protests, calling them a "Himalayan miscalculation" because some participants were not trained in nonviolence. Henceforth, they must be. To purify future actions he fasted, blaming himself for the "miscalculation."

Ironically, the Rowlatt legislation would contribute to Indian independence in an unexpected and tragic way. In the city of Amritsar, a large crowd of Indians had peacefully gathered in an enclosed park, in violation of the Rowlett Acts. A government rifle corps entered the park, blocking its only exit. They fired into the crowd, killing almost 400 and injuring 1,100. British authorities were shamed. Though the Rowlatt Acts were not repealed, they were never again enforced.

1924–1925 The Vykom Temple Campaign against Religious Discrimination

Gandhi strongly condemned discrimination against untouchables, whom Gandhi called the *harijans*, "children of God." High-caste Hindus believed that proximity to untouchables was polluting and had a barricade erected to prevent untouchables from passing in front of a temple. The detour made the lives of the *harijans* that much harder. *Satyagrahis* set up a picket line at the entrance of the forbidden road and remained there for sixteen months, even during a monsoon season in which they stood in shoulder-high water or sat in boats. Picketers were arrested. But eventually, a mix of caste groups joined the demonstrations and collected 25,000 signatures and presented them to the head of the state who ordered Vykom officials to open the road to all.[4]

1930 The Salt March and the Dharsana Salt Works Acts of Defiance

In March of 1930, Gandhi, now sixty-one years old, wrote a letter to the British Viceroy, Lord Irwin, asking him to remove the Salt Law, a state monopoly on the production, sale, and taxation of salt. In his letter, Gandhi pointed out that in India's hot climate, perspiring manual laborers especially required that their salt levels be replenished frequently. The salt tax, he argued, was one example of a great economic injustice of the British occupation. The salt tax helped pay for the high cost of the British administration of the country. The viceroy's annual salary, Gandhi noted, was 5,000 times that of an Indian peasant. The only reply he received from the Viceroy's office was a short note confirming that his letter had been received. Gandhi wrote the Viceroy a second time, giving him notice that Indians would stage a campaign of civil disobedience if the Salt Law was not repealed. He received no response. Gandhi then planned a march that would culminate in mass civil disobedience. With a group of *satyagrahis*, he began a 230-mile walk to the Indian Ocean. They walked for twenty-four days, joined by thousands of supporters as the march passed through villages. Suspense rose: what would the government do? Would the march be stopped by the British army? It was superb theater. Marchers arrived at the Indian Ocean, and thousands of people committed civil disobedience by boiling sea water down to salt. Thousands of Indian leaders were immediately jailed. That would prove unwise since the government was left with no one with whom to negotiate. Gandhi was arrested a week later.

Three weeks later, several hundred *satyagrahis* assembled at the entrance of the Dharsana Salt Works, intending to stop the government's production of salt. Gandhi was not able to participate because at that point he was still in jail. Row after row of *satyagrahis* tried to enter and were clubbed, but did not resist. Foreign journalists witnessed the grisly scene and posted the story around the world. Louis Fischer, an American journalist, described what occurred and its impact:

> When the Indians allowed themselves to be beaten with batons and rifle butts and did not cringe, they showed that England was powerless and India invincible. The rest was merely a matter of time. (Fischer 1954, p. 102)

This resort to violence was a tipping point. Britain had lost its moral legitimacy to rule India. Gandhi insisted to the growing number of satyagrahis that India's freedom was assured if they embraced nonviolence.

Norwegian sociologist Johan Galtung (1930–) is a great admirer of Gandhi, recalling that as a teenager he heard the news of Gandhi's assassination and wept. Galtung went on to become a prominent Gandhi scholar. He provides an excellent summary of Gandhi's nonviolent principles and strategies. Galtung identifies six systemic evils that Gandhi addressed: colonialism, racism, caste oppression, economic exploitation, religious animosity between Hindus and Muslims, and the oppression of women.

Galtung describes what might be called Gandhi's "rules of engagement" (Galtung 1992, pp. 169–209).[5]

1. Do not delay action until perfect conditions exist; act even without perfect knowledge.
2. Refuse to cooperate with evil customs and structures.
3. If imprisoned, manifest a nonviolent spirit toward jailers.
4. Seek to eradicate evil, not those who commit it.
5. Seek to understand an opponent's stance and to empathize.
6. Choose means that are least likely to escalate the conflict.
7. Do not provoke or humiliate adversaries.
8. Remain in contact and conversation with adversaries.
9. Articulate goals clearly and simply and recognize that injustice is dismantled in increments, one step at a time. Exercise patience.
10. Do not assume that opponents cannot change; instead, assume their inherent goodness which will require time to be manifested. Mutual transformation is the goal.
11. Nonviolent warriors must be willing to compromise on nonessentials. They must recognize their own fallibility.
12. Refusing to change one's convictions when evidence warrants is not a virtue; be willing to change even if one is accused of weakness.
13. Be more self-critical than critical of opponents.
14. Conversion rather than coercion is the ultimate goal of resolving conflict.

Gandhi sought to avoid "victories" that merely reversed the power holders' positions, whereby the oppressed become the oppressors.

Galtung describes Gandhian strategies and tactics:

1. Analyze the situations; explain grievances, using the media.
2. Stir the community to agitate.
3. Work to open negotiations.
4. Organize demonstrations.

5. Organize boycotts and strikes.[6]
6. Organize noncooperation with the government.
7. Commit acts of civil disobedience, accepting the penalties.
8. Make community improvement ("village uplift") an integral part of the struggle.

Here is the rich creativity of nonviolent social, political, and economic activism. Galtung concludes: "It is difficult to envisage a more complete challenge to any social order. . . . The miracle is that so much succeeded, not that some tasks were left unfinished" (Galtung 1992, p. 12). The strategies and tactics Gandhi pioneered would be adopted by many activists who followed him. One of them, Martin Luther King Jr., professed that he learned a great deal from Gandhi; indeed, Gandhi and King are hailed as the great nonviolent activists of the twentieth century.

It is important to note Gandhi's affirmation of other faiths. He welcomed non-Hindus to his prayer services, recited scriptural passages from other religious traditions, and included their hymns.[7] Among his closest friendships were those with C. F. Andrews, an Anglican priest, who was a close friend of Gandhi, as was Khan Abdul Gaffar Khan, a Muslim.[8] Khan's people, the Pathans, had long made war on the British to drive them from the Indian Northwest Frontier. Khan worked to create a nonviolent culture, saying of the Pathans, "I want to show the world how beautiful [the Pathans] are, these people from the hills, and then I want to proclaim: show me, if you can, any gentler, more courteous, more cultured people than these" (Easwaran 1989, frontispiece). Khan traveled to some 300 mountainous villages establishing schools and promoting public health and women's empowerment. In 1929, Khan established a movement called the "Servants of God," a nonviolent army that grew to a hundred thousand Pathans. The Servants took an oath to do God's work for humanity, to renounce external and internal violence, and to do two hours of social work each day (Easwaran 1989, pp. 121–122). He wrote: "To me nonviolence has come to represent a panacea for all the evils that surround my people, a powerful, socially benign force equal to but opposite to the destructive force in the Pathan temperament and culture" (Easwaran 1989, p. 196).

In 1930, the British imprisoned Khan for three years, and in 1935 banished him from the Northwest Frontier. Gandhi called the Pathans' nonviolence and fearlessness a source of courage and spiritual power. Both he and Khan recognized the strength of the poor that needed to be unleashed. When Pakistan was created in 1947, Khan was imprisoned there for fifteen years, and his Servants of God were suppressed for "sowing unrest." Khan died in 1988. Sadly, governments often lack wisdom to see constructive and nonviolent allies with whom to achieve justice and peace.

Mahatma Gandhi was a subject of the British Empire. At first, he supported its wars. While Gandhi was living in South Africa, British forces fought Dutch forces for control of several South African states (the Boer War, 1899–1902). Gandhi organized an ambulance corps in support of the British forces. His intention was both humanitarian and to demonstrate the courage and loyalty of the Indian community. He again supported Britain in World War I, believing that the British commitment to freedom and democracy would bring India's independence at the end of the war. But the Rowlatt Acts imposed martial law and British brutality was manifested in the massacre at Amritsar, the beatings of unarmed *satyagrahis* at the salt works, and the arrests of thousands of Indians.

By the time World War II was on the horizon, Gandhi had concluded that all Western nations were unprincipled and pursued their national interests through violence. His stance was that India remains neutral. When Japan's aggression broke out, Gandhi was challenged with the question of how India could defend itself. Gandhi's strategy was noncooperation, rendering India ungovernable and a futile waste of Japanese military resources badly needed elsewhere. However, most Indian politicians supported the Allies, believing again that India's wartime support would be rewarded with independence. The exception was a small number of politicians who sided with the Germans and Japan, in order to force Britain's hand. The British recruited two and a half million Indians into the British Indian Army (BIA).

NONVIOLENT RESISTANCE TO THE THIRD REICH?

When it came to Hitler, Gandhi believed that the Fuehrer could change and made this appeal in 1939:

> Friends have been urging me to write to you for the sake of humanity. But I have resisted their request, because of the feeling that any letter from me would be an impertinence. Something tells me that I must not calculate and that I must make my appeal for whatever it may be worth. It is quite clear that you are today the one person in the world who can prevent a war which may reduce humanity to the savage state. Must you pay that price for an object however worthy it may appear to you to be? Will you listen to the appeal of one who has deliberately shunned the method of war not without considerable success? Anyway I anticipate your forgiveness, if I have erred in writing to you.

The Fuehrer did not respond. Germany invaded Czechoslovakia two months later, and then Poland. Could the growing power of the Nazis be checked by the German people before the Third Reich achieved total power?

The responses of the German Churches reflect the depths of their denial and their motivation for self-protection. In *German Catholics and Hitler's War: A Study in Social Control*, Gordon Zahn examined the pastoral letters of German Catholic bishops to German Catholics prior to and during World War II. What he found was continuous stress on the duty of Catholic soldiers to defend the *volk* and the *vaterland* and the assurance that to suffer and die for the nation was honorable and even holy, mirroring the suffering of Christ. Their emphasis was on defending the greatness of German culture. Zahn found that the German bishops never raised the question of whether Hitler's war was just. Instead, were "official religious controls exerted on the individual Catholic to assure his conformity with the demands of the Nazi's war effort" (Zahn 1979, p. 158).

The exception to support of the Third Reich was the "Confessing Church," which Dietrich Bonhoeffer helped to found in 1938. That Church confessed that Jesus Christ alone was Lord and Savior and condemned the worship of Hitler and Aryanism as idolatry. It was a small movement, but after the war, it was recognized as the expression of German Christianity's true north.

What could other German institutions have done to effectively oppose Hitler? Civil societies such as trade unions, sports clubs, charitable organizations, medical societies, hundreds of such organizations could have used their influence to shape public opposition. Two prestigious institutions that cooperated with the Third Reich were the orchestras of Berlin and Vienna. Hitler loved classical music, intending to make German music and arts celebrations of Aryan culture. At the Reich's orders, both orchestras stopped performing the works of Jewish composers and dismissed Jewish musicians. Terry Teachout writes:

> The Berlin Philharmonic was placed under the direct supervision of Joseph Goebbels . . . exempting [musicians] from military service and guaranteeing their old-age pensions. But there had never been any serious question of protest, any more than there was by the Vienna Philharmonic . . . [S]even of the Vienna Philharmonic's 11 Jews were either murdered by the Nazis or died as a direct result of official persecution. In addition, both orchestras performed regularly at official government functions and made tours and other public appearances for propaganda purposes, and both were treated as gems in the diadem of Nazi culture. (Teachout 2017, n.p.)

One effective protest occurred in Berlin in 1943. The Gestapo had rounded up several hundred Jewish men married to Aryan women. Before they could be deported to the death camps, their wives staged a protest in front of the Gestapo headquarters in Berlin for several days. The government released their husbands because the Reich did not want its persecution of Jews to become more widely known. However, a tragic sequel to their release was the Gestapo's re-arrest of the men at night and their immediate deportation.

There were few organized protests against the persecution of German Jews. After the war, Sabina Bonhoeffer, the twin sister of Dietrich Bonhoeffer, was asked why so many Germans had been silent as Nazi power increased. She recounted what happened to her in 1942, when having learned of the Nazi's "final solution," she tried to tell others. One day in line at a store she spoke up loudly. But others cautioned her to be silent, especially in public, for it was very dangerous. Sabina compared the Nazis to a poisonous snake that would strike its prey from behind. Eventually, it had become too dangerous and futile to try to oppose the Reich.

Most of the German people failed to act. After the war, Martin Niemoeller, a Lutheran pastor, reflected on the passivity:

> When the Nazis came for the Communists I kept silent; I was not a communist. As they imprisoned the social democrats I kept silent; I was not a social democrat. When they came for the trade union people I did not protest; I was not in the trade union. When they came for me there was nobody left to protest.[9]

But outside of Germany active resistance occurred. In Denmark, Jews were protected by Danes and rescued in parts of occupied France.

NONVIOLENT RESISTANCE IN OCCUPIED DENMARK

Germany occupied Denmark from 1940 until the end of the war. At first, the Danish government signed an armistice agreeing to cooperate with the occupation in return for limited autonomy. But the Danish population began to actively oppose the occupation. Danish king Christian X refused to fly the Nazi flag. A teenager named Arne Sejr wrote "The Ten Commandments for Denmark," describing ways Danes could resist in their daily lives, including boycotting products made in Germany and Italy. Danes who cooperated with Germans must be shunned (Musynske 2009, n.p.). Five hundred and fifty underground newspapers sprang up across Denmark encouraging Danes to actively resist. Workers slowed down production. The German Navy desperately needed ships that Danish ship builders in Copenhagen were required to deliver. But workers made "mistakes" that prevented the completion of ships. They began to walk out of the shipyard at noon with the excuse that they needed to tend their gardens at that time since the curfew imposed during the occupation made it impossible to garden after work. Unfinished ships had to be towed to German shipyards. Acts of sabotage began. German vehicles were disabled with sugar in gas tanks. At night empty buildings were torched and railroad tracks destroyed.[10]

The Germans gave the Danish Parliament an ultimatum to stop the resistance. In response, the parliament dissolved itself. Now there was no Danish leadership to enforce compliance with German demands. Eventually, an estimated 45,000 Danes actively protested.

In 1943, German plans were in place to deport Danish Jews. Knowing the Danish opposition, German officials decided to round up Jews clandestinely on the night of Rosh Hashanah, when Jewish families would be together. But when the plan came to light, Danes swiftly spirited almost all Jews in Denmark to neutral Sweden. In 1942 John Steinbeck had published *The Moon Is Down*, a novella that offered hope across occupied Europe that occupations were unsustainable and would be defeated.[11]

THE RESCUE OF JEWS IN SOUTHERN FRANCE

In May of 1940, Germany invaded France. On Saturday, June 23, France surrendered and signed an armistice that divided the country into two zones, a northern and western zone under direct German control, and a so-called "Free Zone" in the south, headquartered in Vichy. Marshall Philipe Petain's puppet government in the Free Zone passed anti-Semitic laws to identify and hand over Jews. When France fell, there were 350,000 Jews in France, half of them foreign born. In Paris, roundups and internments of Jews began in 1940.

The Christian response to Nazism in Le Chambon and the surrounding area was sharply different than in Germany. The day after the armistice was signed, André Trocmé, pastor of the Protestant church in Le Chambon in the Vichy-controlled south, read a declaration from his pulpit:

> Tremendous pressure will be put on us to submit passively to a totalitarian ideology. If they do not succeed in subjugating our souls, at least they will want to subjugate our bodies. The duty of Christians is to use the weapons of the Spirit to oppose the violence that they will try to put on our consciences. We appeal to all our brothers in Christ to refuse to cooperate with this violence. . . . Loving, forgiving, and doing good to our adversaries are our duty. Yet, we must do this without giving up, and without being cowardly. The duty of Christians is to resist violence that will be brought to bear on their consciences. With weapons of the spirit we will resist when demanded what is contrary to the Gospels. We will do so without pride or hate. (Young 2005, p. 1)

The area comprises small towns and farms located on a 3,000-foot plateau. It is 135 miles from Vichy. Many of its people are descendants of

Huguenots, the first in France to convert to Protestantism, for which they were persecuted by the Catholic Church.[12] They regarded the Jews as *le peuple de Dieu*, the first to receive God's promises.

André Trocmé (1901–1971) became pastor of the Protestant church in Le Chambon in 1934. He and his wife Magda (1901–1996) had met in New York after WWI, where he was studying for the ministry and she was preparing for a career in social work.[13] They were familiar with Gandhi and had hoped to visit India. Both were pacifists. André accepted a church position in northern France and in Le Chambon in 1934. In 1938, pastor Édouard Theis and his wife Mildred, also pacifists, arrived. Theis would serve as the first headmaster of the school founded by the Trocmés and Theises, the l'École Nouvelle Cévenole. Roger Darcissac, a parishioner and headmaster of the public school for boys, was also a pacifist. Although most of the congregation did not share their pastors' pacifism, they agreed that they should neither attack German soldiers nor collaborate with them. Whatever image "pacifism" might conjure, what the pastors would encourage over the four years of occupation was anything but passive.

In the winter of 1941, Magda Trocmé welcomed a desperate Jewish woman who knocked on the parish house door. Magda hid her. More Jews arrived and were welcomed and hidden in villages and on plateau farms.[14] The women's work has been called their kitchen project, for it was women who arranged hiding of Jews while their husbands were working in the fields. The École Nouvelle Cévenole proved very useful for hiding Jews because it drew international students with many different accents. The student body swelled from 18 to 350 students during the occupation.

Rescue efforts became increasingly dangerous after the Germans took direct control of the "Free Zone" in 1942. Unannounced raids by the French police and Gestapo began. Being careful and discreet were essential. In London General Charles de Gaulle had established a French government-in-exile and organized a guerrilla force called the *maquis* ("resistance"). The nonviolent people of the plateau had to contend not only with the Gestapo but also with the violent *maquis* fighting a guerrilla war all around them. If the Germans had identified the nonviolent rescuers as *maquis* sympathizers, they too would have been arrested and deported. But the rescuers were saving the lives of Jews without taking the lives of Germans. In 1945, retreating German troops murdered French in towns known to have supported the guerillas. None of the rescuers' towns suffered that fate. In the five years of the occupation, an estimated 5,000 refugees, among them at least 3,500 Jews, found shelter among this stock of caring Protestants—and among some Catholics, some Jews and atheists as well. The Chambonnais exemplified generosity. After the war, Jews expressed both gratitude and awe at the extent to which hospitality was extended to them. The Jews had been encouraged to observe the Sabbath and high holydays. Never was it suggested that their Jewish guests convert to Christianity.[15]

It was a blot on France that an estimated 75,000 Jews were deported to their deaths. Many Frenchmen did not speak out. But it is estimated that an equal number of Jews survived because of those who did care (Henry 2007).

Villagers did not delay but moved quickly into action. They did not wait for assurance that outside groups would help them. As Gandhi said, sometimes action is required without perfect knowledge. They gave little consideration to the danger in which they were putting themselves. They did not weigh helping Jews against protecting their own families. They shared their rationed food.

After the war, Pastor Theis was asked an all-important question: could Russia have used nonviolent means to prevent the war that took ten million Russian lives? He responded:

> It was too late then. Both the Germans and the Russians were *embarqués*, committed to mass murder. . . . Nonviolence involves preparation and organization, methods patiently and unswervingly employed—the Russians knew nothing of all this. Nonviolence must have deep roots and strong branches before it can bear the fruit it bore in Le Chambon. Nonviolence for them would have been suicide; it was too late. (Hallie 1979, pp. 34–35)

Gandhi's and his nonviolent army's determination to achieve justice and reconciliation sometimes failed. Most tragically was what happened on the eve of India's independence. Hindus and Muslims had been stirred by politicians to deathly fear one another. Muslim politicians insisted that a Muslim state, Pakistan, had to be created if Muslims were to be safe. In the last year of his life, Gandhi worked feverishly to put out the fire of growing animosity between Hindus and Muslims and to prevent the partition of India. He called it a "vivisection" that would kill both India and Pakistan. Gandhi spent the last several months of his life trying to overcome sectarianism. "Thirty-two years of work," he said, "have come to an inglorious end" (Fischer 1954, p. 175). But even in the aftermath of the tragic breakup of the country, Gandhi worked for reconciliation, insisting that the Indian government transfer 550 million rupees (the equivalent of $125 million) to the fledgling government of Pakistan. He also insisted that the new Indian constitution guarantee freedom of religion. Then he was assassinated by a Hindu fundamentalist.

Gandhi inspired future activists who learned from him to oppose their adversaries nonviolently. Eknath Easwaran writes of Gandhi's activism:

> Again and again when the violence around him seemed impossible to face, he flung himself into battle without thought of personal consolation or safety, and every time, at the eleventh hour, some deeper power within him would flood

him with new reserves of energy and love. . . . By the end of his life he was aflame with love . . . free from the ego cage of *I* and *mine* to be united with the Lord of Love. (Easwaran 1972, p. 89)

Though later nonviolent activists may not have expressed themselves in this way, they too refused to hate even their most aggressive adversaries. Gandhi's followers liberated India without killing a single Englishman. The Danes and the people on the French plateau rescued Jews without killing a single German.

The idea that he was a saint would have riled Gandhi. He would have wanted to be remembered as a man struggling to find God, to work for justice, and to "turn the spotlight inward" often.

Albert Einstein left Germany as the violence of Nazism was growing, as well as the violence of fascism elsewhere in Europe. Being familiar with the Salt March the year before, he penned a letter to Mr. Gandhi. In it, he expressed his hope that "we can conquer the votaries of violence by nonviolent methods." He wrote that "your example will inspire and help humanity to put an end to a conflict based on violence" (Einstein 1931). The chapters ahead illustrate how Gandhi's example has and will continue to inspire.

FOR DISCUSSION

1. How is "power" to be understood in terms of nonviolence?
2. Do Gandhi's philosophy of nonviolence require a religious foundation?
3. Imagine an issue and an opponent with whom you are interacting. Describe his or her difficult temperament. How would you apply the Gandhian principles to work successfully with him or her?
4. In Gandhi's historical struggles, what conflicts were hardest to resolve? Why?
5. Gandhi was an extraordinary human being. What is required for "ordinary" human beings to follow his way?

Chapter 3

Successful Nonviolent Revolutions

THE PHILIPPINES' "PEOPLE POWER";
POLAND'S "SOLIDARITY"; EAST GERMANY'S
RESISTANCE TO COMMUNISM; SERBIA'S
"OTPOR"; TUNISIA'S "ARAB SPRING";
AND WOMEN'S LIBERATION OF LIBERIA

Erica Chenoweth and Maria Stephan compared the success rates of violent and nonviolent resistance to corrupt regimes. They identified 323 resistance movements between 1900 and 2006 and were able to gather sufficient information to examine 259 of them. Nonviolent campaigns succeeded twice as often Chenoweth and Stephan conclude that "nonviolent resistance is almost twice as likely to succeed," 52 percent as opposed to 26 percent cases of violent resistance (Chenoweth and Stephan 2011, p. 7). Why? They offer several hypotheses. First, nonviolent campaigns attract more participants because they are less dangerous to join. Second, nonviolence "enhances a campaign's domestic and international legitimacy." Third, nonviolent activists are more sympathetically received, especially if regimes use violence against them. Fourth, nonviolent behavior projects reasonableness and a willingness to negotiate. Fifth, regimes reliant on military support can lose it very quickly if soldiers defect.

The campaigns described below illustrate the power of nonviolence. A participant once observed that nonviolent struggles are often underestimated. Regimes ignore them, then become worried and oppress them, then turn to force which undermines the regimes. "First they laughed at us, then they mocked us, then they beat us, then we won." The outcomes of nonviolent victories are more likely to be stable governments that respect rights and uphold democratic principles. The nonviolent means they displayed are more likely to produce just social order. The following nonviolent revolutions describe the contexts in which campaigns developed, their strategies, and why they worked.

"PEOPLE POWER" IN THE PHILIPPINES

Ferdinand Marcos won the presidency in 1965, and for two decades his family and cronies amassed millions of dollars. Opposition to his corruption grew, and in 1972, Marcos declared martial law, which lasted until 1980. His most powerful political opponent was Benigno Aquino, who was most likely to challenge Marcos in the 1986 election. But Marcos had imprisoned Aquino for eight years, but then allowed him to go to the United States for medical treatment. On the day Aquino returned to the Philippines, he was assassinated on the airport tarmac. Cardinal Jaime Sin of Manila presided at Aquino's funeral, declaring him a "national martyr."

The Catholic Church was the sole power that Marcos had to fear and had been unable to silence. Sin and the Catholic Bishops Conference of the Philippines were his nemesis, but he did not dare to attack them directly. The bishops issued several letters increasingly critical of Marcos. Cardinal Sin encouraged Benigno's widow, Corazon Aquino, to run in the 1986 presidential election, with Salvador Laurel, another candidate for the presidency, as her running mate, in order not to split the vote. Fearing widespread voting fraud by Marcos, the cardinal established vote monitoring offices to tally vote totals and report instances of fraud. The bishops wrote a pastoral letter encouraging voting for candidates who were honest and would protect human rights. When asked if voters could accept bribes offered by Marcos for their votes, the bishops said yes; after all, it was their own money that had been stolen by Marcos. Their only obligation was to vote their consciences. Marcos lost the election but declared himself the winner and was inaugurated three days later. Trying to curry favor with the bishops, Marcos's wife Imelda desperately sought an audience with Cardinal Sin to plead for the Church's backing. Instead, the Church issued a pastoral letter claiming that the Marcos government was illegitimate. Aquino spoke at a rally of two million people in Manila. In the face of this crisis, Filipinos staged strikes, boycotts, and withdrew their money from banks owned by Marcos's cronies.

But a potential violent force that could undercut nonviolent efforts was the New People's Army waiting in the wings to stage a coup. In addition, several military officers were planning a coup. But their plot was discovered. Marcos made a mistake by waiting twenty-four hours to arrest the officers, misjudging his control. What Cardinal Sin did next would save the officers' lives and bring the Marcos regime down. It was a Saturday and the Cardinal directed priests in Manila at the Saturday evening Masses to urge the faithful to assemble the next morning on the causeway separating the Presidential Palace from the defense headquarters. On Sunday morning several thousand Filipinos responded, blocking Marcos's forces from advancing on the defectors. Marcos's military forces refused to attack the crowd. Marcos's power collapsed that day in the face of "people power." Ironically, the military officers planning the violent coup were saved by the nonviolent masses.

Corazon Aquino assumed the presidency a few days later, ending two decades of dictatorship.[1] The New People's Army did not have a chance to play a role that might have led to a government no better than Marcos's had been. The ousting of President Ferdinand Marcos in 1986 is a case study of a disciplined citizenry overcoming a dictatorship without firing a shot.

POLAND'S AND EAST GERMANY'S VICTORY AGAINST COMMUNISM

Poland was occupied by Nazi Germany from 1939 to 1945. After the war, the Soviet Union emerged and the Polish Communist party took control of Poland. Poles lost their rights, as did all citizens of the nations in the Soviet bloc. In the 1950s, 900 priests, several bishops, and the cardinal of Poland were imprisoned. By the late 1960s, the country faced economic collapse. In 1970, workers at the Gdansk shipyard went on strike and marched in protest to the Communist Party headquarters. A Molotov cocktail was thrown through a window, starting a fire. Police opened fire, killing an estimated 300 workers.[2]

The government clamped down harder. But in 1979, a Pole became Pope John Paul II. On his trip home that year he lectured the government on the protection of rights. In 1980, a second strike was organized in the shipyard. This time the lessons of 1970 had been learned. Workers did not leave the shipyard, in order to avoid a clash with government forces. The movement called "Solidarity" was born. Workers chose strictly nonviolent tactics. Among the strike organizers were Lech Walesa and Alana Piérkowska. On the first day of the strike, she stood at the factory gates with a megaphone urging workers leaving at the end of their shift to remain and join the strike. They stayed. Citizens handed food over the fences, and priests offered Masses. Piérkowska was one of the many women who worked in the shipyard and participated in the negotiations that followed. Solidarity made twenty-one formal demands of the government, including:

1. guaranteeing free trade unions independent from Communist Party control, the right of workers to strike, and freedom of speech and the press;
2. reinstating workers fired after the 1970 strike and release of political prisoners;

3. permitting citizens (that is, non-communist party members) to participate in reform programs;
4. selecting factory management personnel based on qualifications, not party membership;
5. eliminating privileges for the state police, security services, and members of the Communist Party;
6. providing living wages to workers and larger allowances for families to buy essentials;
7. allowing men to retire at 55 and women at 50 and guaranteed pensions; providing paid maternity leave for three years and daycare for workers' children; and
8. observing Sunday as a day of rest.

After tough negotiations that the government had never faced before, it bowed to the demands. Lech Walesa described his convictions throughout the strike: "I am a believer, which is why I forgive blindly. The point is not to smash your head open in one day, but to win step by step, without offending anyone" (Craig 1987, 204). Mary Craig writes that Walesa "used words honestly and gave them a truthfulness that years of doublespeak had taken from them." The Gdansk strike soon spread to 400 other Polish factories.

But the victory of the strikers was short-lived when in 1981 the government imposed martial law, banned Solidarity, and imprisoned 5,000 Poles. But the Church kept Poles hopeful during this bleak time. In 1981, a young Catholic priest, Jerzy Popiełuszko, had been assigned as chaplain at a Warsaw University and a steel mill. He heard students' frustrations and saw workers' poverty. In 1982, Cardinal Josef Glemp, the Archbishop of Warsaw, initiated "Masses for the Fatherland" to pray for change. Fr. Popiełuszko was assigned to organize and officiate at the masses. He presided at them in Warsaw for two years, preaching increasingly harsh sermons aimed at the Communist government. He condemned its dishonesty and encouraged people to tell the truth. "Truth," he said, "contains within itself the ability to resist and to blossom in the light of day, even though the government tries to hide it" (Brian 2016, p. 35). A government that survives only by lies and violence will fail, he said. Gandhi would have agreed that truth, *sat,* was the most powerful force when pursued vigorously and nonviolently. Popiełuszko urged nonviolent struggle:

A regime that needs weapons to stay in power dies by itself. Its violence is proof of its moral inferiority. The responsibility of Polish Christians is to tell the truth about human dignity and the necessity of freedom. Freedom is a value that God has inscribed in man since his creation. As children of God we cannot be slaves. (Brian 2016, p. 61)

He asked the people to pray for soldiers "that they may never stain their uniforms and their honor by raising a hand against their nation" (Brian 2016, p. 82). Popiełuszko's message was love:

> Violence and hatred were conquered by the Lord's love. Let us therefore be powerful in love, by praying for our brothers who have gone astray, without condemning anyone, but while unmasking evil. We will go to the resurrection, to victory, through the cross; there is no other path. (Brian 2016, p. 88)

Popiełuszko's Masses drew ever-larger crowds. His homilies were recorded, smuggled out of Poland, and broadcast in Europe and throughout Poland, to the anger of the government. Cardinal Glemp feared for Popiełuszko's life and suggested that he leave the country and go to Rome to study. Popiełuszko refused, saying that he would not leave his country in such perilous times. Popiełuszko was about to experience an ultimate form of self-suffering (*tapasya*). He was arrested and interrogated several times. Then came anonymous death threats. Finally, in October 1984, he was kidnapped and murdered. His body was recovered in a river eleven days later, beaten beyond recognition. When his death was announced, crowds gathered in Warsaw churches. Among the prayers they said was the "Our Father." At the phrase "forgive us our trespasses as we forgive those who trespass against us" priests paused and repeated the words, to emphasize the call to forgive those who had killed Fr. Popiełuszko. Thousands of Poles turned out for Fr. Popiełuszko's funeral. In his eulogy, Lech Walesa expressed deep gratitude for Jerzy Popiełuszko's great courage, saying he had kept Solidarity alive during its darkest years. There was no violence that day to legitimate police violence.

The Communist government still believed it could retain power. But it continued to lose ground over the next five years and by 1989 was desperate to hold on to power. Its appeals to Moscow for tanks but was refused; the Soviet Union was itself on the verge of collapse. Polish officials were told to deal with their own problems themselves. It was too late. An election was called, and Lech Walesa won, becoming the first democratically elected president of Poland.

East Germany's nonviolent revolution bore similarities to Poland's.[3] At the end of WWII, Germany was partitioned into East and West Germany, as was Berlin. West Germany thrived as a democracy with a robust economy; East Germany was ruled by a Communist party and remained poor. By the 1960s, East Germans were increasingly opposing the government. Their government was hostile to the West; if a European nuclear war were to break out, East Germany would be the first target of short-range nuclear missiles.

East Germans were increasingly outspoken. The Lutheran Church was a calming force amid the tense political atmosphere. In the 1960s, it had initiated an annual program called "Ten Days of Peace," culminating in a national

"Day of Repentance." Now, in 1989, demonstrations and marches began in the city of Halle, protesting the poverty of the country. Activists found an imaginative way to stage marches while avoiding police intervention. Since marches were outlawed, protestors called them "religious processions," and moved from one church to the next, stopping to pray at each one. Citizens also did what was most worrisome to the government: they gathered to talk about the regime's failures and to propose reform. They demanded talks between the Communist bloc and the West to deescalate the arms race.

Throughout the growing citizen activism, the Lutheran Church urged activists to proceed nonviolently. When large crowds finally gathered in Halle, the Church used loudspeakers calling on crowds to remain nonviolent. By 1989, the communist government had lost popular support and collapsed. An irony was the regime's request to Church officials—whom it had loathed for years—to use their facilities to mediate a peaceful transfer of power. Protests were spreading throughout the Soviet bloc, gathering momentum from Poland's and East Germany's successes. By 1991, nonviolent protests had spread to Moscow and the Soviet Union soon collapsed.[4]

SERBIA'S OTPOR ("RESISTANCE")

After World War II, the Socialist Federal Republic of Yugoslavia was created, consisting of Serbia, Croatia, Albania, Bosnia-Herzegovina, Kosovo, and Montenegro. Ethnic animosities were long-standing but had been contained, at least until the Soviet Union collapsed. Slobodan Milosevic was president of both Serbia and the former Yugoslav Federal Republic. He deployed the Yugoslav army to keep the federation intact. But in rapid succession, Albania, Croatia, and Bosnia declared independence, and their sovereignty was recognized by Western nations. These small nations soon waged ethnic wars on one another; Kosovars (Muslims living in the Serb province of Kosovo) became targets of Serbian repression and expulsion. Milosevic, later called the "butcher of the Balkans," supported the uprising of Serbs in Croatia and Bosnia, intending to annex part of their territories to be part of "greater Serbia." Croatia was fighting to defend and extend a "greater Croatia." The Serb army attacked Muslims in Bosnia-Herzegovina. Paranoia, fear, and hatred led to massacres of civilians, destruction of entire towns, and ethnic cleansing—that is, genocide. The world witnessed widespread rape, a military tactic to dehumanize and traumatize women, humiliate men, and assert ethnic dominance. One hundred and fifty thousand people lost their lives in the Balkan Wars, the worst death toll since World War II. None of the belligerents were innocent, but Serbia was responsible for the majority of the atrocities. Two Serb generals were eventually tried and convicted in 1999 for war crimes and crimes against humanity by the International Criminal Court in The Hague.

In 1999, NATO nations bombed Belgrade for seventy-eight days hoping to depose Milosevic. The bombing campaign had a reverse effect, rallying Serbs around Milosevic. At that point, a nonviolent movement within Serbia called Otpor ("resistance") arose. Its founding members were mostly university and high school students. Otpor did not intend to stir Serbian nationalism once more. Its focus was on the suffering of Serbs under Milosevic's rule. Otpor was committed to a democratic Serbia. Srdja Popovic accused him of having taken away the best years of his generations' lives (Popovic 2000).[5] He also expressed Otpor's determination not to remain passive, as the older generation had, saying: "We are not victims but activists" (Popovic 2000). Through Otpor's rallies, flyers, and pamphlets, the movement grew. Though at first small, Otpor's leaders projected an image of a large and powerful movement, which persuaded people to join. Otpor's symbol was a black clenched fist. Its leaders appeared at rallies in black. Their methods remained strictly nonviolent. Seeing the potential of Otpor to oust Milosevic, the United States Institute of Peace supported Otpor with seminars on nonviolent strategies and also provided funds for computers. Otpor established satellite headquarters across the country; if the Belgrade office was shut down by the government, the movement would continue.

Otpor relentlessly called attention to Milosevic's incompetence, often through street theater mocking him. When people realized they could laugh at him in public, they began to lose their fear. After all, how could the government arrest thousands of people for what was not a crime? Otpor knew how to assemble a crowd. On New Year's Eve of 2000, it organized a rock concert in Belgrade with pop music the regime had banned. The concert concluded with the solemn projection of images of those who died in Milosevic's wars as the crowd stood in silence.

Milosevic moved up the presidential election, confident that he held sufficient power to win. Otpor members campaigned across Serbia feverishly; their slogan was "His [Milosevic's] time is up." Otpor pressured the anti-Milosevic political parties to give their support to a single candidate to challenge Milosevic. Otpor also established a computer network to track vote totals. Milosevic made a mistake, assuming that he did not need to campaign. The day after the election he declared himself the winner. But Otpor had tracked the voting and announced the real vote count. Protests broke out. Milosevic's security forces struck back, arresting and beating hundreds of protesters. A month later, a hundred thousand Serbs from across the country converged in Belgrade's parliament square demanding Milosevic's resignation. Again, Milosevic sent troops. But this time they defected. Not a shot was fired, and Milosevic was out.

In 2007, three leaders of OTPOR established the Centre for Applied Non-Violent Action and Strategies (CANVAS). They published *Nonviolent Struggle: 50 crucial points*, a workbook describing how to "organize, strategize, and carry out nonviolent action, so that you can win your rights, overcome repression, resist occupation, achieve democracy, and establish justice" (Popovic, Milivojevic, and Djuinovic 2007, p. 11). A crucial factor for the success of struggles everywhere is convincing large numbers of people to withdraw their cooperation and refuse to be obedient.

TUNISIA AND THE BEGINNING OF THE ARAB SPRING[6]

The uprising in Tunisia was triggered by the self-immolation of a poor street vendor, Mohamed Bouazizi, who had dropped out of high school to support his family. One day in December 2010, the police confiscated his cart and refused to return it. He took his own life. His death was symbolic of the hopelessness created by the country's poverty, the government's corruption, and "draconian repression" (Clancy-Smith 2013, p. 15). In January 2011, protests began in Tunisian cities. In Tunis, police and security forces killed an estimated fifty unarmed demonstrators.[7] Asaad al-Saleh quotes a student who wrote that the demonstrators "stood like an army ready to face the enemy" (Ghafar 2015, p. 28).

But when the chief of the Tunisian armed forces refused President ben Ali's order to attack the protestors, his government collapsed. Ben Ali, who had held power for twenty-four years, living lavishly with his family and cronies, fled to Saudi Arabia. Liberation was at hand because young Tunisians had overcome fear and organized massive demonstrations of students and workers. For the first time, social media was used to organize protests and convey truthful information to Tunisians and the world.[8] As was the case in Serbia, the energy of the young was critical. They were motivated and impatient for change. They saw their parents' suffering and sense of hopelessness. The younger generation was idealistic and determined not to live as prisoners in their own country. Youth are often more likely to be risk-takers. Most are not yet supporting families. In Tunisia as in Serbia, the dangers of political activism did not stop them—even though they knew that many would suffer. They deserved much credit in Serbia and Tunisia.

It is instructive to contrast the successful Arab Spring in Tunisia with its failure in Egypt. The protests that began in Cairo in January 2011 lasted for eighteen days, attracting thousands of young Egyptians and members of political and religious groups that had not previously collaborated. The campaign for democracy seemed hopeful. It succeeded in removing Egyptian president

Hosni Mubarak, who had enjoyed strong military support. But strong anti-democracy forces still were in place, namely, in the army and security forces. A fuller account of the complexities that weakened Egypt's Arab Spring is provided in Appendix 1.

WOMEN'S LIBERATION OF LIBERIA

In 1822, 15,000 freed slaves from the United States settled in Liberia and the Caribbean. In 1847, Liberia declared its independence and made Monrovia its capital.[9] By the 1920s, foreign companies were extracting Liberia's resources, paying Liberia almost nothing. Firestone, the U.S. tire-maker, had a 100-year lease on a million acres, growing rubber trees. At its height, 14,000 Liberians and Nigerians worked for Firestone under hazardous conditions for meager wages.[10]

The extraction of Liberia's resources contributed to the poverty and political instability of the country. Liberia struggled to modernize its economy and overcome corruption as warlord rivalries divided the country into violent factions. William Tolbert was elected as president in 1971 and assassinated in 1980 in a coup led by Samuel Doe, who initially had the support of the United States. Doe promised that military rule would be replaced with civilian rule by 1985, which did not happen. In 1992, the National Patriotic Front of Liberia led by Charles Taylor advanced on Monrovia and overthrew Doe, torturing and murdering him, videotaping, and broadcasting it to the country. Taylor promised reform but his brutality was soon worrisome. A political group called the Association for Constitutional Democracy was formed to moderate Taylor's violence. But his aggression spilled into Sierra Leone, where he fueled a civil war by supplying guerrillas with guns in exchange for diamonds. In 1997, Taylor won a fraudulent election against Ellen Johnson Sirleaf.

Liberia had suffered two civil wars (1989–1995 and 1997–2003) that claimed an estimated 500,000 lives and displaced one million Liberians. Child soldiers were recruited, rape was widespread, and brutality committed by rival groups was routine. In 2002, another violent group formed to remove Taylor, misnamed the Liberians United for Reconciliation and Democracy (LURD). Since 1994, a women's peacemaking organization called the Mano River Women's Network for Peace had been working to stop the regional violence along the Liberia, Sierra Leone, and Guinea borders. In 2002, a women's peace movement formed in Monrovia, protesting the continuous warfare of Taylor, LURD, and tribal warlords.[11] The women's demand was simple: we are tired of war; we want peace. They united across religious (Christian and Muslim), ethnic, and class identities. They gathered daily at a major Monrovia intersection wearing white scarves, singing, and dancing, rain or shine. They demanded Taylor's resignation. Taylor ignored them. They also devised an unusual strike, denying their husbands sex until they put down their weapons and negotiated for peace. In early 2003, several African nations succeeded in bringing Liberian rivals to a peace conference in Accra, Ghana. But the negotiators were enjoying themselves in their Accra hotels, and negotiations went nowhere for six weeks. Then alarming news came from Monrovia. LURD had reached Monrovia and were fighting Taylor's forces in the streets.

The women who had come to Accra from Liberia and their sisters living in exile in Ghana, a thousand strong, surrounded the conference hall and physically blocked exits and windows, threatening not to allow anyone to leave until a peace accord was reached. A peace accord was signed, and Charles Taylor was prohibited from holding political office. A few days earlier the Sierra Leone high court had indicted Taylor for war crimes. As he left Liberia in exile, he described himself in messianic terms and pledged to return to lead the country.

The women of Liberia continued to play a critical peacemaking role. They assisted the United Nations and NGOs in the first steps in rebuilding the country: demobilization, disarmament, and the reintegration and rehabilitation of soldiers. They also worked to reform the national police system and planned a reconciliation program.

The damage done to Liberian women during the civil wars was extensive. Their suffering was typical of women in many contemporary war zones. In 2006, Ellen Johnson Sirleaf was elected president of Liberia and became the first female head of state in Africa. She was committed to elevating the status of women, who had suffered so much. In her inaugural speech she said:

> Liberian women endured the injustice of being second-class citizens. During the years of our civil war, they bore the brunt of inhumanity and terror. They were conscripted into war, gang raped, and forced into domestic slavery. (Johnson 2009, 333)

Women's activism and Johnson Sirleaf's election to some extent opened doors for Liberian women. But throughout the country, beyond the Presidential Palace, the oppression of women continued. Women's equality had not yet been achieved. If insufficiently acknowledged in Liberia, these women were recognized by the international community and awarded the UN prize for human rights. Women's liberation in Liberia had been twofold. Women have begun to liberate themselves and their country from violence.

****

People's power was a critical source of nonviolent liberation in Poland, East Germany, and the Philippines. So too was the influence of Christian

Churches, which the people trusted. A decisive factor in the victories in Serbia and Tunisia was the energy of youth. Women-power brought justice and finally peace to Liberia. In all these cases, nonviolent activists created the tipping point at which the larger populations were convinced to join.

American sociologist Gene Sharp, building on Gandhi's insights, prescribes many strategies and tactics for successful nonviolent revolutions.[12] Sharp's writings have been translated into thirty languages. Among his books are *Exploring Nonviolent Alternatives* (1970), *There Are Realistic Alternatives* (1973), *Civilian-Based Defense* (1990), *Nonviolent Action: A Research Guide* (700 pages of references, published in 1997), and *From Dictatorship to Democracy: A Conceptual Framework for Liberation* (the fourth U.S. edition, 2010, is in PDF format and downloadable for free). His research informed the organizers of the Serbian campaign as well as the activism of young Egyptians. *From Dictatorship to Democracy* describes how dictators gain power, hold power, and lose power.

A principal theme in Sharp's work is that the seemingly absolute power of dictators is very fragile. Even though they deceive the population with false claims about enemies of the state and with promises of stability and security, they undermine the rule of law, brutally eliminate their opposition, and siphon government funds. Dictators surround themselves with opportunistic advisors who assure them of their invincibility and shield them from growing popular discontent. Sharp reminds activists that leaders only maintain their power if the people consent and cooperate. Dictators must keep their opposition isolated, unorganized, and afraid to speak out. Sharp lists many civil entities (often called "civil societies") with the potential to swell the opposition: unions, religious organizations, sports clubs, cultural associations, and others—the list is long (Sharp 2010, 21). Such civil societies might have opposed the rise of Hitler. Sharp observes that

> these centers of power provide the institutional bases from which the population can exert pressure or can resist dictatorial controls. In the future, they will be part of the indispensable structural base of a free society. Their continued independence and growth therefore are often a prerequisite for the success of the liberation struggle. (Sharp 2010, p. 22)

Sharp writes that tyrants want their subjects to have no confidence, no power, and little spirit. Sharp's prescriptions for success include:

1. learning how to withdraw support;
2. being patient;
3. avoiding impulsivity which fails to consider cause and effect—the relationship between the means employed and the ends produced;

4. developing problem-solving skills;
5. recognizing how fear, hubris, anger, and ideological blindness obscure vision; and
6. being willing to experiment with innovative strategies.

When Filipino troops refused to obey Marcos's orders on that Sunday in 1986, and when Serbian soldiers refused to stop the crowd from entering the parliament building on that day in 2001, both regimes were doomed. When it was clear that the regimes had stuffed the ballot boxes, their legitimacy evaporated. The lesson is that when enough people withdraw their cooperation by protesting, insisting on fair elections, and by other nonviolent means, societies can be reformed and rebuilt on democratic foundations. After the opposition succeeds in ousting dictators with strikes, boycotts, sit-ins, and other tactics, activists then have the task of rebuilding. In contrast to violent coups, which often produce more violence, nonviolent campaigns are much better positioned to do the work of healing communities rent by violence.

There remains that work of training the next generation in nonviolence. A successful nonviolent struggle is never a permanent victory. The nonviolent activism of one generation must be renewed by the next. Succeeding once does not guarantee the continuity of nonviolent power structures. Consider what occurred in the Philippines thirty years after the overthrow of Marcos. Rodrigo Duterte was elected president in May 2016. He had run on a platform of being tough on drugs, which most Filipinos supported. But Duterte's "war on drugs" quickly became a "reign of terror" on poor people. Within a few months, 7,000 Filipinos suspected of using drugs or having drug ties were murdered by Duterte's security forces. There were no arrests or trials, only extrajudicial killings, often in the streets of Manila.

At first, Duterte's support remained high; his victims were mostly anonymous and poor. When the Catholic Church began to speak out, he dismissed it as corrupt, in contrast to Marcos's fear of alienating the Church. The bishops wrote a pastoral letter condemning Duterte's supposed war on drugs as a "reign of terror against the poor." Duterte was revealed to be a sociopath; he claimed his methods would send him to hell and told others to "come join me" (Rauhala 2017, n.p.). He said that those who killed on his orders bore no moral responsibility. The Church began doing what it could, assisting victims' families, giving faces to the victims in a large photo display in front of a church in Manila, and opening its doors to provide sanctuary for witnesses at risk. The Church organized a "March for Life" in Manila that attracted 20,000 Filipinos, who prayed and condemned the regime's violence. Archbishop Socrates Villegas, President of the Filipino Bishops Conference, asserted: "If the response of violence is also violence, then we are only doubling down on violence" (Villegas 2017). In 2020, the Archbishop called for a fifteen-day fast for the healing of the nation (Villegas 2020). As of 2020, there had yet to be an end to Duterte's rule.

Chapters 4 and 5 continue to shine a light on nonviolent campaigns waged by blacks and other people of color in the United States, as well as the nonviolent overthrow of apartheid in South Africa.

FOR DISCUSSION

1. What were the most effective means of toppling the dictatorships of Marcos and Milosevic?
2. What new tactics of Otpor were especially useful?
3. What advantages might women have over men as successful nonviolent activists?
4. What contributes to leaders overestimating their power and how can nonviolence movements capitalize on that?
5. What do dictators often do to "legitimate" their regimes? What has been an effective way to expose their illegitimacy?

Chapter 4

Systemic Racism from the Civil Rights Struggle to the Black Lives Matter Movement

The struggle for racial equality in the United States has not yet succeeded, despite the successes of Civil Rights movements led by Martin Luther King, Jr., the Student Nonviolent Coordinating Committee (SNCC), and other decades-old racial equality organizations. Today, activism for racial equality has new energy, reflected in the Black Lives Matter movement. Because of the murder of another black man, George Floyd, by the police in 2020, a degree of white soul-searching and solidarity with blacks not seen before arose.

U.S. CIVIL RIGHTS MOVEMENTS IN THE 1960S

In the 1960s civil rights movement, African Americans chose nonviolent means to resist legally sanctioned racism. Two organizations had been working for black equality since early in the century. The National Association for the Advancement of Colored People (NAACP), a biracial organization was founded in 1909, with W. E. B. Du Bois as its first president. Its emphasis was on legal challenges to segregation. The Congress of Racial Equality (CORE), founded in 1942, was made up of two-thirds of white activists. CORE was of equal importance and committed to nonviolent means.

Black men had frequently been lynched by white mobs throughout the Reconstruction and Jim Crow eras. In 1955 Emmet Till, a teenager from Chicago, was visiting his cousins in Mississippi when he committed the "crime" of talking "fresh" to a white woman. The woman's husband and brother-in-law murdered Till but were found innocent by an all-white jury. The murder of blacks was a catalyst for a mass movement. Several months after Till's death, Rosa Parks was arrested in Montgomery for refusing to give up her seat on a bus to a white passenger. Local pastors led by Martin Luther King, Jr. formed the Montgomery Improvement Association (MIA) to challenge bus segregation, organizing a bus boycott. They met a wall when they tried to negotiate with the city for desegregation of buses; city officials filed a lawsuit to end the MIA's boycott. Fifty-five thousand Montgomerians chose to walk rather than ride the buses. The KKK attempted to intimidate them. King was arrested and his house bombed. An angry black man challenged a policeman: "Now you got your .38 and I got mine; so let's battle it out." Another called for shooting whites "to show them we mean business." King urged the black community not to retaliate but to remain nonviolent, which they did. They walked for 381 days until the U.S. Supreme Court ruled that segregated buses were unconstitutional.

The campaign succeeded because of careful planning and the thousands of committed nonviolent participants. They had gathered at weekly church meetings to be sustained in their resolve, to be reminded that transforming a racist society was a righteous cause, and to remain nonviolent. King told participants that the campaign would require great sacrifice, saying "a river of blood will be shed and it must be our blood. . . . To our most bitter opponents we say: 'We shall match your capacity to inflict suffering by our capacity to endure suffering'" (King 1963, p. 56). This was Gandhian *tapasya*. The years ahead would be very bloody.

In 1959, King visited India to learn more about Gandhian nonviolence. When he returned, he gave a sermon at the church he pastored, the Dexter Avenue Baptist church. It was entitled "Palm Sunday Sermon on Mohandas K. Gandhi." King made a connection between Gandhi and Jesus: "More than anybody else in the modern world [Gandhi] caught the spirit of Jesus Christ and lived it more completely in his life." In *Stride Toward Freedom*, he wrote:

> Gandhi was probably the first person in history to lift the love ethic of Jesus above mere interaction between individuals to a powerful and effective social force on a large scale. . . . Gandhi, a Hindu, sharpened the meaning of Christian discipleship. (King 1958, p. 97)

King endorsed six principles of nonviolent social struggle:

- Nonviolent resistance is active and not passive.
- The purpose is to change the heart of oppressors, not to humiliate and defeat them.
- The ultimate goal is reconciliation to create the Beloved Community.
- Achieving justice requires suffering without retaliation.

- Nonviolence of the spirit is also required.
- At its heart nonviolent resistance is love, *agape*; suffering love character-izes Jesus' and his disciples' way of life.

The Montgomery campaign sought to liberate the white community as well.[1] King called for the creation of a "Beloved Community" of black and white equality, mutuality, and harmony.

More challenges to segregation through boycotts, voter registration drives, marches, protests, civil disobedience, and lawsuits began across the South. King and the other pastors founded the Southern Christian Leadership Conference (SCLC) in 1957 to oppose segregation. In 1962, they announced "Project C" (Confrontation) in Birmingham, one of the most segregated cities in the South.[2] When blacks marched, they were attacked by police dogs and knocked down with water cannons. Children marchers filled the jails. The whole world saw it. But the local press and white clergymen criticized Project C as ill-timed, claiming that Birmingham was making steady, if slow, progress toward desegregation. In response, King asserted in his "Letter from a Birmingham Jail," that 340 years was too long to wait for racial justice, that there was no "right time" to oppose segregation: "justice delayed is justice denied."

In the summer of 1963, 250,000 blacks and poor whites converged on the national mall in Washington, D.C., protesting racism and poverty. There King delivered his "I Have a Dream" speech. In 1967, at the Riverside Church in New York City, King denounced the Vietnam War for its racism, people of color being sent in disproportionate numbers to kill other people of color. Besides the immense loss of lives was the squandering of money necessary for Johnson's "war on poverty" to succeed (Washington 1992).

King had for some time had a premonition of his own death. He was assassinated on April 4, 1968, while working with garbage men in Memphis seeking to unionize. The day he died he had telephoned his church secretary with the title of the following Sunday's sermon: "Why America is going to hell." What might have been his message? Perhaps he meant that by resistance to the Beloved Community, his vision of a nation of mutual love and support, whites were creating a hell.

Although King's life is celebrated annually, Americans often miss the full depth of his critique of America. He decried America's "evil triplets": racism, militarism, and unregulated capitalism. Vincent Harding argues that King would today have called Christians to account:

> What does it mean when the Christian community now identifies itself with
> empire . . . and goes to war in the armies of the empire? . . . What does it mean to
> have democratic citizenship responsibility and have the identity of the children

of God? . . . Where do you stand in relationship to the sufferings and oppression of the world? And where do you stand in relationship to our country's contribution to that suffering? I think the challenge is still very, very present. (Harding 1996, pp. 148–149)

Theologian Cornell West, in his collection of King's sermons and writing, describes the real, radical King:

He was staunchly anti-colonial and anti-imperialist. His revolutionary commitment to nonviolent resistance in America and abroad tried to put a break on the escalating militarism run amok across the globe. . . . Jim Crow was never reducible to individual prejudice or personal bias. Empire, white supremacy, capitalism, patriarchy, and homophobia are linked in complex ways, and our struggles against them require moral consistency and systemic analysis. (West 2015, pp. xii)

STUDENT NONVIOLENT COORDINATING COMMITTEE (SNCC)

In the 1960s, black consciousness and black power movements were growing in both the United States and Africa. The younger generation of blacks wanted progress more quickly. They would devise more confrontational and dangerous campaigns. In Nashville, James Lawson, a black man, and Glen Smiley, a white, members of the American chapter of the International Fellowship of Reconciliation, offered workshops on nonviolence to prepare students for lunch counter sit-ins. Lawson had spent a year in prison for refusing to serve in the Korean War. He was paroled to the Methodist Church and served as a missionary in India where he became acquainted with Gandhian principles and strategies. In 1960, he earned a degree from Boston University and enrolled in the Vanderbilt School of Theology. He was expelled when he began to train students for sit-ins. Lawson and Smiley told the students that attackers were "victim[s] of the forces that have shaped and filled their anger and fury" (Lewis 1998, p. 87). King called the workshop participants "the best organized and most disciplined in the South" (Lewis 1998, p. 117). Eventually, some 130 sit-ins were organized across the South.

The Student Nonviolent Coordinating Committee (SNCC) was organized in 1960. Diane Nash, a white student at Fisk University, told students from fifty-eight black colleges and twelve white schools that struggling for desegregation was "applied religion . . . designed to bring about a climate in which there is appreciation of the dignity of man and in which each individual is free to grow and produce to his fullest capacity" (Carson 1981, p. 21). SNCC's mission statement expressed its purpose and nonviolent commitment:

Nonviolence as it grows from the Judaeo-Christian tradition seeks a social order of justice permeated by love. . . . Through nonviolence, courage displaces fear; love transforms hate. . . . nonviolence nurtures the atmosphere in which reconciliation become actual possibilities. (Sellers 1975, p. 35)

Dr. King spoke to the gathering, telling them that "our ultimate end must be the creation of the beloved community and that without the spirit of nonviolence [activism] may become a new kind of violence" (Sellers 1975, p. 39). Ella Baker challenged the delegates to grow a movement addressing more than lunch counters but the wide range of injustices black people suffered (Sellers 1975, p. 36). The mood was to quicken the pace.

There were many admirable activists in SNCC. Two may be singled out: John Lewis and Cleveland Sellers. Lewis was born in 1940 in rural Troy, Alabama, one of ten children. His father owned 300 acres of cotton, but the family was in, Lewis's words, "dirt poor" (Lewis 1998, p. 87). Lewis had been attracted to the ministry and at nineteen went North to Nashville to a black seminary. In his second year, he applied to an all-white university and was rejected. Lewis wrote to King to offer his rejection as a test case. King agreed but Lewis's parents were frightened by the possible consequences. Lewis didn't proceed, but King saw in him a fearless activist. Lewis said he learned from King that "it is a moral responsibility of men and women with soul force to respond and struggle nonviolently against the forces that stand between a society and the harmony it naturally seeks" (Lewis 1998, p. 87). Lewis helped organize sit-ins at lunch counters and boycotts of segregated stores in Nashville, suffering serious injuries several times at the hands of the police, the national guard, and white mobs. From 1987–2020, Lewis has represented Georgia in the U.S. House of Representatives.

Cleveland Sellers was born in 1944 in Denmark, South Carolina. In 1960, he heard that students at the University of North Carolina-Greensboro had organized a lunch counter sit-in, so he organized a sit-in in Denmark. He was only sixteen when he joined the SNCC. He was fiercely committed to SNCC being in the vanguard of the struggle.

An early SNCC action was its Nonviolent Action Group's sit-in in a Washington, D.C., federal building to force the federal government to use its power to push for integration in the Southern states. SNCC and other civil rights organizations together conducted some of the most dangerous civil rights campaigns yet undertaken. In 1961, black and white "Freedom Riders" attempted to ride interstate buses from Washington, D.C., to New Orleans. Organized by CORE, SCLC, and SNCC, the goal was to challenge segregation laws by integrating buses and using "whites only" facilities in bus terminals. The Freedom Riders were subjected to some of the worst violence of the 1960s civil rights actions. In the Montgomery and Birmingham bus stations white mobs clubbed riders as police watched. A bus was firebombed on a lonely stretch of highway in Alabama. Organizers called for discontinuing the action for fear of riders being killed, but they refused. Lewis wrote:

> *Satyagraha* means "holding onto truth." Truth cannot be abandoned even in the face of pain and injury, even in the face of death. Once the truth has been recognized and embraced as in this case, the truth of the absolute moral invalidity of racial segregation and the necessity of ending it [by] backing away is not an option. (Lewis 1998, p. 143)

Between May and September 1961, over 300 Freedom Riders in integrated groups made a total of forty-seven trips between cities in Georgia, Alabama, Mississippi, and Louisiana. Almost an equal number of blacks and whites participated. Forty percent were under twenty, and 40 percent were women. Ninety percent were from the Deep South, while riders came from thirty-nine states and ten foreign countries. They all had nonviolence training. Among the Freedom Riders were

- Larry Hunter, 19, from Georgia, who refused to be drafted in 1968 and went to Canada; charges against him were dropped when he returned in 1976.
- Miller Green, 18, from Mississippi, who said: "Who do you get to go to war? You get nineteen-year-olds."
- David Fankhauer, 22, from Indiana, whose parents were active in the Fellowship of Reconciliation.
- Morton Linder, 23, from Pennsylvania, who wrote: "When I got out of jail . . . that's when I tried to figure out why I had gone. I read Gandhi and I read Martin Luther King. I think it was a feeling of—maybe of guilt, maybe of obligation. . . . it was just a window of time when I could do something like that. Maybe I wouldn't have a chance to put my body on the line later on."
- Chela Alexander Weiss, 25, from Vienna, Austria, whose parents had escaped the Nazis in 1940. He wrote: "Once all this stuff started happening down South, I just couldn't believe it. One of the motivations for joining CORE and volunteering to go on the Freedom Rides was I did not want to be one of those "good Germans who just looked the other way. . . . I'm not going to stand by."
- William Leons, 26, whose family was originally from the Netherlands and had lost his father in the Holocaust. His mother hid Jews and was deported to a concentration camp but survived.
- Theresa Walker, 33, and Wyatt Tee Walker, 32, from New Jersey, Theresa was beaten during the Birmingham campaign (1963) and hospitalized. Wyatt was executive director of SCLS in 1961. He wrote: "When I was a

pastor [in Virginia] I used to carry a gun. I was waiting for some racist to have a confrontation with me so I'd have an excuse to shoot him. . . . I met Martin Luther King, I came under his influence and he made me put up my gun." (Etheridge 2008, pp. 123, 190, 195)

The courts eventually ruled that segregated buses violated the federal Interstate Commerce clause. But President John Kennedy and Attorney General Robert Kennedy were worried about the violence suffered by the Freedom Riders and urged organizers to focus on registering black voters instead. Lewis agreed that "the central front is that of suffrage. If we in the South can win the right to vote, it will place in our hands more than an abstract right. It will give us the concrete tool with which we ourselves can correct injustice" (Lewis 1998, p. 180).

SNCC, SCLC, CORE, and the NAACP focused on registering Mississippi blacks to vote, calling on people from around the country to join the effort. Sellers urged help from the North, saying "political and social justice [in Mississippi] cannot be won without the massive aid of the country as a whole" (Sellers 1975, p. 56). The voter registration drive took activists into rural areas that afforded them no protection from hostile segregationists. Between 1961 and 1963, 150 incidents of violence against voter registration workers occurred. SNCC, a small organization, was spread thin. In Mississippi, the center of the voter registration drive, it had only 130 organizers in its offices to coordinate and protect volunteers. Several workers were murdered, including blacks, James Chaney and Medgar Evers, and whites, Michael Schwerner and Andrew Goodman. But thousands of voters were registered. Assessing Freedom Summer, Lewis wrote:

We did succeed in our objective of educating and organizing a significant number of black voters in Mississippi . . . more than 17,000 black men and women filled out registration forms . . . . Within the next decade 300,000 black Mississippians would be registered, and more blacks would hold public office in Mississippi than in any other state in the Union. (Lewis 1998, p. 143)

In March 1965, SCLC organized a march from Selma to Montgomery to demand the protection of the voting rights of blacks. On "Bloody Sunday" marchers were attacked by police and the Alabama national guard as they attempted to cross the Edmund Pettus bridge in Selma. Lewis marched and was knocked unconscious, suffering brain trauma. Three participants died. Marchers tried again two days later but again were attacked. Two weeks later, thousands of supporters from around the country joined the fifty-four-mile march, arriving in Montgomery five days later. SNCC member James Meredith began a "March Against Fear" through Mississippi and was shot but survived. The march continued with King in its ranks. Decades after the 1965 federal Voting Rights Act was passed, John Lewis was still leading the fight for greater federal voting rights protection. In 2012, he told an audience: "Your vote is precious, almost sacred. It is the most powerful nonviolent tool we have to create a more perfect union."[3]

SNCC remained nonviolent, even as it was vilified, and its members harassed. The FBI and southern politicians denounced it as a group of communists, anarchists, and fomenters of hatred for America. FBI director J. Edgar Hoover called it the country's greatest threat. Its leaders were beaten, jailed, and some were murdered. Harvard psychiatrist Robert Coles interviewed Freedom Summer staff and volunteers, reporting clinical signs of depression from battle fatigue, exhaustion, despair, frustration, and rage. By 1970, SNCC was all but dead. H. Rap Brown was its fifth and last director. With no resources, many members in prison, scattered, or dead, SNCC allied itself with the Black Panther Party for Self-Defense (BPPSD).

That same year four Kent State white students were shot and killed by the Ohio National Guard during a campus rally against the Vietnam War. In contrast, an event was organized by Cleveland Sellers on the campus of South Carolina State University in Orangeburg, South Carolina. Sellers was helping a student campaign to integrate a local bowling alley. One evening the South Carolina National Guard and local law enforcement agents (together numbering almost a thousand) surrounded the college campus where the student activists were staying and opened fire on them. Three were killed, and twenty-seven wounded, including Sellers who suffered a gunshot wound. Nine students were indicted, although none had been armed. Sellers was the only one convicted for "refusing to disperse when ordered" and was sentenced to a year in prison. On appeal, his case was dismissed. But the headlines and outpouring of grief for the white students killed and injured while protesting the war on the campus of Kent State was in sharp contrast to the shootings of black students killed while protesting segregation. Few people ever knew about the Orangeburg massacre.

Sellers and Lewis had both denounced the war in Vietnam, Lewis calling it illegal, immoral, and criminal. How could the United States fight for democracy in Vietnam, he asked, when its own citizens were not free? He wrote, "I did not agree with the reasoning behind a 'just' war, and this war was not even that" (Lewis 1998, pp. 273–274). Lewis applied for conscientious objector status. His all-white draft board, whom Lewis said "had no idea about the history and philosophy of nonviolence," denied his application. But after further review Lewis was granted CO status, with the official comment that he was morally unfit to serve his country (Lewis 1998, p. 359). He told his draft board:

I will fight as the rest of the black brothers have for the liberation of black people till my death, I will fight for that. We will not stop because we can't. I take solace in the face of the hardships before me because I know that we are right and those who oppress us and our people are wrong. Most important, I believe that Dr. King was eminently correct when he said, 'The moral arm of the universe is long, but it bends toward justice. (Sellers 1975, p. 180)

He was the first black man in Alabama to be a conscientious objector. Sellers were arrested, found guilty of draft evasion, and imprisoned. When released from prison, Sellers was destitute, depending on friends for food and living in a dilapidated apartment in Baltimore.[4]

MALCOLM X AND THE BLACK PANTHER PARTY FOR SELF-DEFENSE

Was Malcolm X a violent man encouraging a black uprising? Did the Black Panthers use violence against white America? Were they calling on blacks to retaliate with violence or were they calling out American society for its violence toward people of color? Clearly, they were responding to white violence and working to liberate the black community from white oppression. Their analyses and goals ought not be summarily rejected because of their fiery voices.

Consider their life experiences. Malcolm Little's childhood was seared by racism. Huey Newton and Bobby Seale, co-founders of the BPPSD, grew up amidst police brutality. Little was born in Omaha, Nebraska in 1925, the fourth of eight children. His father was a minister preaching "black improvement" and "back to Africa." The family was driven out of Omaha by the KKK and resettled in Lansing, Michigan. There their home was burned to the ground and Malcolm's father was killed when he was run over on street-car tracks, where he had most likely been dragged. Malcolm's mother was eventually institutionalized in a mental hospital. At fifteen, Malcolm was put in a foster home and the next year went to Boston to live with his sister. He moved to New York where he worked various jobs back in Lansing and then in Harlem. John Lewis describes his first visit to Harlem in 1963:

The one thing I will never forget . . . was the great sense of anger and hopeless-ness I felt in Harlem. It was very different from the South . . . with [its] sense of community and purpose. In Harlem I saw boarded-up buildings, metal grates on store windows, and a different kind of poverty . . . a starker, dismal, urban kind of poverty. (Lewis 1998, p. 206)

Malcolm was soon selling drugs and committing armed robberies. He spent six years in prison and there converted to the Nation of Islam (NOI). Released from prison, he took a new name, Malcolm X, and became minister of a New York mosque. In 1958, he married Betty Shabazz, with whom he had six daughters, including twins born the month before his assassination in 1965.

The Honorable Elijah Muhammad, leader of the NOI, sent Malcolm to Africa in 1959 to share the message and vision of African American and African solidarity. He addressed legislatures and heads of fifteen African and Middle Eastern countries. Upon his return he founded the Organization of Afro-American and African Unity. In 1962, Malcolm X broke with Elijah Muhammad when the leader's sexual promiscuity came to light. That year seven blacks were shot by Los Angeles police outside an NOI mosque when they were falsely accused of robbery. One died, but none of the police were charged. Malcolm X's distrust and condemnation of white America grew. He condemned the political, social, and economic systems that oppressed blacks. He called whites "blue-eyed devils," urging blacks to either return to Africa or to remain in America but live separately from whites.

Malcolm was highly intelligent and an eloquent speaker. He debated Ivy League professors on world history and religion, despite an eighth-grade education. But he sometimes made rash claims he later regretted, once saying that the deaths of 100 people in a plane crash was a divine judgment. Malcolm and King met only once. He had a harsh judgment of King's campaigns.[5] In a debate with CORE's James Farmer, Malcolm called nonviolence "idiocy" and offered an analogy: "if a dog were biting a child, would we not be obligated to kill the dog?" He insisted on self-defense and retaliation: "If we bleed, they will bleed." "Islam" he argued, "is a religion that teaches us never to attack, never to be the aggressor—but you can waste somebody if he attacks you. . . . When the white man becomes nonviolent, I'll become nonviolent" (Malcolm X 1964, n.p.). As long as America was a land of racism it would not be saved, he argued. As it stood, the United States continuously perpetrated violence abroad. So why was violence at home unacceptable?

Malcolm made the hajj (pilgrimage) to Mecca in 1964. There he underwent a change. His encounter with blond blue-eyed Muslims caused him to reconsider the white race:

> I have always said that whites were blue-eyed devils, but I have been to Mecca and I have seen whites with blue eyes, with whom I felt a brotherhood, and so I can no longer say this—that all whites are evil. (Gallen 1992, p. 74)

Malcolm had for many years been a separatist, believing that the only hope for blacks to thrive was to live apart from whites. But Malcolm's separatist views moderated. Near the end of his life Malcolm reconsidered his many angry words. He believed his fiery speeches was necessary at the time and did not regret them. But he did regret that his NOI rhetoric stirred up many black people without providing a constructive program for their liberation. He declared: "I'm not dogmatic about anything anymore" (Goldman 1979, 232). In an interview, he said: "I don't intend to let anyone make my mind to be set on anything that I can't change it according to the circumstances and conditions that I happen to find myself in" (Gallen 1992, p. 59).

How much he might have changed cannot be known, for Malcolm was assassinated by a member of the NOI in February 1965 at the age of thirty-nine. A few days before his death, he circulated a document outlining a constructive plan of action for black communities. In it he no longer espoused black nationalism. He was about to publish the document when he died. Unfortunately, it never saw the light of day (Goldman 1979).

We cannot do justice to the complex personality of Malcolm X. He offered dark prophecies about the fate of America, frightening white Americans. He called on blacks to rise up in awareness of the strength of their blackness. Malcolm X was labeled a fanatic, a communist, and an anarchist. Malcolm X had indeed said that violence is the only language racists speak and therefore blacks must also use the language of violence to defend themselves. When whites called for protecting themselves, blacks heard the call: "Keep blacks intimidated and subjugated by violence." Malcolm X had never urged violent uprisings. Instead, he was a victim of violence. One week before his death, his house was firebombed. His family was homeless, reminiscent of the burning of his family's home in Lansing when he was four years old.

Neither Sellers nor Lewis agreed with Malcolm. Sellers declared himself a pan-Africanist but not a separatist: "I consider myself a Pan-Africanist. I am convinced that the destiny of blacks in this country is inextricably linked to Africa" (Sellers 1975, p. 230). King, with his global perspective, would have agreed. Lewis rejected Malcolm's call for separatism and reaffirmed his own vision of an "interracial democracy, a Beloved Community" in America (Lewis 1998, p. 328). If Malcolm had been given more years, especially after his experience at Mecca, perhaps his views might have converged with those of Lewis.

In 1966, Huey Newton and Bobby Seale, students at a community college in Oakland, California, founded the BPPSD. Its purpose was to overcome the pervasive police violence against black communities. Newton and Seale composed the Black Panther's demands:

1. freedom and power for black communities to determine their destiny;
2. guaranteed employment;
3. monetary reparations;
4. decent housing;
5. education that includes black history;
6. exemption from military service for black men;

Chapter 4

7. "an immediate end to POLICE BRUTALITY and MURDER";
8. release of incarcerated black men and black juries to try black people;
9. the provision of material and political necessities to empower people of color worldwide (Seale 1970).

The BPPSD's first mission was to confront the violent elements in the Oakland Police Department. Its inaugural action, chosen to achieve maximum press, was its small membership's march from Los Angeles to the California State Assembly building in Sacramento. They entered the building brandishing shotguns, bandoleers, and pistols. When ordered to disarm, Newton said, "You put your [weapons] down, then we'll put ours down." Newton was quick to point out that it was legal to carry firearms; the State Assembly quickly changed that law.

In fiery speeches, Newton called for an armed revolution to shake the country to its roots. Seale claimed that black activism was "beginning to control the police"—or so he hoped (Seale 1970). But the opposite was actually happening: the Black Panthers became the targets of some of the worst police violence in the country, much of it coordinated by the FBI. The Black Panthers' vision was inspired by Malcolm X's call for blacks to defend themselves. The BPPSD was caricatured as ultraviolent, intent on killing policemen and overthrowing the government. J. Edgar Hoover, the director of the FBI, called the Black Panthers the greatest internal threat to the country. When Bobby Seale was asked whether nonviolence was the better course, he redirected the question: "Nonviolence on the part of whom? We must defend ourselves by any means necessary."

On an evening in October of 1967, Newton was stopped by police. Gun fire was exchanged. One policeman was killed, another injured, and Newton critically wounded. He was found guilty of manslaughter and sentenced to three years in prison. While he was in prison forty-five chapters of the BPPSD sprang up across the country, boasting 5,000 active members. Over time Newton's tone was moderated and constructive. Police departments, he said, must learn "to be civilized and to value human life." Black communities needed to exercise oversight of the police. He claimed that the Black Panthers were dedicated to law and order. In a prison interview in 1968, Newton was reaching out, saying

> we've asked in the past and the opportunity is still open for the [Los Angeles] police chief and mayor to negotiate with the BPPSD and we're willing to talk. We would like to have peaceful solutions to the crucial problem in the black community (Newton 1968).

In a later interview, Newton embraced nonviolence, saying: "It was very wrong and almost criminal for some people in the Party to believe that the

Black Panthers could overthrow even the police force. Only a nonviolent revolution was worth fighting" (Lader 1979, pp. 268–269).[6]

Yet the lasting image of the Black Panthers is that of dangerous criminals. But it was the FBI's war on the Black Panthers that doomed the movement. In Chicago, the FBI raided an apartment riddling it with bullets, killing the leader of the Chicago chapter of the BPPSD. The historical record reveals almost no retaliatory physical violence by the BPPSD. Again, it was violent rhetoric that alienated white America. King, Lewis, and Sellers were critical of divisiveness. Most black communities found the Black Panthers to be too extreme. Both Malcolm and the founders of the BPPSD eventually rejected violence and even expressed regret for their rhetoric that for many whites justified violence against blacks. The irony is that despite their calls for black self-defense "by whatever means necessary," it was the U.S. government that engaged in deadly violence against them. The vision of black power and activism was constructive. Black consciousness arose with the hope that black power could change America. But white Americans condemned Malcolm X and the Black Panthers and closed their ears to their message. The medium had overshadowed the message. Malcolm and the BPPSD may have doubted King's claim that black liberation would be achieved by self-suffering. But they were prophetic witnesses, accusing America of its racial sins, and seeking to build flourishing black communities.

The activism of blacks was a window of opportunity for whites to join the struggle against racism. But after the assassination of King, violence exploded within black ghettos. In Detroit, Newark, Chicago, Los Angeles, and Washington, D.C., whole black neighborhoods were torched. President Johnson created the Kerner Commission in 1968 to examine why it had happened. In its report, the commission attributed much of the unrest and anger to the fact of black poverty, inferior housing, substandard educational opportunities, and lack of health care. Equally to blame, it concluded, was pervasive police violence in black communities and the resulting lack of trust. The Commission reported that a study by the University of California-Los Angeles found that "seventy-four percent of Watts's residents believed that police used unnecessary force. . . . An Urban League study of inner-city Detroit reported that eighty-two percent of residents said that the police engaged in brutality" (Kerner Commission 1968, p. 158). The Commission noted that some police departments engaged in the "harassment of youth . . . as a proper crime prevention technique" (Kerner Commission 1968, p. 159). Insulting behavior, intimidation, and violence against black men created deep resentment. Fifty years later, the Report's recommendation for police constructive presence in black communities is still unrealized.

There were shining moments in the struggles for racial equality in the United States. Black pastors, students, working people, organizations, and intelligentsia were joined by a small cadre of whites. As noted, many younger blacks disagreed with Martin Luther King's approach and, with his blessing, adopted more confrontational methods. But when violence occurred it was not by blacks but by whites. Events in America's streets make it clear that struggles for racial respect and equality are far from won.

BLACK LIVES MATTER

Ta-Nehisi Coates found in Malcolm X a man who spoke

> like a man who was free, like a man above the laws that proscribed his imagination. I identified with him. I know that he had chafed against the school, that he had almost been doomed by the streets. But even more I knew that he had found himself while studying in prison, and when he emerged from the jails, he emerged wielding some of the old power that made him speak as though his body were his own. (Coates 2015, p. 32)

The struggle for racial equality in the United States continues. Legalized racism was overcome in the United States as Jim Crow laws were declared unconstitutional and the Civil Rights Act and Voting Rights Act were passed. But structural racism in the United States continues. The income and wealth of blacks are a small fraction of whites' economic power. Black children attend inferior schools. Black unemployment is very high. For example, in Milwaukee, Wisconsin, over 50 percent of black men are unemployed. In 1980s, the "war" on drugs across the United States targeted black communities; black men are ten times more likely than whites to be incarcerated. The police violence that led to the formation of the Black Panthers continues.[7]

The Black Lives Matter campaign was born in Oakland, California, in 2013, a few blocks from the birthplace of the Black Panthers Party, with the same goal of overcoming police violence. Today cell phones capture killings of (mostly) black men almost daily. For several years, the Black Lives Matter movement remained a black movement and faced a backlash with whites retorting that "all lives matter" and "blue lives matter." But that suddenly changed on May 25, 2020, when George Floyd was murdered by a policeman in Minneapolis. A passerby caught on her camera a video—of Floyd in handcuffs and lying face down in the street, an officer's knee on his neck. Floyd begged for air for nine minutes as he lay dying. What millions saw caused an explosion of anger at police brutality and the demand for change. For the first time in U.S. history, massive numbers of white people joined the Black Lives Matter campaign. Large protests erupted throughout the country, in Europe, and beyond. It is yet to be seen whether the deaths of George Floyd and many others by the police will trigger a sustained racial reckoning in the United

States. Will white America awaken to the fact that racism is not confined to police conduct but is pervasive in American society. Coates writes:

> Americans are pretending that there is a real difference between their own atti-
> tudes and those of the ones appointed to protect them. The truth is that the police
> reflect all of [their] will and fear, and whatever we might make of the country's
> criminal justice policy, it cannot be said that it was imposed by a repressive
> minority. (Coates 2015, p. 26)

Remarkably, blacks, as slaves and then as citizens, have not retaliated for the brutal victimization they have suffered. There is not black-on-white violence. (The only record of black-on-white violence during the slave era was the Nat Turner insurrection in 1831, so unimaginable that it sent shock waves of fear through slaveholders.) During the civil rights era, mass actions by black Americans remained nonviolent. The only violence that has now arisen is black-on-black violence, violence turned in on the black community, resulting from impoverishment and hopelessness in black neighborhoods.

The Black Lives Matter movement has become the voice for yet again defending the dignity of people whose humanity had been denied since slave ships left West African shores. The next chapter considers the struggles for justice by other peoples of color in the United States and South Africa. Later chapters return to unachieved racial justice in America.

FOR DISCUSSION

1. Who was W. E. B. Du Bois?
2. The Civil Rights movement of the 1960s is hailed as a breakthrough for the freedom of black Americans. In your opinion, how true is that?
3. What would be King's message and activism if he were alive today?
4. In what ways were Malcolm and the Black Panthers successful? If you believe that they failed, why?
5. As noted in the next chapter, King was willing to consider that war against South African apartheid might be just. If this was so, why did he not accept the violent language and threats made by Malcolm X and the Black Panthers against U.S. racism?
6. Who was H. Rap Brown?
7. Many African American men and women have been killed at the hands of the police. Why do you think the murder of George Floyd in May of 2020 caused an outcry on a scale never seen before?
8. Ta-Nehisi Coates refers to the woundedness of black bodies. Why does he describe it in terms of "bodies"?

Chapter 5

Nonviolent Struggles of U.S. Farm Laborers, Native Americans, and Black South Africans

U.S. migrant farm workers and Native Americans continue to feel the indignities of racism. Their struggles for justice have been almost exclusively nonviolent. While struggles against racism were occurring in the United States, racism in the form of apartheid (separation of the races) in South Africa was raising fears that a bloody civil war was coming.

LA CAUSA: JUSTICE FOR MIGRANT FARM WORKERS

I know a fella. Brang'im in while I was in the jail house. Been tryin' to start a union. Got one started. An' then those vigilantes busted it up. An' know what? Them very folks he bee tryin' to help tossed him out. . . . Says, "Git out. You're a danger on us." (Steinbeck 1939)

The fields are cold for the sun is not yet up when labor contractors drop off migrant workers in the fields. By ten in the morning, the heat is scorching. The migrants work quickly; their pay depends on how much they pick. Most of them are of Mexican heritage, with Filipinos and other Asians among them. Their lives are hard, and they are poor. They have no power to negotiate contracts with growers. Instead, labor contractors hire, fire, and set their wages.

César Chávez (1927–1993) and Dolores Huerta (1930–) knew these realities well. Chávez had worked in the fields since he was a child. His family moved from Arizona to California during the Depression when they were unable to pay property taxes and lost their farm. Contrary to what many Euro-Americans may assume, the Chávez family were American-born. Like hundreds of thousands of families, they went West in search of work. César recalled moving so often that he attended thirty-seven schools before dropping out in the seventh grade. Chávez joined the navy in 1949, where he had more bitter tastes of racism, calling the experience "the two worst years of my life." In 1951 he was back in the fields with his wife Helen. Most of Dolores Huerta's extended family were also migrant workers, facing humiliation, poverty wages, exposure to poisons, and the intimidation and violence of growers.

If they had the bargaining power of a union, farmworkers could negotiate contracts for fair wages and safe working conditions. They could demand protection from sexual assault, an end to child labor, protection from pesticides, and they could afford health care and other necessities. Chávez and Huerta slowly recruited migrant workers, a difficult task since migrant workers were always on the move, could not afford modest union dues, and were too tired at the end of the day to get involved. Most of all they were intimidated by growers and labor contractors from forming a union. Chávez and Huerte had driven up and down the California coast for years, recruiting workers and in 1962 succeeded in forming a union, the United Farm Workers of America (UFWA). Chávez and Huerte were a force. He was soft-spoken and charismatic—though the Chávez family came to be known as the "strikingest family" in California. Huerta was a political force. As a co-organizer and voice of the UFWA, she had the ability to pressure politicians in Sacramento to support the migrants' cause, sometimes even bringing workers to camp out in legislators' offices. A California State Senator said: "You always knew when Dolores was in town" (Bratt 2017).

The UFWA struggled to pressure growers to sign labor contracts by marching, boycotting, striking, and picketing. In 1965, it organized farmworkers to walk out of the fields rather than harvest the grapes of forty growers. Workers picketed two of the largest growers of table grapes. Union organizers were threatened, and several were killed. Workers picketing in isolated fields were an easy target.

Union members were accused of being communists, and the union members were harassed and often forced to show proof of citizenship. The UFWA assisted families of strikers and established clinics and credit unions. Meanwhile, the California labor department, the farm bureau, banks, and water authorities—the whole chain of agribusinesses—sided with growers. Government unemployment benefits and food assistance were cut.

In 1966, the UFWA organized a 340-mile march to Sacramento to protest the refusal of table grape growers to negotiate contracts with the union. The union then hatched a very ambitious plan: it would convince grocery chains and consumers around the country to boycott California table grapes, neither selling nor buying them. The union sent representatives with little money in their pockets to fan out across the country to convince grocery chains. They requested British wholesale fruit companies and consumers to do so as well.[1] Growers' profits plummeted. Chávez was jailed in 1970 for calling an "illegal strike." The judge offered to free him in exchange for calling off the strike; he responded, "I will never call it off." Dorothy Day, Robert Kennedy, and Coretta King visited him in jail and supported the strike. After five years of struggle, the UFWA negotiated contracts with DiGiorgio and Perelli-Minetti table grape growers. The farmworkers had won binding contracts.

Most Latino farmworkers are Roman Catholics; banners with images of Our Lady of Guadalupe were prominent at marches. Chávez was deeply informed by the Gospel writing:

> Jesus' life and words are a *challenge* while they are Good News. They are a challenge to those of us who are poor and oppressed. By [Jesus'] life he is calling us to give ourselves to others. . . . He is calling us to "hunger and thirst for justice. . . . Jesus does not promise that it will be an easy way to live life and his own life certainly points in a hard direction. (Stavans 2010, p. 135)

The Sermon on the Mount, Chávez said, was ever on his mind. But while black churches of the South were the spiritual home of the civil rights struggle, the Catholic churches in California valleys seldom supported farm laborers. Church leaders were much more comfortable with and beholden to the wealthy growers. Chávez challenged them:

> We don't ask for more cathedrals. We don't ask for bigger churches or fine gifts. We ask for its presence with us, beside us, as Christ among us. We ask the Church to *sacrifice with the people* for social change, for justice, for love of brother. (Stavans 2010, p. 87)

Only gradually were a few priests assigned to minister to farmworkers.

In conviction and action, Chávez stood with Gandhi and King. On several occasions, he fasted to purify the movement and to be in solidarity with suffering farmworkers. He saw suffering for *La Causa* as something to be embraced: "To be a man is to suffer for others. God help us to be men!" (Stavans 2010, p. 135). Chávez expressed eloquently the power of nonviolence to activate and enlist the community:

> Nonviolence forces one to be creative; it forces any leader to go to the people and get them involved so that they can become force with new ideas. I think that once people understand the power of nonviolence—the force it generates, the love it creates, the response it brings from the total community—they will not be able to abandon it easily. (Stavans 2010, p. xx)

Even when they picketed on remote farms and were beaten and sometimes shot, they responded nonviolently. Even when law enforcement agents looked the other way when they were beaten, *La Causa* activists did not retaliate. Chávez had deep insight into the dynamics of nonviolent activism:

I don't subscribe to the belief that nonviolence is cowardice, as some militant groups are saying. In some instances, nonviolence requires more militancy than violence. Nonviolence requires you to abandon the shortcut, in trying to make a change in the social order. Violence, the shortcut, is the trap people fall into when they begin to feel it is the only way to attain their goal. . . . When people are involved in something constructive, trying to bring about change, they tend to be less violent than those who are not engaged in rebuilding or in anything creative. Nonviolence forces one to be creative; it forces any leader to go to the people and get them involved so that they can come forth with new ideas I think that once people understand the strength of nonviolence—the force it generates, the love it creates, the response it brings from the whole community—they will not be willing to abandon it easily. (Chavez 1969, p. 64)

This is the philosophy of nonviolence in a nutshell.

The prominent leadership roles of women in the nonviolent movements, especially in Poland, Serbia, Liberia, SNCC, and in *La Causa* must be emphasized. Dolores Huerta is among the greatest activists in American history. It should be noted that Coretta King protested against the Vietnam War long before her husband joined the antiwar movement. The power of women will be examined at greater length in chapter 8.

The struggle to unionize continues, for without unions, workers have no leverage. Though they put food on American tables, they remain all but invisible. Protecting the dignity of farmworkers—both domestic and foreign—is a constant challenge. What they need is consumer solidarity to champion their cause.

NATIVE AMERICANS RECOVERING THE CENTER

In the early morning hours of November 20, 1969, eighty Native Americans met at a bar in Sausalito, California, late at night, and set off across San Francisco Bay to Alcatraz Island. Identifying themselves as "Indians of All Tribes," they came without weapons to occupy and gain title to Alcatraz, the site of the famous prison that had been abandoned since 1963. Richard Oakes, the spokesman for the group, described the shameful reality that motivated the takeover. The Statue of Liberty, he said, was the eastern gateway to the United States, representing the ideals of freedom, inclusion, opportunity, and prosperity. But Alcatraz, the western point, represented the near-extinction of the First Nations, by theft of their lands and the several hundred treaties the U.S. government broke.

The takeover of Alcatraz was symbolic of the Indians of All Tribes' demand for self-determination and dignity. They issued the "Alcatraz Proclamation to the great White Father and his People," asserting, "We have a right to use our land for our own beliefs" (Blansett 2018, p. 128). They remained on the island for eighteen months and offered to buy it for $24 in beads and cloth, equivalent to what whites had paid for Manhattan Island in the late 1600s.

The activists' plan in taking over Alcatraz was to demand that an 1868 treaty Indians negotiated with the federal government be honored. The treaty stipulated that government property once belonging to Indians be returned to them if no longer in use. But when the Indians tried to negotiate the return of Alcatraz Island with the Department of Interior, it was clear that the government had no intention of returning the island. The Indians were told that a competitive bidding process would determine the future use of Alcatraz. Some developers wanted to turn it into a theme park. The Department of the Interior wanted to make Alcatraz part of the national park system, a tourist attraction, which it is today.

A brief look back tells the story of what European colonists wanted and what Indian tribes sought to keep—land. Father Jon Sobrino, a Jesuit liberation theologian in El Salvador, has analyzed how social evil progresses. Referring to the Ten Commandments, Sobrino observes that the powerful take what does not belong to them, violating the Seventh Commandment, "Thou shall not steal." Then they justify what they have done by lying, claiming that they are only taking empty land, violating the Eighth Commandment, "Thou shall not bear false witness." Finally, when the poor cry out against their impoverishment and try to recover what is theirs they are murdered, violating the Fifth Commandment, "Thou shall not kill."

Native Americans' attempting to defend themselves were caricatured as savages, but the real savages were elsewhere. The "Trail of Tears" in the 1830s is the story of brutality inflicted by the U.S. Cavalry. Tribes were driven out of the Carolinas and marched through winter under military escort to the territory of Oklahoma. Several thousand died along the way.

Native American men, women, and children were massacred on several occasions. In 1863, the Cavalry attacked the winter village of the Northwest Band of Shoshone at Bear River (Idaho), killing 250 men, women, and children. In 1864 at Sand Creek (Colorado), Cheyenne and Arapaho villages were attacked by 700 soldiers. The death toll was estimated at 133 Indians and nine soldiers. At Salt Creek (Texas) in 1872, fifty-two Comanches were killed and 124 captured, mostly women and children. In December 1890, soldiers surrounded a camp of the Lakota's at Wounded Knee (South Dakota). They disarmed the Lakotas, except for one deaf Lakota who discharged his rifle in the confusion. The Cavalry opened fire, killing more than 200 men, women, and children.[2]

The Comanches, known as extraordinary horsemen and archers, were defeated in October 1871 near Fort Worth, Texas, marking the U.S. government's last battle against the First Nations. There had been some white defenders of the Indians, including Sam Houston, the first president of the Republic of Texas, who worked with and admired them. When Comanche leaders appealed to him to establish boundaries to protect their land, he replied: "If I could build a wall from the Red River to the Rio Grande . . . white people would go crazy trying to devise a means to get beyond it" (Gwynne 2010, p. 128).

By the end of the nineteenth century, most of the North American tribal lands were gone; an estimated 130 million acres, from the Eastern seaboard to the Ohio valley, from the deep South, to the great plains, the southwest, and the northwest.

Only a few whites had an appreciation for native peoples, their spirituality, and their regard for the land as a sacred trust. To most whites, land was only a commodity. By the terms of the Dawes Act (1887), Indian lands could no longer be held in common but were required to be surveyed and titled to individuals. In the nineteenth and twentieth centuries, 367 treaties were negotiated with the U.S. government, all of which the government broke. Tribal chiefs were incredulous that the U.S. government would lie and betray their trust. In one negotiation, the government offered to buy tribal land for fifty cents an acre. When the offer was rejected, the government tripled the offer, but with a threat: accept the offer or the land will be taken with no compensation.

Other laws were passed to deal with the "Indian problem." The Indian Removal Act (1830) was the first effort to control Native Americans by confining them to reservations, thus restricting their ability to gather food off reservations (Gwynne 2010, p. 74). From the 1870s, Christian groups organized off-reservation boarding schools to assimilate Indian children into white society, forbidding children to speak their native languages. The Termination Act (1953) declared that tribal identity was no longer legally recognized. The Indian Relocation Act (1956) moved Indians off reservations to assimilate them into white society. But facing discrimination, some returned to their reservations which had less and less to offer them. Young Indians found themselves between two worlds.

The Indians of All Nations who took over Alcatraz proposed establishing "Thunderbird University" on the island, as well as a cultural center and a museum.[3] Their vision was never realized, but more actions followed. A group of Oneidas came ashore in Milwaukee to claim an abandoned Coast Guard station. That too failed, but Indian women established a Native American primary school in the city (Krous 2003). Troy Johnson documented sixty-three occupations and protests between 1969 and 1975 (Johnson 1996, p. 240).

The American Indian Movement (AIM) was established in 1968, its members linked with those who had occupied Alcatraz. In 1973, AIM organized an action called the "Trail of Broken Treaties," with a mobile school traveling between reservations telling the story of the First Nations. Activists also occupied the Bureau of Indian Affairs in Washington; the BIA had been a source of animus for Indians since its creation in 1819.

A sense of humor has come to help Indians deal with the U.S. government, as Otpor had done in Serbia. A good joke can make a sharp point. "If there's an earthquake, head for the BIA building because it never moves." When the Indians of All Nations arrived on Alcatraz, Richard Oakes told the white caretaker that if he cooperated the Indians would set up a Bureau of Caucasian Affairs and make him commissioner. Another joke was that Indians were polled about the Vietnam War. Fifteen percent wanted the United States out. Eighty-five percent wanted the United States out of America. Yet another joke lamented that the greatest mistake of Native Americans was lax homeland security.

The fact that there are such a large number of tribes makes forging Indian unity a challenge. There are militants and traditionalists, urban Indians, and reservation Indians. The two most prominent unifying organizations are the National Congress of American Indians, which has been able to attract a large number of member tribes, and the National Indian Youth Council, which Vine Deloria refers to as the SNCC of Indian activism (Deloria 1969, p. 17).

Their programs work to preserve Native American cultures, strengthen tribal self-governance, and enhance tribal development. The chief mission of the struggle is the health of reservations, which must be resurrected to be well-functioning communities and spiritual centers.

Violence by Indians seeking liberation is almost unheard of, while prejudice and violence against them is the norm. Of the sixty-three actions from the occupation of Alcatraz until the occupations and demonstrations in 1975, only two incidents involved violence. In 1973 on the Pine Ridge reservation, the site of Wounded Knee, occupiers and FBI agents exchanged gunfire. Two Indians were killed, 237 arrested, and three dozen weapons confiscated. In 1975, also on the Pine Ridge reservation, gunfire was exchanged, killing two FBI agents and one Indian. Kirkpatrick Sales quotes Henry Spellman, who lived with a tribe for many years, observes that

> they might fight [a war] for seven years and not kill seven men. . . . Organized violence, in short, was not an attribute of traditional Indian societies, certainly not as compared with their European contemporaries, and on the basis of this imperfect record what is most remarkable about them is their apparent lack of conflict and discord. (Sale 1990, p. 319)

Traditionally, when adversaries were killed in the war, villagers mourned their deaths as they did for the loss of their warriors. Ceremonies of purification were necessary for those who took lives. Tink Tinker writes, "From our Native perspective, the euro-christian (*sic*) warrior cultures and their persistent war-making savagery has left the whole world in radical imbalance for more than five centuries" (Tinker 2015, p. 211). Oppressed people always face the question of whether violence can be an effective means of change. Vizenor writes that most Indians view violence as alienating white society although a small minority believe that "the use of violence has made the job of moderates working within the system more successful" (Nabokov 1999, p. 379).

In 1990, Canadian Mohawks resisted the takeover of a pine forest and Mohawk cemetery on which a town wanted to build a golf course. The Canadian military arrived in gunships and used tear gas to disperse Mohawks and remove their barricades. Peter Blue Cloud wrote to the military officer who led the military invasion, and to the Canadian people:

> Will you ever begin to understand the meaning of the soil beneath your very feet? From a grain of sand to a great mountain, all is sacred. Yesterday and tomorrow exist eternally upon this continent. We natives are the guardians of this sacred place. (Nabokov 1999, p. 437)

To its credit, the Canadian government returned sovereignty to a tribe, giving them control of public services and timber, mining, and fishing rights on land in British Columbia, land half the size of Rhode Island. But the struggle continues. In northern Wisconsin, non-Indians have on occasion used violence to stop a tribe from exercising its treaty right to spearfish for food before sports fishermen were allowed on the lakes.

In North Dakota, the Sioux protested fracking that poisons their water. Everywhere Indian tribes protest environmental degradation. Vine Deloria writes:

> Luther Standing Bear's prediction that the white man cannot live in peace until he comes to understand and love this land still stands as a warning to our wasteful consumer society. The land itself must be seen to have a measure of dignity and respect and when it does not receive these accommodations, human beings who live on the land are accordingly incomplete. (Nabokov 1999, p. xix)

The heart of nonviolence is the protection of the earth. The essence of Indian nonviolence is respect and care for all of creation. Of all the nonviolent campaigns this book examines, it is the indigenous people's struggles that most reminds us of injustice to the earth and the imperative that it be healthy for the sake of "the next seven generations." Nonviolence toward the earth and one another are essential for a future.

Tragically, every form of justice—commutative, criminal, social, and reparative—has been denied to Native Americans. From Alcatraz Island Richard Oakes read this statement:

> We invite the United States to acknowledge the justice of our claim. The choice now lies with the leaders of the American government—to use violence against us as before, to remove us from our Great Spirit's land [or to act justly]. Nevertheless, we seek peace. (Oakes 1969, n.p.)

ENDING APARTHEID IN SOUTH AFRICA

What prevented a civil war in South Africa, a war between four million privileged whites and twenty-two million impoverished blacks? In 1652 Dutch colonists, mostly farmers ("Boers," in Dutch), arrived on the southern tip of Africa, the Cape. British colonists followed in the early 1800s. While Britain outlawed slavery throughout the Empire in 1833, the Boers rejected the claim of racial equality. They left the Cape, going north and establishing what they considered to be their God-given promised land. When gold and diamonds were discovered, British military forces and miners came north to stake claims. A war broke out (the Boer War, 1897–1903) in which British forces burned Boer farms and herded civilians into the world's first concentration camps. But liberal peace terms gave rural Boers majority representation in the new parliament, leading to the establishment of the Boer's Union of South Africa in 1910 and so began the systematic denial of the rights of black South Africans.

Nowhere was color consciousness more pronounced than by Afrikaners (as the descendants of the Boers are called). The white government legally classified all South Africans by their color. They were either "white," "colored" (mixed race), "Asiatic" (Indian), or Bantu (black). "Bantu" was a derogatory term they used, lumping all black people together rather than acknowledging different tribal identities. The Afrikaners' dream of "Afrikanerdom" was simply for a country of white supremacy. The ideology of "apartheid" (separation of the races) gave whites total control, blacks having only the capacity for manual labor. Blacks labored in gold, coal, and diamond mines. They worked in factories, on farms, and as domestics in white homes. They were prohibited from living in white areas unless deemed necessary workers; of course, they were needed by the thousands but required to leave white areas at night to sleep in "townships." The Pass Laws required black males sixteen and older to carry government-issued passes at all times, the same odious passes once applied to Indians, until Gandhi succeeded in eliminating them for the Indian community in 1914. Blacks were barred from professions and from owning land. Their education was limited to learning specified trades.

Not all English-speaking whites shared the vision of absolute white supremacy, but nonetheless benefitted from apartheid. The churches of those of English extraction tolerated apartheid. Afrikaners, however, belonged to the Dutch Reformed Church (DRC) that gave religious sanction to apartheid and ordained only those of the same view. In effect, South Africa had a "state theology." When the staunchly apartheid political party, the Nationalist Party (NP), won the 1948 election by a landslide. Daniel Malan, an ordained DRC minister, became prime minister. The four prime ministers who followed were all from the NP. The same year, 1948, also saw the promulgation of the UN Universal Declaration of Human Rights and the establishment of the World Council of Churches. Both would become strong opponents of apartheid.

By the early 1950s, opposition to apartheid was growing and the government was becoming more oppressive. The African National Congress (ANC) had been founded in 1912 with the vision of a multiracial, democratic South Africa, although other blacks were calling for an end of white rule and "Africa for Africans." The ANC organized "Freedom Day" on May 1, 1950, and called for a one-day national strike to "stay-at-home" and "pray-at-home." A "Defiance" campaign began in 1952 with thousands turning in their government passes. In 1954, 20,000 black women marched to protest the pass laws which now applied to women as well as to men. In 1955, the ANC and South African Communist Party (SACP) organized a meeting on the fifth anniversary of Freedom Day. For two days an assembly of blacks, coloreds, Indians, pro-democracy whites, and communists met to write a new constitution, the "Freedom Charter." The Freedom Charter contained an eloquent vision of human and civil rights. It proclaimed that South African blacks were "robbed of their birthright" and called for "a democratic state, based on the will of the people, [to] secure [for] all South Africans their birthright without distinction of color, race, sex, or belief." The constitution contained a guarantee of equal rights for women. On the second day of the assembly, South African security forces raided the meeting and arrested all 155 participants, including Nelson Mandela, who was to become the symbol of resistance to apartheid. Mandela was sentenced to five years in prison. He escaped and went underground, helping to established *Umkhonto we Sizwe* ("Spear of the Nation"). *Umkhonto*'s goal was to destabilize the government and end apartheid by means of sabotaging government offices and infrastructures. It intended to do so without human casualties.

For the next four decades, the government "tightened the screws" with more laws to squash opposition: the Suppression of Communism Act (1950) criminalized membership in the Communist Party; the Public Safety Act (1953) gave the government broad police power and the authority to declare states of emergency; the Criminal Law Act (1953) making opposition to the government illegal; and the Unlawful Organizations Act (1960) made black political organizations illegal. The ANC was banned in 1960 and more apartheid laws followed, including the prohibition of inter-racial marriage and sexual contact between the races.

Blacks were then classified as belonging to one of eight "tribal" groups, their classification determining which Bantustans (reservations) were now their "homes." Beginning in 1955, the government sent transports into black townships to carry residents and their few belongings to the Bantustans. Three and a half million blacks were removed from towns and relocated in Bantustans, only 13 percent of the country's land, with its poorest soil. Working-age blacks remained in white areas to work in daylight hours. They sent their meager wages to their families in Bantustans and returned there for the Christmas holidays. Primarily women, children, and the elderly lived in these desolate places without able-bodied men, although many women were also forced by economic necessity to migrate to white areas to work as domestics. All of this contributed to the breakup of black families.

To suppress opposition, the Sabotage Act (1962) classified sabotage as a crime punishable by hanging. The Indefinite Detention Terrorism Act (1967) permitted imprisonment without charge of a crime. At one point, 1,500 South Africans were in detention indefinitely. Banning individuals also silenced opposition. Banned persons were not permitted to travel outside a prescribed area, and sometimes could not even leave their homes. They were under constant police surveillance, and prohibited from meeting with no more than two people—sometimes only with their immediate families, and from speaking in public or publishing. Violation of the ban meant imprisonment.

In 1960, government troops opened fire on unarmed civilians who were protesting in the Sharpeville township. Seventy-two people were killed, and 200 were wounded. In 1970, blacks were stripped of South African citizenship and instead classified as citizens of Bantustans. In 1976, the army killed sixty children protesting a new government law requiring education to be conducted in Afrikaans.[4]

Black South Africans outnumbered whites seven to one. A slogan of U.S. protestors during protests of the Vietnam War was, "They [the United States government] got the guns but we got the numbers." The "guns" possessed by the apartheid government were an extensive network of military and police forces, security services, and intelligence services, giving the Afrikaner government hold on the country comparable to the Nazis control of Germany. South Africa was a police state, using brutal means of controlling blacks: torture, murder, "disappearances," kicking in doors and taking people away, and dispersing crowds by means of armored carriers. Would there be an armed uprising by those who had "the numbers"?

In 1963, the ANC and SACP had established a "nerve center" on a secluded estate fifteen miles from Johannesburg where they would produce bombs and plan *Umkhonto* attacks. But government security forces invaded the estate on July 11, 1963, and found bomb-making materials and a cache of documents revealing plans and names of activists throughout the country. Three whites and five blacks were arrested without resistance, and no weapons were found. Those not rounded up fled the country. *Umkhonto* was destroyed, although some of its members continued to plant bombs for another decade to the frustration of security forces. Among the names found was that of Nelson Mandela. He and seven others were charged with high treason, punishable by death. Bram Fischer, an Afrikaner and Oxford-trained lawyer, and a member of the South African Communist Party, headed the legal defense team. Mandela gave a four-hour statement to the court at the close of the trial, saying in part:

> I do not deny that I planned sabotage. It was the result of a calm and sober assessment of the political situation . . . of tyranny, exploitation, and oppression of my people by whites. . . . When we took this decision the ANC heritage of nonviolence and racial harmony was very much with us. . . . Sabotage was a way to release growing anger that would lead to civil war. We felt that the country was drifting toward civil war. . . . We viewed the situation with alarm. Civil war would mean the destruction of what the ANC stood for. (Frankel 1999, p. 239)

All defendants were found guilty and sentenced to life in prison. The sole violence the guerilla movement had committed was sabotage that served mainly to keep hope alive that blacks still had some ability to strike back. Martin Luther King, Jr. had this to say about the South African sabotage campaign:

> Clearly there is much in Mississippi and Alabama to remind South Africans of their country, yet even in Mississippi we can organize to register black voters, we can speak to the press, and we can in short organize the people in nonviolent action. But in South Africa even the mildest form of nonviolent resistance meets with years of imprisonment, and leaders over many years have been restricted and silenced and imprisoned. We can understand, in this situation, people felt so desperate that they turned to other methods, such as sabotage. (King 1964, n.p.)[5]

Bram Fischer, despised by fellow Afrikaners, was arrested in 1966 and charged with high treason. At his trial, he defended the SACP as not interested in "establishing a dictatorship of the proletariat but of equality and dignity for all the people of South Africa."[6] He said that the SACP did not share the Soviet Union's ideology of violent overthrow but was committed to the defense, liberation, and equality of black Africans. He did not believe in the defense of blacks "by any means necessary." Bram was found guilty and also sentenced to life in prison. The ANC and SACP members were all labeled anarchists, communists, and terrorists committed to the overthrow of the government. ANC, PAC, and SACP members had taken risks that altered the course of their lives.[7] There seemed to be no light at the end of the tunnel.

Few Afrikaners and English-speaking white South Africans had allowed themselves to see the brutality toward blacks and the poverty in which they were forced to live. A documentary about the black boycott of white stores in the township of Elizabethtown featured an interview of a white woman who said she had never been in a black township and had no knowledge of life there, although she lived only a short distance from the township. White consciences could only remain untroubled by not looking (Ackerman and Duval 2000, n.p.).[8]

Steve Biko was one of the many young activists killed by government forces. Inspired by the SNCC in the American South, he had helped to found the South African Student Organization (SASO). SASO was a forceful advocate of black consciousness and provided health, literacy, and development projects in the townships, mirroring Gandhian work for "village uplift." In 1977, Steve Biko died of head injuries while in police custody.

Trevor Huddleston, an Anglican priest, had come from England in the 1940s to pastor a church and administer a school in Sophiatown, a black township outside of Johannesburg. It was older than other black townships, and black culture had thrived there. Its population had swelled as other townships were destroyed, creating a giant slum. In 1956, Huddleston published *Naught for Your Comfort* that described the crimes police committed in Sophiatown (Huddleston 1956, p. 64). A man who forgot his pass was kicked in the stomach so many times by a policeman that he died. A worker moving too slowly was beaten to death. The foreman who killed him was exonerated by the court. Huddleston had testified and was warned by the judge at the trial never to impugn the character of a white man. When the government decided to move blacks further away from white areas, squatters' tin and cardboard shacks were razed.

Huddleston related a story that he believed made a strong moral judgment on English-speaking Christians who supposedly opposed apartheid. One day a young Afrikaner made a delivery to Huddleston's school. He asked what the school was for, and Huddleston explained that it was a boarding school that prepared black South Africans for college. The young man said that was a waste of time because blacks needed only an elementary education. Reverend Huddleston asked him why blacks were considered inferior and denied equal opportunities. The young man replied that the separation of the races was God's will; that only at the "eschaton"—the end time when Christ returned—would the races be united. Huddleston was surprised how thoroughly the doctrine of apartheid was held by Dutch Reform Church members. "In a way the young man was correct," Huddleston wrote, because "the DRC cannot conceive of a relationship between whites and blacks *in this world*" (Huddleston 1956, pp. 74–75). Huddleston wished that English-speaking Christians would be able to articulate as clearly the Christian truth of the unity of the races *in this world* that the Gospel commands.

Huddleston condemned the years of passivity:

> The church sleeps on—though it occasionally talks in its sleep and expects (or does it?) the government to listen. He said that "the church's silence, indifference, and submission [was] deafening." (Huddleston 1956, p. 189)

He left South Africa shortly after publishing his book, writing "I weep because we have failed so utterly to uphold principle over prejudice, the rights of persons against the claims of power" (Huddleston 1965, 189). Only slowly did the Anglicans, Presbyterians, Methodists, Lutherans, Congregationalists, and Roman Catholics come to condemn apartheid. A few members of the DRC began to protest their church's stance. One was theologian Beyers Naudé. In 1968, he founded the Christian Institute, committed to ending apartheid. Initially, he worked with whites but then turned the Institute's energy to empowering blacks. Naudé and the Institute were banned in 1977, the DRC continuing to support apartheid.

What was the impetus for the DRC to finally change its stance on apartheid? One factor was the establishment of the World Council of Churches (WCC), which today is comprised of over 350 denominations. The WCC opposed apartheid and in 1960 met with eighty South African church leaders to encourage them to do the same. The DRC attendees signed the resolution condemning apartheid but recanted when their church leaders condemned it. In 1968, the South African Council of Churches (SACC) was established, calling apartheid a "false faith," and contrary to the unity of all people that God wills. In 1970, the WCC announced "A program to Combat Racism." By that point, the government was so incensed with the WCC that it refused to allow its officials to enter the country. The SACC and Southern Africa Catholic Bishops Conference (SACBC) wrote that white South Africans should consider refusing military service and that the government must respect the right of its citizens to claim conscientious objection. Instead, the government sentenced conscientious objectors to prison.

The *Kairos Document* (1985), signed by 150 church leaders, distinguished three kinds of theology: "state theology" legitimizing apartheid, "church theology" focusing primarily on the spiritual life of individuals, and "liberation theology" bearing prophetic witness by joining the struggle for human rights and justice. The Document said that while church theology decried violence on all sides if it remained neutral it was accepting the racist regime's legitimacy. Neutrality enabled the status quo of oppression to continue. The *Kairos Document* demanded action:

> [Churches] must move beyond a mere "ambulance ministry" of participation . . . Church actions and campaigns must be in consultation, co-ordination, and cooperation with the peoples' political organizations rather than be a "third force." . . . It must mobilize its members in every parish to begin to think and work and plan for a change of government in South Africa. . . . We pray that God will help all of us to translate the challenge of our times into action. (World Council of Churches 1985, n.p.)

Frank Chikane, president of the SACC, condemned the hypocrisy of debating whether the oppressed were morally permitted to use violence while daily the oppressors maintained their power by violence. He warned that if the state refused to dismantle apartheid, it could not expect its long-suffering victims to defend themselves nonviolently.[9] The SACC and SACBC were banned in 1980 but continued to be headaches for the government. In 1989, both of their headquarters were bombed. That year 30,000 marched in Cape Town led by Anglican bishop Desmond Tutu; 25,000 marched in Johannesburg led by Chikane. Denis Hurley, the Catholic Bishop of Durban, was arrested for claiming that the military had invaded Namibia. (He was exonerated and sued the government for defamation and won.) The government literally barred church doors, but the South African Supreme Court ruled it was suppression of religious freedom. In 1990, the DRC was expelled from its own World Alliance of Reformed Churches that had labeled "apartheid" a heresy. Only then did the DRC renounce apartheid and ask forgiveness for years of injustices committed against black South Africans.

Between 1950 and 1989, opponents of apartheid had used various Gandhian forms of resistance with increasing intensity: marches against the pass laws, protests against all sorts of oppressive measures, boycotts, strikes by workers demanding unions, community self-improvement organizations to engage larger numbers of people, and alternative governmental structures established in the townships. The goal was empowerment. Popo Molefe, a member of the ANC, proposed a two-part strategy to empower the black population and its white supporters. Grassroots organizations should work on local issues and then broader political organizations should be developed to coalesce popular pressure for a free South Africa. Molefe was arrested and received a ten-year prison sentence.

Desmond Tutu, Anglican Archbishop of Johannesburg, urged those struggling against apartheid to remain nonviolent. As had Gandhi, Tutu insisted that the means of struggle must be consistent with the end of a just and peaceful South Africa. Tutu was awarded the Nobel Prize in 1984. The only violence was some black-on-black, when blacks considered to be collaborators were killed.

Chapter 5

In 1987, a book by American theologian Walter Wink was widely circulated (Wink 1986). Wink argued that an armed struggle against apartheid would not qualify as a just war because of wide-scale deaths of civilians that would surely occur. An armed struggle would indeed have horrific consequences. South African Defense Forces would destroy townships in their hunt for "terrorists," fill prisons, and increase black outrage. A civil war would destroy what little blacks had. In the end, even if a civil war succeeded, the resulting carnage would make rebuilding an overwhelming task that would take decades. Many blacks would flee to neighboring countries, perhaps producing millions of refugees.

In the mid-1980s, approximately 650 South African organizations joined forces as the United Democratic Front (UDF). The coalition included unions, civil society organizations, and banned organizations, including the SACC, the SACBC, and the ANC. The overwhelming opposition to apartheid could no longer be contained, even though a huge part of South Africa's defense budget was for internal control. South Africa also became economically vulnerable as the international community imposed economic sanctions. After thirteen years of advocacy by the United States Congressional Black Caucus, Congress passed—over President Ronald Reagan's veto—the Comprehensive Anti-Apartheid Act (1986), prohibiting new loans to and investments in South Africa and banning the sale of computers to the government, and imports of South African products. Between 1986 and 1988, thirty-six corporations ended their South African operations. Of all the justice struggles described so far, this time external economic pressure played a major role.

It became clear that apartheid could not survive. In 1989, President F. W. de Klerk announced the repeal of apartheid laws, lifted the bans on organizations and individuals, and permitted the return of those who had been exiled. In the early 1990s, a new constitution was written and approved by the South African parliament. In the 1994 election, Nelson Mandela, the great proponent of a peaceful transfer of power, was elected as president. Ahead lay the monumental tasks of education, employment, housing, and health care for millions of black South Africans and the opening of economic and political institutions for their participation.

What can be learned from the South African struggle, one of the largest and longest nonviolent struggle of the twentieth century? What gave the population hope? The ANC and SACP took risks that cost their members dearly. The minimal sabotage campaign was a warning to the Afrikaner government that opposition would increase if apartheid was not dismantled.[10] The churches finally stood up, moving beyond merely preaching the unity of all people and condemning racism. Only when church leaders and their members took to the streets and withdrew support of the government did their solidarity become a force. The South African opposition was blessed with wise leaders; only a few of the most well-known have been mentioned here. In far-off Bantustans, the news of black liberation came slowly. The cheering reverberated when Nelson Mandela walked out of prison in February 1990, after twenty-seven years. A day like no other came in April 1994 when black South Africans voted for the first time in their lives and elected Mandela as president.

This and the past chapters have focused on nonviolent struggles against racism. Throughout these tumultuous struggles, the oppressed managed to keep in mind an important distinction: racist ideology was evil, but not the racists themselves. It was racism and not racists that must be attacked.

Afrikaner Bram Fischer described his transformation. He recalled having black playmates in his childhood but how his friendships with blacks ended in his adolescence. As a young adult, he was on a local racial affairs panel and had contact with blacks. When a black man shook his hand, he said that he was "repulsed," which troubled him greatly. He recalls:

> That night I spent many hours in thought trying to account for my strange revulsion, when I remembered I had never had such feelings toward my boyhood friends. What had become abundantly clear was that it was I who had changed, and not the black man. I came to understand that color prejudice was a wholly irrational phenomenon and that true human friendship could extend across the color bar once the initial prejudice was overcome. (Frankel 1999, p. 337)

The following two chapters examine U.S. violence and how Americans can work to overcome it. What happened in South Africa proved that a nonviolent future is possible. Working for change is difficult but its rewards are great.

FOR DISCUSSION

1. Consult the website of the United Farm Workers of America. What issues are they currently addressing? How would you assess the state of migrant farmworker campaigns today? How does the UFWA assist undocumented farmworkers?
2. What programs currently assist Native American tribes? Access their effectiveness. Look up Native American Studies school curricula.
3. Gandhi campaigned against South Africa's pass laws and other forms of oppression against Indians in South Africa. Why do you think he did not extend his campaigns to free black South Africans as well?
4. What anti-apartheid actions were most effective in bringing about the downfall of apartheid? By what activity could you imagine yourself being involved in U.S. anti-apartheid?

Chapter 6

Violent America

Conflict resolution theorists have examined nonviolent activism from Montgomery to Serbia, East Germany to Tunisia, and South Africa to the fields of California. Nonviolent methods are being practiced to prevent violence in many places of conflict. But the manner in which the United States engages the world is often violent. At home, violence is decried, but except for some civil rights greats, and small communities dedicated to nonviolence, it is not part of the American way. This chapter considers the violence of U.S. foreign policy and in its domestic life. The next chapter explores possibilities for increased commitments to nonviolent activism.

In the 1970s, Latin American theologians and philosophers adopted a form of social analysis they called "see, judge, act" for evaluating social, political, and economic structures. They identified how class differences, autocratic governments, and economic systems exploit the poor. They asked how structural systems could be reformed. Seeing and judging the American reality is the task of this chapter. What is in plain sight and how must it be judged if change is to happen?

EMPIRE

Here is a brief sketch of America's formative decades. English colonists were the first to arrive in North America. The second wave of immigrants were Irish and continental Europeans who were pushed west from the eastern seaboard in search of land. Indigenous peoples encountered these pioneers wanting their land. In the South, the importation of slaves would make "King Cotton" the largest U.S. export and slaveholders the country's first millionaires. With seemingly endless resources, wealth was to be found everywhere.

In 1821, John Quincy Adams, then Secretary of State, declared that the new nation would "not go chasing monsters around the world" but only protect the new nation from foreign aggression. But the U.S.' dynamic was expansion. The doctrine of Manifest Destiny asserted that North America belonged to Euro-Americans. In 1849, the United States defeated Mexico in a short war and paid Mexico $15 million as compensation for the annexation of one-fourth of Mexican territory that would become the states of California, Arizona, Texas, New Mexico, Nevada, and parts of Utah and Colorado.

The defeat of Spain in the Spanish-American war of 1898 allowed for the expansion of U.S. power in the Caribbean and across the Pacific. In 1914, the [Theodore] "Roosevelt Corollary" asserted that the United States had the right to replace South American regimes that failed to act "with efficiency and decency in social and political matters." The U.S. Marines occupied Nicaragua from 1912 to 1934. After World War II, the United States contended with Soviet and Chinese communism. It supplied arms to pro-U.S. Latin American nations to battle communist elements and socialist governments, less because they were undemocratic and more because they threatened the freedom of U.S. corporations to extract their resources. The U.S. Central Intelligence Agency (CIA) overthrew the nascent democratic government of Guatemala in 1954 and the democratically elected socialist government of Salvador Allende in Chile in 1971. The United States supplied military aid to Honduras and El Salvador, where leaders were rewarded for their loyalty to the United States. Again, the motivation for United States intervention was at its root economic, keeping countries open for American business.

When the Soviet Union collapsed in 1991, the United States was the world's sole superpower. For many Americans, "superpower" sounded positive, a power capable of exporting good government, championing rights, improving the condition of women, ending poverty by creating capitalist economies, and bringing violent and corrupt political criminals to justice. The list of supposedly "just causes" for intervention was long. But "superpower" masked the reality that the United States was an unrivaled empire. Like earlier empires, it would use violence to maintain its dominance. In 1997, a conservative Washington think tank proposed *The Project for the New American Century* (1997). It called for intervention across the Middle East to replace hostile states and urged an increase in the country's military defenses." To project U.S. strength, more defense spending was necessary to add more military bases to the 134 that the United States already had around the world. More resources were needed to fight on "multiple fronts" simultaneously.

As discussed in chapter 1, Afghanistan was invaded in October 2001 to hunt for the masterminds of 9/11. In 2003, Iraq was invaded, under the pretext that Hussein had weapons of mass destruction. *New York Times* columnist

Thomas Friedman wrote that "the real reason Iraq [was] invaded was because we could . . . and because [Saddam] deserved it and because he was right in the heart of that world" that we wanted to control (Friedman 2003). A high-ranking government official declared simply: "We're an empire now and when we act we create our own reality. . . . we'll act again, creating other new realities."[1] The United States was fighting terrorism in forty countries. George Kennan, former ambassador to the Soviet Union and later to Yugoslavia, called for realism in U.S. foreign policy, urging it to "withdraw from its public advocacy of democracy and human right," which he called "vainglorious and undesirable" because it was not true. The United States played a role in the failure of some of the nonviolent movements examined in previous chapters. For example, it supplied military hardware to Egypt and Israel for years. The United States and NATO tried to topple Milosevic, as noted in chapter 3, but it was Otpor's nonviolent campaign that succeeded.

In 2019, the Department of Defense announced plans to refocus its military strength away from the Middle East to the Russian and Chinese geopolitical spheres. The goal was to "project" U.S. military power in case either country considered aggression against its neighbors. A supporter of this new development is Reihan Salam, a defense analyst. While admitting that the 2019 $716 billion defense budget was bloated, he argued that the "great power competition" requires more military spending" (Salam 2020).[2] He warns that "United States military forces no longer enjoy unchallenged priority in every theater. . . . [and that] the United States sets out to do much more [through its military interventions] than do its potential rivals" What does "much more" mean? Salam echoes the logic that led to the U.S. quagmires in Southeast Asia and the Middle East. He nevertheless concludes that

> if our goal is to prevent China and Russia from dominating their neighbors, it helps to have United States troops forward-based in potential flashpoints so they're capable of blunting an enemy's advances, giving war-winning forces time to gather on the horizon. (Salam 2020)

Salam nevertheless criticizes "egregious waste," "mindless buying," corrupt military contracting, and the militarizing of foreign policy by vastly under-funding the State Department (Salam 2020).

The 2019 defense budget was $716 billion, representing 54 percent of federal discretionary spending. The combined defense budgets of the five nations with the next largest military budgets (China, Saudi Arabia, Russia, the United Kingdom, and Germany) were $335 billion. Together, they spent less than half of what the United States spends. The U.S. military budget does not include the cost of intelligence agencies. Two of them were established after World War II: the National Security Council (NSC) and the CIA.

After 9/11, the number of spy agencies grew to seventeen. Likewise, the military budget does not include the funding of the Veterans Administration.

Department of Defense (DOD) officials testify before Congress annually that new weapons systems are essential for the security of the country. Congress and the president do not question their claims, defense industry lobbyists—some 200 of them—help secure military contracts, and legislators are pressured to win contracts for their districts and states.

The president has nearly total discretion to initiate U.S. military intervention. The War Powers Act of 1973, passed by a joint resolution of Congress after the experience in Vietnam, was intended to prevent "presidential wars" by limiting interventions to ninety days without congressional approval. But once troops are on the ground, Congress is pressured to approve "supplemental military appropriations"—above and beyond the DOD budget.

MILITARY CONTRACTING

Wars are economic bonanzas for weapons producers. Especially since 9/11, corporations producing anti-terrorism weapons easily win government contracts. Azhar Azam writes that "in major conflicts around the globe, U.S. arms manufacturers have been the definite winners" (Azam 2019). Defense spending goes to 4,200 defense contractors employing two and one-half million workers, that is, 2 percent of the American workforce and 20 percent of all workers in the manufacturing sector.[3] John Tirman examined defense contracting twenty-five years ago. In 1995, $380 billion was awarded to contractors to produce military equipment and services for the DOD and foreign governments. Tirman reports that of the sixty-member government watchdog agency, the Defense Trade Advisory Group, fifty-seven come from defense industries (Tirman 1997, p. 10).

U.S. weapons manufacturers produce 60 percent of the world's arms. In 2018, the Stockholm International Peace Research Institute study of the arms trade reported that of the $420 billion' worth of weapons purchased around the world, U.S. companies had 60 percent of the market. In 2018, four of the five largest arms producers were U.S. corporations with sales of $148 billion.[4] By far, the largest markets are in the Middle East. Israel and Egypt buy billions of dollars of jet fighters and anti-aircraft systems. The largest U.S. customer is Saudi Arabia, which purchased $100 billion mostly of fighter jets in 2019 and is contracted to buy $300 billion more weapons over the next ten years.

Moral questions abound. Most critical is the sheer destructiveness of new generations of weapons. John Bellamy Foster writes:

Given the unprecedented destructiveness of contemporary weapons, which are defused ever more widely, the consequences for the population of the world could well be devastating beyond anything ever before witnessed. (Foster 2003, p. 6)[5]

The numbers of civilians killed and injured as a result of the greater destructiveness of weapons are growing. Saudi Arabia used American-made fighter jets against the Houthi people in Yemen; the fighter jets were refueled by U.S. air tankers. In addition, once weapons are sold, there is no way to prevent them from changing hands. The United States armed Afghanis in their war against the Soviet Union in the 1980s. Later, the Taliban used these arms against the United States. Countries also use weapons purchased from the United States against their own people. For example, helicopters and AK47s sold to Turkey have been used against its Kurdish population.

When the question of the morality of manufacturing weapons arises, weapons' manufacturers point to the economic benefits to the country because of the jobs that are created. They also use the rationale that if the United States did not sell weapons, then other countries would supply the demand. Oscar Arias, former President of Costa Rica (a nation that has never had an army), debunks the second argument:

> [Drug cartels] could argue that exporting mind-altering drugs to the United States is justified because the production of cocaine and marijuana creates jobs in their own agricultural, commercial, and industrial sectors. Moreover, it could be claimed that, if these drugs were not exported from Colombia or Bolivia, they would simply be supplied by other countries. (Tirman 1997, pp. 283–284)

Another question, but one not asked, is how much is weapon-spending stealing from the U.S. poor? That question leads to American domestic policies.

"WARS" ON THE HOME FRONT

Military language has seeped into the U.S. government's strategies for addressing domestic problems. In the 1960s, the United States declared "war on poverty." Fighting poverty obscured the systemic causes of poverty. Instead of examining the causes of poverty, the war turned on the poor themselves, characterizing them as lazy welfare cheats, not taking responsibility for their own lives and a burden on society. Poor people themselves became the problem. But most Americans in poverty are children, single mothers, the handicapped and ill, the elderly, those without health insurance, and veterans. By the late 1960s, the funding for the war on poverty was diminished by the cost of the war in Vietnam.

In the 1980s, the "war on drugs" and "war on crime" began. Aggressive laws were passed that imposed harsher punishments. Drug users (specifically people of color) and other felons went to prison and "truth in sentencing" laws kept them there. This ground does not need to be covered further; it is a well-known reality and one to which many Americans do not object. What were other options rather than criminalizing drug possession and filling prisons? Would the better policy have been to reduce the demand for drugs by providing drug rehabilitation? The United States now has the largest prison population in the world. And the grandchildren of those poor in the 1960s are just as poor.

The Homeland Security Agency established after 9/11 gave surplus military equipment to state and local law enforcement agencies. The "war on crime" became militarized. But the structural injustices that propel crime were insufficiently addressed.

Another war is being waged on the home front is a gun war. Gun violence has become part of daily life. A woman interviewed at the scene of a mass school shooting said "I'm not surprised. It was bound to happen eventually. My only surprise is that I am not surprised." Many high school students say they now accept the possibility that their schools will one day be targeted by a shooter. In response to the gunfire plaguing our society, citizens acquire more guns to defend themselves. Handguns and assault rifles are everywhere. According to the Gallup Poll, there are an estimated 250 million guns in the United States owned by 30 percent of the population. The largest number of gun owners are White men (Saad 2019).[6] Mass killings are the real terrorism in the United States. Terrorists are not foreigners but are homegrown, some angry and alienated, others White supremacists who kill people of color, of different faiths, or different sexual orientations.

Patrick Blanchfield urges Americans "not only to ask how to get rid of guns and what is going on in shooters' minds, but also to consider other questions we should be asking that we don't want to be asking."[7] The crucial question, he argues, is how we have

normalized and made acceptable public opinions that "others" are outsiders and dangerous. Such opinions drive the behavior of a few on the fringes, but they have led to social acceptance of the unacceptable, to toxic expressions of American identity. (Blanchfield 2019)

If we only mourn the victims and wonder how to stop this terrorism, we "will adopt the almost naïve, kind of childlike wonder—where could this possibly have come from?"

To date, wars against poverty, drugs, crime, and guns have all been lost.

CITIZEN ACTIVISM?

Citizen activism is essential to overcoming American violence. The civil rights movement in the South worked nonviolently, but many protests against the Vietnam war took other forms. Protestors turned to violence in their anger; violence split the country with the older generation usually more supportive of the war, at least until it became clear that the war was unwinnable. In 2003, nonviolent U.S. protest occurred on the eve of the second Iraq War. Massive protests occurred at home and in Europe. But when the war broke out, protestors gave up.

Mass protests do not materialize in the United States. There are several explanations. First, most U.S. citizens do not suffer the oppressive conditions that have led to nonviolent revolutions in Eastern Europe, Africa, Asia, and the Middle East. Americans who are economically secure do not protest the poverty of others. Second, Americans do not live under a dictatorship or a foreign occupation. The U.S. government does not suppress the rights to free expression and of assembly for most of its citizens, although at times these rights have been suppressed. The relative security of the middle class has a sedating effect. Many Americans pursue their private interests at the expense of civic engagement and concern for the common good. Those most affected by the fraying social safety net have little time and energy to do more than try to feed their families although some of the most energetic activists come from oppressed communities.

Military spending robs domestic program for job training, health care, adequate housing, nutrition, and education. The mortality rate for African American newborns is three times that of whites. The mortality rate for pregnant African American women is five times that of a pregnant white woman. The poor rely on food banks. In the richest country in the world, half of African American children live in households below the poverty line, as do one-fifth of all children in the United States. Indicators of the nation's health—levels of poverty, infant mortality, murder rates, and incarceration—paint a picture of social illness.

In *Habits of the Heart: Individualism and Commitment in American Life*, Robert Bellah and his colleagues asked people about their priorities (Bellah, Robert N., Richard Marsden, William M. Sullivan, Ann Swidler, and Steven M. Tipton 1983). One respondent said that in his college years he was politically active, but now with his law practice and family, he had little time for anything else though perhaps he might become involved in the Boy Scouts when his son got older. Bellah summarized the trend: Americans are very busy and most pay little attention to the wider community. They are consumed by work and the desire for upward mobility. Indicators of success are tangibles: ever-larger homes, expensive automobiles, and glamorous vacations. Life becomes a competition in which the finish line is a retirement of leisure. But self-promotion eclipses the common good.

Perhaps a telling feature of American life is the "home entertainment center" with a wall-to-wall video screen and surround sound. Viewers are distracted as they consume sporting events, violent video games (enjoyed primarily by men and boys), violent movies, docudramas about crime, reality TV, and interviews with celebrities. Merely watching is an invitation not to think but simply to allow themselves to be passive recipients of whatever producers want them to see and to buy. The more viewers consume this diet, the less able they are to differentiate entertainment from what is going on around them. Nguyen writes

> No matter the horrors Americans may see on their screens—the beheadings, the suicide bombings, the mass executions, the waves of refugees, the drone's eye view of war—the viewers who are not physically present at those events are anesthetized into resignation. This too is the "society of the spectacle" . . . a society in which all horror is revealed and *nothing is done on the part of the average citizen to resist it.* (Nguyen 2016, p. 14, italics in original)

In *Amusing Ourselves to Death: Public Discourse in the Age of Show Business*, Neil Postman analyzes the effect of television (Postman 1985). Print media, long the source of information, is being replaced by electronic media in which "news" is delivered in short sound bites. The images move so fast that they cannot be absorbed. Postman observes that news addresses many topics but is delivered in ways that require minimal ability to comprehend. Network news is now "a format for entertainment, not for education [or] reflection" (Postman 1985, p. 87). He concludes:

> When a population becomes distracted by trivia, when cultural life is redefined as a perpetual round of entertainment . . . then a nation finds itself at risk. Americans have moved far and fast in bringing to a close the age of the printed word and have granted TV sovereignty over all of their institutions. (Postman 1985, pp. 155–156)

To that may be added the many social media platforms that compete for attention. An example of how news and entertainment are fused is the way the first Iraq War (1991) was reported by one of the major network news. Each night during the war, coverage began with the image of a waving flag and patriotic music. A masthead read "America at War Day 1," then Day 2, and so on. Falling bombs, statistics of the number of bombing runs, and video of one incredibly accurate missile (replayed continuously) filled the screen. The bombings were celebrated as if they were Fourth of July fireworks. The war was a Super Bowl in which our team trounced the opponent. Almost the sole commentaries on the war were those of retired air force generals who described the types and lethality of U.S. aircraft and missiles. In this patriotic programming, there was no place for thoughtful discourse. There was no analysis of the justification for the U.S. war with Iraq, how it could have been avoided, or what the possible fallout would be. It was only about the euphoria of winning.

Marianne Williamson writes that "in a world where selfishness is the accepted ethos, a commitment to social justice is a rebellious form of being" (Williamson 1997, p. 87). And rebellion is viewed suspiciously. Citizenship requires taking a wider view and being concerned with the common good, with meeting the needs of others, and especially of the least well-off.

Although social problems are obvious, how many citizens will make time to fix them? Why do so few Americans commit themselves to the well-being of the larger American and world societies? How can the violence woven into the American fabric be undone? One way is by means of sustained nonviolent activism. Violence is undone by learning skills of activism and the virtues that sustain activism.

COVID-19, COMPASSION, AND THE COMMON GOOD

Passivism prevents citizen activism supporting any kind of social change. But as the United States battled the COVID-19 pandemic in 2020–2021, a deep polarization in American society happened that threatened the concept of citizen cooperation in addressing social justice issues.

The COVID-19 pandemic ravaged the world in 2020–2021. By the end of 2020, the estimated number of infection-carrying individuals was ninety-three million, and the death toll was around two million. In poor nations without any access to protective gear, hospital capacity, and later, vaccines, the numbers exploded into 2021. The United States reported 35,000 deaths by April 2020. The number had risen ten times by December, and by the winter of 2021 the death toll was over 560,000.

As reassuring as the signs "We are all in this together" were, we were actually not. White-collar workers were fortunate to be able to work from home in a safe environment. But those with low-paying service jobs did not have that option, continuing to work in dangerous conditions. Many lost those jobs as well. Factories and businesses shuttered, and the number of the unemployed reached 22 million by late spring 2021. Schools closed, which forced students to be taught remotely, forcing parents, mostly mothers, to drop out of the labor force. Unemployment increased the rate of childhood poverty, already high in the United States. Food pantries were overwhelmed and were forced to close when food was gone. Life changed abruptly, leaving millions unable to feed their families, pay bills, rent, and mortgages.

Yet, the suffering was not shared. Some reaped windfall profits. Online retailers, streaming services, and producers of essential goods made record profits. The Pentagon designated defense industries as an "essential critical infrastructure workforce" that were "protecting those in uniform" on par with health care workers, first responders, pharmacists, grocery store workers, and other truly essential workers. By law, the government could have redirected defense industries to produce the much-needed equipment to fight COVID-19, but that did not happen.

Race was the key determinant of who were most likely to contract and die from the virus. In Chicago, blacks constitute 32 percent of the population, but they accounted for 70 percent of COVID-19 deaths. Health conditions, such as diabetes, heart disease, asthma, and hypertension, contracted by blacks because of unhealthy living conditions and unavoidable exposure to the virus contributed to morbidity. U.S. surgeon general Jerome Adams attributed his own poor health to the "legacy of growing up poor and black in America," repeating the saying that "when whites get a cold, blacks get pneumonia."

How the country should contain the virus became a highly divisive issue, and many stopped raising the subject with those they assumed disagreed with them. What to do in the face of COVID-19 became a hotly divisive issue. Two camps emerged. The majority of Americans complied with the precautions laid out by epidemiologists. Even though only a few knew anyone who had died from the virus, they nonetheless recognized how deadly it was.

But a vocal number of Americans rejected the call to take precautions, claiming their right to personal freedom. They refused to agree that governments had the power to mandate mask wearing and limit or close businesses. Government officials were labeled "socialists." In some places, public health officials were threatened, and their advice was declared to be "only opinions."

Responses to COVID-19 differed along political party lines. Many Republicans intent on reopening the economy, encouraged by President Trump, made that the priority. Trump refused to wear a mask, leading millions of his base to do the same. Unknown numbers of those who attended his campaign rallies in 2020 contracted the virus. Trump developed a mild case of COVID-19 and recovered, boasting to his supporters that he "never felt better" and urging them not to fear the pandemic, as getting the U.S. economy on track would boost his chances of reelection. Some said the numbers of deaths were inflated; others asserted that the pandemic would quickly run its course. President Trump downplayed COVID-19, accusing the media of creating "false news" and a "hoax." Democrats were more likely to embrace the strategy of first bringing the pandemic under control. In this sense, the response to the pandemic was politicized. But the intransigence too reflected a deep polarization. The sides were poles apart, refusing to speak to each other.

At the height of the pandemic, health care workers desperately tried to save lives of the COVID-19 patients, overwhelming hospitals. Nurses and doctors could only ease the pain of those dying on ventilators. Family members could not be present, for a fear of spreading the virus. Medical personnel were traumatized. In 1947, Albert Camus published *The Plague,* a fictional account of how a community responded when the bubonic plague ravaged a city in French Algeria in the 1930s. A central character is Dr. Rieux, who for months feverishly cares for the stricken. Rieux is asked how he continues to serve day after day unfailingly. He responds:

> There is no heroism in all this. It's a matter of common decency. One could always refuse to face this disagreeable fact, shut one's eyes to it or thrust it out of mind, but there is a terrible cogency in the self-evident. How for instance, continue to ignore the funerals on the day somebody you loved needed one? (Camus 1947, p. 147, 154)

The microbe is natural, observes Rieux, but "all the rest—health, integrity, purity (if you like)—is a product of the human will, of a vigilance that must never falter." What stands out in the stricken city are the risks and sacrifices of its citizens to protect each other. Where was the compassion in those in the United States insisting on their freedom to behave as they chose and downplaying the effects of the pandemic? What was the relationship between demands of the common good and protecting the freedom of individuals?

The *Cambridge English Dictionary* defines "individualism" as "the idea that freedom of thought and action for each person is the most important quality of a society, rather than shared effort and responsibility." Alexis de Tocqueville visited the United States in the 1830s and described his impressions in *Democracy in America* (Tocqueville 1835 and 1840). He characterized the country as one of "competitive individualism" which fosters commerce. He warned that individualism "disposes each citizen to isolate himself from the mass of his fellows and withdraw into the circle of family and friends" (Tocqueville 1830, p. 506).

The common good is goods and conditions that all people require to flourish. The common good is not the private goods of individuals taken together; many people who do not have access to goods would be left out. The common good is not the "greatest good for the greatest number" for that leaves out the needs of the "lesser number." The common good includes what all members of a society need to thrive. Those who chose to "strike out on one's own," taking their chances with COVID-19, did not account for the possibilities that they might spread it to others or become infected themselves, requiring scarce medical resources.

COVID-19 was not the only reflection of the fissures in American life. As noted in chapter 4, in the wake of George Floyd's death, masses of Americans denounced police violence against blacks and demanded police reform. Large protests in the United States and internationally went on for weeks. Most marchers were peaceful, but tempers flared on occasions, and protestors destroyed property. Police, the national guards, and paramilitaries attacked "Black Lives Matter" protestors in several instances. President Trump asserted tough—that is, violent—enforcement of law and order. He blamed Democratic local and state officials for being weak in handling protests. Over and over, the message was that the protesters had contempt for their country and the police. At the same time, leading up to the 2020 presidential election, Trump repeated the baseless claim that Democrats had rigged the election. When he lost, a mob of his supporters attacked the U.S. Capitol on January 6, 2021, to prevent Congress from certifying the election of Joe Biden. Five people died. A mix of hate groups, neo-Nazis, and white supremacists were the country's homegrown terrorists.

Isabel Wilkerson writes of those who in disbelief say:

"This is not America," or "I don't recognize my country," or "This is not who we are. But this is who we are," whether we have known or recognized it or not. (Wilkerson 2020, p. 4)

The crucial need is to bridge the deep chasm in American life in order to address issues of justice. Regarding COVID-19, the poles were often stark:

- Controlling the spread of the virus requires/does not mean sacrificing personal freedom.
- Poverty made people of color much more likely to die from the virus/maintaining good health is a personal responsibility.

Divides were just as stark in many other issues such as public health, climate change, policing, incarceration, and foreign defense spending. The COVID years revealed again the disconnect.

A survey by the Pew Research Center in 2014 found a widening gap between conservatives and liberals between 1994 and 2014:

Partisan animosity has increased substantially over the same period. In each party . . . the share of a highly negative view of the opposing party has more than doubled since 1994. Most of these intense partisans believe the opposing party's policies "are so misguided that they threaten the nation's well-being." (Pew 2014)

In *Together: The Healing Power of Human Connection in a Sometimes Lonely World*, Vivek Murthy, former U.S. surgeon general, reports that a poll in 2018 found that 79 percent of those polled believed that "the negative tone and lack of civility in Washington will lead to violence" (Murthy 2020, p. 160). In Congress and state legislatures, the tone of opposing views has become shrill, the truth twisted to score points, and divisions among constituents deepened. Murthy observes that broad disconnection contributes to "loneliness, alienation, and anger violently expressed" (Murthy 2020, p. 140). That proved prophetic on January 6, 2021. Do citizens at the grassroots offer a better hope for restoring civility and dialogue?

Ways must be found to gather people of different opinions to engage in nonthreatening conversations. We naturally feel most comfortable talking with those who share our views. But encounters across divides may reveal that others are not so different than us. If peoples in other times and places have sat down with those who were threatening their lives, cannot Americans find common ground? Those who are assumed to be far apart may develop the goodwill it takes to collaborate. A remedy is civility and inclusion that happens when people listen to and respect one another. Listening is more effective than presenting data confirming that one is right and the other wrong. It is more important to learn to understand why views are different and to find ways to build the common good.

FOR DISCUSSION

1. What specific campaigns to reduce U.S. military spending do you think might work?
2. Why has civic activism declined in the United States?
3. What do you think are the most effective means of drawing Americans into nonviolent activism?
4. Suggest a concrete way to bring people of opposing views into conversation on a specific justice issue.
5. Given that today's social media is here to stay, by what means can Americans be more critically informed rather than only entertained?
6. This account of the U.S. way of life should also highlight the good which Americans do? Identify some of the strengths of the nation. How can they best be "exported" without trying to impose them?

Chapter 7

Nonviolent Citizen Movements for Justice

Henry David Thoreau was a staunch critic of the Mexican American War. He protested, refused to pay his taxes, and went to jail. Thoreau also opposed slavery. In his essay "Civil Disobedience" (1846) he called for a nonviolent "revolution of one" to abolish slavery, writing

> If one thousand, if one hundred, if ten men whom I could name, __ if ten honest men, __ ay, one HONEST man, in this state of Massachusetts, *ceasing to hold slaves,* were actually to withdraw from this copartnership, and be locked up in the county jail therefore, it would be abolition of slavery in America. (Lynd and Lynd 1995, p. 7)

He continued that "the only place in a slave state in which a free man can abide with honor is prison." Thoreau hoped to stir consciences. But prophetic witness does not provide direction for action. When it came to abolition, William Lloyd Garrison created an abolition movement. He vowed: "I will lecture, circulate tracts and publications, form societies, and petition our state and national governments" (Lynd and Lynd 1995, p. 16). While Thoreau was a voice crying in the wilderness; Garrison was an organizer. This is the difference between prophets and practitioners, those who condemn and those who actively work for reform. The first part of this chapter considers a number of building blocks for effective citizen activism. The second part suggests how movements can overcome U.S. violence abroad and at home.

BUILDING BLOCKS

Motivating People to Participate

Americans in general are not inclined to join movements. How can they be motivated to be involved? There are several possible motivations. Many citizens belong to religious communities that stress justice and compassion (as will be discussed further in the next chapter) and warn against worshiping idols, embodied in empires. Another reason for activism is the political freedoms Americans enjoy. The U.S. Constitution's Bill of Rights guarantees freedoms of speech and assembly. Many other peoples do not have such rights and often risk their lives struggling for human rights, justice, and freedom. U.S. citizens have the means and responsibility to influence their government's behavior and the health of American society. Involvement in movements—other than the U.S. civil rights struggles examined in chapters 4 and 5—is low-risk. The principal risk Americans face when they express opposition to the status quo is disapproval by others. The Chambonaise defied the Germans and criticized those who would not speak out or resist the Vichy government's policies. They called them the "what will [others] say people," afraid of not holding prevailing public opinions.

Another argument for resisting violence is that it may worsen. For example, presently in the United States, supremacist groups are committed to making America a "white Christian nation." They are attacking people of color, people of other religions, and people not of heterosexual orientation. Can they be ignored in hopes that they will disappear?

Another reason for acting is concern for the world that the next generation will inherit. If problems are not addressed now, what will our children face? What will they think of their parent's failure to act? Inaction is acting, not making a decision is deciding, not being racist oneself does not work to overcome systemic racism. The Holocaust happened to a great extent because good people remained silent as the persecution of their Jewish neighbors worsened. Many have warned that the harm done by evildoers is as much the result of the passivity of good people. Blueprints for action must be at hand.

Movement Leadership

Leaders possess convictions and commitments that are admired and attractive to others. Leaders project optimism that goals can be attained. They are collaborative in setting goals, welcoming the contributions of others. It is a temptation for leaders to impose their vision, to insist on making major decisions, and to dictate strategies. They are tempted to want to micro-manage the movement. They may behave that way because they have invested so much in the work. Activism controlled by only a few can expect participation to dwindle when participants are only seen as numbers and not contributors. Movements are by definition composed of many people whose variety of ideas enrich movements. Movements must model democracy. Leaders don't allow adversaries to dissipate the movement's energy. Finally, leaders who display humility and acknowledge failure are being honest. Displaying their fallibility humanizes them. Movements acknowledging mistakes can right their course.

Youthful Participation

The Otpor movement in Serbia was begun by the young generation in Belgrade. Youth bring idealism, energy, new thinking, and creativity to the able. Psychologist Alison Gopnik reports that her research finds there is a "burst in creativity in the social world in adolescence. . . . I think there is a lot of reasons to believe that adolescents are often at the cutting edge of social change. And part of that is this capacity to think about all the different possibilities about the way the world could be."[1] The future of the young is at stake. They may change the views of their elders. Still young, they may have fewer family responsibilities and more time for social commitments. Today, young people are conspicuously leading the environmental and gun control movements. As they persuade their parents to join, movement participation grows.

John Paul Lederach, who has facilitated negotiations in Northern Ireland and Nicaragua, describes what keeps participation strong:

> In my view, the single most important aspect of encouraging an organic perspective on peace-building politics is creating a genuine sense of participation, responsibility, and ownership in the process across a broad spectrum of the population. People must move from sitting back and reacting toward a proactive engagement that helps shape and define the process. (Lederach 1998, p. 242)

Channeling Energy into Concrete Strategies and Tactics

Goals must be clear and easily describable. Multiple goals may be commendable but may be too much to tackle simultaneously. A movement spreads itself thin by tackling too many issues at once. Accomplishing small goals at first are confidence builders. They can instill confidence that more victories will follow. For instance, in Montgomery, desegregation was the issue. But the planners chose one goal at first: desegregation of the busses. Later came Freedom Riders' action to integrate all interstate transportation and then the immense task of Freedom Summer's initiative to register thousands of blacks to vote. All of these actions challenged segregation, but they were incremental. Each victory moved the needle toward greater optimism and more participation.

How will one's resources be most effectively used? Will focus be civil disobedience? What will be most effective at a particular time: marches, demonstrations, strikes, boycotts, student staying home from school, shop closings, government workers not reporting to work, refusal to pay taxes, for other actions? Tactics are specific actions, the when, where, who, how. What will be boycotted? Who will strike and how will their families be provided for if strikers are arrested? How long will it last? When is the best time?

Gandhi learned that training people for nonviolent action was critically important. When Indians arrived at the Dharsana Salt Works to interrupt salt production, they were prepared for the possibility of being attacked and were resolved not to fight back. Their ability not to defend themselves was not what human beings instinctively do. But by remaining nonviolent, they displayed greater power than their attackers. King reminded the foot soldiers of the Montgomery movement to be prepared to suffer. King saw the necessity of offering workshops on how to respond nonviolently if attacked. That was especially important on the days after the buses were first integrated and white reactions might be inflammatory. As noted in chapter 4, in Nashville, the Fellowship of Reconciliation conducted seminars on the theory and practice of nonviolence. With that preparation, students were equipped with the strength not to respond if they were verbally or physically attacked. The natural response is to fight back. Retaliation would have damaged the movement, conveying a picture of the sit-ins as simply a fight between hoodlums on both sides. Instead, protestors were judged by many as courageous and committed to a legitimate goal. Recall that Gandhi once organized a mass march that became violent when an element untrained in nonviolence killed policemen. He vowed hence forth that all participants be satyagrahis.

Influencers

John Paul Lederach describes two levels of contributors to movements. Nearest to movements are local authorities who are well known and know the justice issue over which a group is struggling. They should be reached out to. At a higher level are national or international authorities, whose influence is less powerful because they speak in generalities rather than to specific situations and are not part of the community (Lederach 1998, p. 242).

Forming Coalitions

The larger and more organized a movement becomes the more power it wields. In an age of easy access to other organizations through the Internet, identifying allies is not difficult. A caveat is that other organizations need to share the philosophy of nonviolence. In South Africa, 650 organizations joined forces in 1983, forming the "United Democratic Front" which the apartheid government could not resist for long.

Working with Adversaries

Being educated in the facts and issue makes the positions of activists more compelling. When opponents are confronted with the facts, they are less able to deny the justice issues, although they will try. The essential need is to put forth a convincing argument difficult for adversaries to counter. Negotiating with opponents is unlikely to succeed quickly. As King said, those with power and privilege do not give them up voluntarily. Victory may take months or years. Patience is all-important. Indian independence took three decades, the South African victory over apartheid six decades, and the success of Solidarity in Poland ten years. The race struggle in the United States is still going on fifty years after the Civil Rights Act and Voting Rights Act were passed. A strategy of those in power is to outlast oppositions, counting on them losing support and energy to imply to wait it out until activists give up and go away. Movement leaders should anticipate what is likely to occur if they try to bargain. Typically, someone low on the organizational chart, with no decision-making power, meets with movement representatives. At the end of the meeting, the company representative will say that he or she does not have the authority to act on the movement's demands but promises to convey the information to decision-makers. Nothing further happens. Movements must determine who the decision-makers are and insist on negotiating directly with them. It may be a good strategy to work with several adversaries simultaneously. If negotiation with one succeeds, there may be a domino effect. Even when negotiations stall, it is important to keep channels of communication open.

Not Burning Out

Resmaa Menakem advises preparing yourself for action, "first settle your own body and nervous system" (Menakem 2017). Otherwise, activists are driven by constant tension. Menakem observes that

> It is easy to get caught up in social activism to the point where you allow yourself little or no downtime. But no human body can be activated all the time. Your body's abilities are finite. . . . Listen to your body, Give it adequate rest, recovery, leisure, relaxation, and rejuvenation. Help it settle, over and over. All of this is required, not optional. (Menakem 2017)[2]

HOW NOT TO CONDUCT
AN ENVIRONMENTAL CAMPAIGN

Activism fails for different reasons. Consider what happened at a critical moment in a demonstration to protect the environment. In July 2019, a group of activists gathered in downtown Salt Lake City to protest a proposed transportation hub that they claimed would cause severe environmental harm, especially to the poor living in the area. They gathered in front of the building housing the planners of the hub, where their spokesperson, calling herself an anarchist, told the crowd that damage to the environment was connected to other injustices: the mistreatment of immigrants, past crimes against indigenous people, police brutality, and capitalism. All were part of the violent American system, she said. "Rise up. Rise up. There is no more putting this off," she urged the crowd. At that point, the demonstrators stormed the building, banging on walls and windows and throwing furniture. Police arrived and fights broke out. Five protestors were arrested.

Afterward, both sides accused the other of violent behavior. A group calling itself "Civil Riot" said law enforcement "served and protected the wealthy and their property, not the majority of the people." The police defended their escalation of force when physical property is destroyed, and peoples' safety is at risk. The governor described the protestors as "borderline terrorists," and part of a "radical fringe element growing out of control in the country." Another official said: "This was more than people standing up for a cause they believe in; this was having no tolerance for a difference of opinion. This was bullying, intimidation, and violence and will not be tolerated."

This incident illustrates the failure to engage in serious discussion of the demonstrators' legitimate environmental concerns. Instead, they demanded that a number of different issues must be addressed. In the chaos that ensued the environmental cause was eclipsed.

Below are concrete goals, strategies, and tactics that citizen movements might develop to transform U.S. violence abroad and at home. They are only suggestive, for movements themselves must choose goals and how best to achieve them.

CHALLENGING U.S. VIOLENCE ABROAD

War Reparations

In the aftermath of the U.S. wars in Iraq and Afghanistan, the United States had an obligation to repair the damages it had done, the harm it inflicted on civilians and the infrastructure destruction it caused. Humanitarian organizations tried to extend aid but had very limited capacities. When the government did not acknowledge its responsibilities to repair the damages, citizen movements may find ways to respond, even in limited ways.[3] What might they do both to help and to call attention to the need to repair damages done? Campaigns might be organized to repair hospitals, water treatment plants, fire stations, and so on. Committing to meeting the medical needs of specific war victims whose names and faces become known humanizes themz are humanized. When people see firsthand the harm war does, they are less likely to passively watch as future war-making is on the horizon. The very first question is why the United States goes to war and incurs these tragic damages in the first place. In addition, when citizens commit their own resources, they may rightly ask critical questions: is not repairing the damage the responsibility of the U.S. government? isn't that rightly part of the defense budget which taxes pay for?

Defense Spending

Decades of citizen disapproval of bloated military spending have not coalesced into protests. At the federal level, the executive branch and the Department of Defense face no real criticisms of runaway spending. For the most part, defense budgets are approved intact. Members of Congress vote against budget line items. What are credible strategies to radically reduce military spending? How can grassroots movements effect change? Criticizing defense spending may appear unpatriotic or at least futile. A hopeful development was the creation of the Quincy Institute for Responsible Statecraft in 2019. It is a think tank dedicated to reforming U.S. foreign policy and the rush to war. It works to avoid violence through a foreign policy that

- ceases to conceive of the United States as the world's police force;
- undertakes military action only as a genuinely last resort, recognizing that "force ends human life, displaces people, devastates communities, and damages the environment"; and
- engages American citizens in a "robust and inclusive debate about America's role in the world"; and recognizes that the purpose of U.S. foreign policy and defense policy is "securing the safety and well-being of the

American people while respecting the rights and dignity of all [across the world]."

At a local level, it might be possible to focus on one defense budget line item. Is something being funded that is redundant, unnecessary, or forced on the Pentagon by defense industry lobbyists? For example, fighter jets cost between $66 and $117 million in 2021. How many inner-city clinics could be funded instead? How is improved health a better investment? The more concrete the comparison the more compelling an argument becomes. U.S. military contracting has produced some of the greatest corporate wealth and abuses in American history. The U.S. government and foreign governments buy billions of dollars of military hardware from U.S. weapons makers.[4] How might citizen movements advocate for reform? Citizen activists might

- Act as watchdogs to stop foreign weapons sales that violate U.S. laws. In August 2020, the U.S. secretary of state approved the sale of $8.1 billion worth of fighter jets, on the pretense that the sale was a "national security emergency," when in fact the weapons were to be used for the continuation of Saudi Arabia's bombing campaign against the Houthis in Yemen (Shesgreen 2020).[5] Congress had tried unsuccessfully to stop the sale. (In 2019, British activists went to court and won a judgment that British arms makers were selling weapons banned under British law.[6]) Movements that seek to challenge the sales of weapons to be used against civilians will find an ally in Amnesty International's Office of Strategic Litigation.
- Organize boycotts of weapons makers who also produce consumer products. Recall the United Farm Workers grape strike that won support across the United States and led to an effective boycott of table grapes. Nestle corporation stopped selling baby formula in Africa when the product's dangers were recognized. Responding to a student-led campaign, U.S. colleges and universities refused to buy clothing made in foreign sweatshops. For some companies, profits from military sales may not be worth the bad publicity and loss of domestic sales.
- Identify and publicize those corporations that produce the most inhumane weapons. A current case is the production of land mines that were banned by a treaty signed in 1997 by over forty countries. Although the United States was not a signatory, it has not used landmines in thirty years nor have they been manufactured since 2002. In 2019, the Trump administration resumed the purchase of land mines as part of its new Russia-China military focus.[7]
- Research and publicize the long-term economic effects on communities that depend almost solely on military industries for employment and the tax base; they are at the mercy of Pentagon spending decisions. A city

manager in Connecticut expressed worry that if the military no longer wanted Sigorski Helicopter his city would be in financial crisis.

The claim is often made that a reduction in military spending will free up funds for underfunded domestic programs. That may not necessarily happen. But again, if a single military expense can be identified, especially one that can be easily demonstrated to be wasteful and then tied to a specific domestic need with a similar cost, that might gain public support. It is a very concrete and easily explained goal.

OVERCOMING VIOLENCE AT HOME

Systemic Racism

Racism has been called America's "original sin" (Wallis 2016). For its victims, it is a chronic and fatal disease. Racism also drives U.S. interventions abroad, as King pointed out in "A Time to Break Silence" (1967). People of color and blacks are disproportionately sent to war.

Racism is the foundation of damage to the lives of African Americans. It is the leading cause of poverty and poor health, incarceration, and police violence. What goals can citizen movements undertake to address poverty-level wages, inadequate schooling, the incarceration of black men, and broken families and communities? What is required of white Americans to respond to racism? Diversity workshops point out how whites make missteps when interacting with African Americans and how to respect and appreciate other cultures. But many whites believe that they know all about racism and that racial prejudice existed in the past but not any longer. They are resentful that it continues to be brought up. For their part, African Americans are weary of explaining their experiences of racism. Understanding racism requires conscience raising, a "Racism 101."

Joy DeGruy examines the psychological damage done to African Americans from the arrival of slave ships four centuries ago until today (DeGruy 2005). DeGruy analyzes what she calls the "post-traumatic slave syndrome." A syndrome is a condition that has a life of its own and is not easily overcome. Traumas continue to occur with a triggering event that wounds deeply and causes the debilitating experience to return and reinjure again, physically, mentally, and spiritually. How is racism still wounding blacks? DeGruy describes three symptoms of post-traumatic slave syndrome. First is "vacant esteem," the lack of a sense of one's potential to contribute to the community. Malcolm X made the powerful observation: "The worst crime whites have committed against blacks was to make blacks hate themselves." As other black leaders have done, Malcolm X worked to overcome self-hatred. It produces nihilism. African American men, especially young men, believe that their lives will be short and end violently. In some cases, they hasten their own deaths by violent confrontations with the police, called "suicide by cop." The second symptom is anger, again especially in black men, when they are prevented from prospering and achieving goals. It often takes the form of self-destructive anger toward others as well as anger turned in on themselves. The third symptom is "racist socialization," the daily experiences of being treated as subordinate and as inferior. What African American male is not diminished by the way he is perceived by white society? "If I stand, I am loitering. If I walk, I am prowling. If I run, I am escaping." Prejudice creates hopelessness.

A TRUE STORY OF POST-TRAUMA SLAVE SYNDROME

"James" is an African American serving a 22-year prison sentence. Here is the story of his life to date. James's grandparents came North in the 1950s, where his grandfather found a good factory job. But the factory closed in the 1980s, and he never found another well-paying job. His daughter, James's mom, quit school. She bore three children. She was a single mom and worked in a fast-food restaurant for minimum wage and had little time with her kids. James hit the streets early. There he found belonging. He became a runner for a drug dealer and eventually was dealing to help his mom and also to have necessary status symbols—shoes and jewelry. He began to carry a gun to defend himself from possible rivals and because the neighborhood was dangerous. He shot and killed a man who tried to rob him and went to prison for twenty-two years. James's story is that of millions of black men. In his Milwaukee zip code, 50 percent of black men will spend time in prison at one time or another. James has two years of his prison term left. He has been recognized as a good worker at his work-release job, determined, and hopeful. He wants to begin a new way of life.

Movements to overcome racism require conceiving goals for overcoming post-traumatic slave syndrome. How can barriers to positive self-esteem be overcome? DeGruy urges self-care within black communities. In *Race*

Matters, Cornell West offers the same prescription: recognize the depth of the damage done by the ongoing trauma and find ways of healing within the black community (West 1993).

Slaves built the American economy. Wealth was produced by stolen black bodies. Ta-Nehisi Coates makes the case for reparations due to the descendants of American slaves (Coates 2014). Coates documents how in every economic period in the history of the United States, African Americans produced wealth and were cheated out of fair compensation.[8] Whites owe blacks reparations.

Without reparative justice, the United States will remain two nations, separate and unequal. Slavery, legal subordination, and discrimination today make a powerful case for reparation. Today, some white institutions have acknowledged how much slavery benefited whites. They have pledged monetary reparations to the descendants of slaves, admitting that whites prospered from slave labor and the theft of African American property. Reparations recognize the decades of violence that have left a deep scar on African Americans. Racial harm may be most effectively described by black conversation partners.

The call for reparations has been met with great resistance (Yancy 2018). What goals might movements embrace to commit resources to repair the damage suffered by African Americans? What goals are realistic? That is a discussion still to be had.

African Americans, other people of color, and many whites do not make a living wage. African Americans make 57 cents for every dollar whites make. The ratio of white wealth to black wealth is 12:1. The "Network" advocacy group describes twelve reasons for the great gap between the white and black wealth (Network Lobby for Catholic Social Justice 2019). It describes the exploitation of blacks, from slavery, to post–Civil War re-enslaving of freed slaves through terror and laws intended to severely punish them. Their economic deprivation continued well into the twentieth century through federal laws such as excluding farm and domestic workers from organizing unions and permitting white unions to deny black membership. In addition, after World War II, almost no African American veterans were given access to GI funds to further their education. In addition, they were denied mortgage loans to veterans after World War II, leaving them no alternative than to sign private contracts to buy homes at several times their value. Poverty continues to rob African Americans of their dignity. They do not desire government help, but without it, they cannot feed their families. From the effects of the poverty he witnessed throughout India, Gandhi was right that poverty is the worst violence. The condition of black poverty, which has continued from one generation to the next, requires proposing concrete reparations can overcome America's "original sin."

Incarceration

The prison population in the United States is the highest in the world. Michelle Alexander reports that in 1980, 300,000 Americans were imprisoned; by 2000, the number had risen to two million, and in 2007, the number had tripled to more than seven million (Alexander 2011). As noted in the previous chapter, very disproportionate number of blacks are incarcerated, not for violent crimes but for drug offenses, crimes for which whites seldom get prison time, The Network Lobby for Catholic Social Justice reports that

the War on Drugs has exacerbated the racial wealth gap through practices that inherently target Black and Brown communities. Although rates of drug use and selling are similar across racial lines, black men are up to ten times more likely to be stopped, searched, arrested, prosecuted, convicted, and incarcerated for drug law violations than white men. (Network Lobby for Catholic Social Justice 2019, p. 26)

The "revolving door" phenomenon sends many blacks released from prison back to prison not for again violating laws but for violating arbitrary parole rules. Michelle Alexander concludes that "the War on Drugs has ushered in a new era of unprecedented punitiveness" (Alexander 2011, p. 60). Alexander urges a new national consensus for reform of the penal system. Reforming prisons can take many forms. The approach might be

- rethinking the "war on crime";
- demonstrating how the U.S. prison system fails to rehabilitate;
- working to eliminate private prisons in particular, which warehouse prisoners;
- publicizing the costs of incarcerating millions of Americans, especially the privatization of prisons in the 1980s, a very profitable business. There is an incentive to keep them full.[9]

While citizens object to some government spending, they seldom complain about the costs of the prison system. There are also human costs: ask most citizens whether prisons rehabilitate, and they readily will say no, prisons are warehouses. Activism for prison reform can grow out of two compelling arguments: the system does not prepare prisoners to be productive citizens and the system is very expensive and is failing. Again, concrete examples of administering, building, and staffing prisons in activists' own back yard is the place to start.

Gun Control

The right to own firearms is protected by the Second Amendment. But an armed society in which everyone has the right to "conceal and carry" guns, and in many states to openly carry guns, is unheard of in other first world countries. For decades, the U.S. Congress has refused to pass legislation to protect citizens from gun violence. Registering guns to keep them out of the hands of certain people has loopholes. The recent proposal to deny guns to the mentally unstable (called "red flag laws") is unworkable and encroaches on civil rights. Gun owners may believe they are safer by owning guns, but guns are used in domestic disputes, and are the leading means of committing suicide. Rival gang members make war with one another, killing innocent people in the crossfire. Almost daily mass shooting occurs. The costs of gun violence are the deaths of breadwinners, medical treatment, rehabilitation, and sometimes lifelong care for permanently disabled victims of gun violence.

The argument for the right of citizens to gun ownership—except for hunting—reflects a culture of individualism rather than concern for the common good. There are two other consequences of a country flooded with guns. Law enforcement agents are afraid that those they confront have guns. Officers often reflexively shoot, only to learn that victims were unarmed. Paramilitaries amass weapons, often military assault weapons, to commit hate crimes as they "defend white Christian America." They are our homegrown terrorists.

For effective gun control in the United States, movements must develop greater power to challenge the National Rifle Association, which to date has been unassailable. A broad coalition is necessary to put a stop to a culture of guns. Many anti-gun organizations have arisen to work for gun control, often after mass shootings. But to successfully compete with the NRA requires sustained grassroots advocacy. Finding allies is necessary to build strength. The NRA knows that public outcries for gun control are not sustained, while the NRA's advocacy is long-term.

Environmental Protection

If carbon emissions continue to warm the earth at the present rate, the damage will be irreversible. There is little time left. Polarization at governmental levels, especially the federal level, has stymied action.[10] What can be done? Here are some possible suggestions.

• During the Nuclear Freeze Movement, the Union of Concerned Scientists created a "doomsday clock." Might such a clock remind us that time is running out?
• Citizens can become aware of their own carbon footprints. The carbon footprint of the military should also be publicized.
• Corporations have often been proactive in reducing carbon emissions. Recognition of their initiatives and working with them is important and encourages other businesses to follow suit.

These suggestions for nonviolent citizen activism are only skeletal. To be successful requires much ingenuity, creativity, and energy. Reform may seem overwhelming. But activism is the only way to transform the world that our children and their children will inherit. Working for change need not deplete energy but can be energizing as we join with others. Pierre Sauvage, one of the Jews who survived the Holocaust because his parents found refuge in Le Chambon, asked the towns people how they were able to persevere for five years. They told him it was nothing out of the ordinary but simply what people do when the need arises. He concluded from his interviews that undertaking difficult commitments does not exhaust people but energizes them (Sauvage 1990).[11]

But we cannot ignore the fact that in the U.S. context working for justice exacts a price. Arundhati Roy writes that "there is no option, really, to old-fashion, back-breaking political mobilization" (Roy 2004, p. 40).

Finally, all activism is hard work. It is time-consuming. It means risking inviting others to join. It means learning to compromise. It means exerting energy to keep pressure for justice on.

FOR DISCUSSION

1. Have you been involved in a social justice campaign? In what ways was your experience positive? Negative?
2. What may have prevented you from participating in a movement?
3. Choose one of the U.S. social problems, foreign or domestic, that is identified here. Suggest your own vision of the goals, strategies, and tactics through which it can be addressed.
4. In what sense is voting the most effective means of social change in the United States? Do you think it is in any way insufficient?

Chapter 8

Nonviolence, World Religions, and the Virtues

Buddhist monks in Burma (now Myanmar) joined the largely nonviolent protests against the ruling junta in 1988. But though regarded as exemplars of nonviolence, in 2015, many monks joined in the persecution of the Rohingya people—persecution so severe that it was called genocide. Tragically, religious convictions too often feed animosities that trigger violence. That has certainly been true for Christians who regarded their faith as the true faith and persecuted Jews, Muslims, and Indigenous peoples for centuries.

But a deeper consideration of conflict reveals factors oftentimes more to blame than religious differences for poisoning communal relationships. While religious differences are claimed to be the source of violence, root grievances are much more often political (denial of rights and freedom) and economic (impoverishment and theft of resources such as land). Hindus and Muslims murdered each other in the frenzy of 1947, Muslims afraid that they would be oppressed under a Hindu majority in independent India. Protestants with British loyalties and Catholics who wanted to be part of the Irish Republic killed one another. National identities and fear of oppression fueled the conflict.

The brief exploration of the following seven spiritual traditions will not fully describe their teachings. Instead, two questions are posed. First, what are their central moral teachings? Second, what do they teach about nonviolence?

HINDUISM

Recall that for Gandhi the search for the divine was seamlessly joined to the struggle for justice, a life journey he called *satyagraha*. That path required *ahimsa* (nonviolence). It also required *tapasya* (the willingness to suffer for others). These virtues would produce *moksha* (liberation). Several Hindu texts confirm the centrality of nonviolence. The Upanishads say that self-control and inner discipline are the way to *sat*, the experience of ultimate reality. Not to practice self-discipline perpetuates ignorance and harm to others. Keshav Kashmiri's reflection on the Bhagavad Gita reminds us of the wisdom of recognizing that others

> are like us in that they are also battling their lower natures. . . . We are all on the same side in the inner war and the Gita's call for nonviolent [struggle] in this war is the strongest foundation for sustainable peace. (Kashmiri)

Lord Krishna's advice to Arjuna in the Bhagavad Gita, not to hesitate in warring against his relatives, may sound like a legitimation of war. Indeed, Arjuna is of the warrior caste with a duty to fight when required. Gandhi's interpretation of the story is that Arjuna faces an inner struggle for self-control in order to live a virtuous life.

Hinduism counsels peace, understood as recognizing what is common in all human beings that produces unity. Gandhi believed that only nonviolence makes this possible. Violence is human passions out of control, with individuals, communities, and nations in a state of chronic warring. The practice of *tapasya* is suggested in this ancient teaching: "Oh how he abused me and beat me. How he defeated me and robbed me. Bind ourselves in such thoughts and you live in hate. . . . Cut the bonds to such thoughts and live in peace." (*Upanishads* 3–4)

BUDDHISM

The Buddha taught that the way to enlightenment, to "awakening," was the practice of loving-kindness. Eleanor Rosh, a Buddhist and professor of Buddhist psychology, provides a comprehensive summary of Buddhist ethical teaching and its prescriptions regarding violence and nonviolence:

- Buddhists must practice empathy.
- Whereas in the West justice often becomes revenge, true justice aims at healing both victim and perpetrator.[1] This is restorative justice.
- Successful struggle is not about winning but about reconciling opposing sides.
- Spontaneity of action means acting from what knowledge one has rather than awaiting full knowledge.
- Overcoming the I-thou duality which leads to judgment is necessary.

Rosch asserts that powerlessness can prove to be a powerful force for healing (Rosch 2015, pp. 161–163).

King Ashoka, who reigned from 268 to 232 BCE in northern India, converted to Buddhism and became committed to nonviolence. He renounced war, urged peacefulness, and emphasized commitment to social welfare. His instructions on the ways of nonviolence are carved on what became known as the Pillars of Ashoka, one of the oldest sculptures in India.

Today, the Tibetan Dalai Lama extols the practices of nonviolence. He rejected violence, even as Buddhists were being persecuted and driven from Tibet by the Chinese. Thich Nhat Hanh, a Vietnamese monk, is a widely known teacher of Buddhist spirituality and the centrality of nonviolence in the tradition.

Rosch offers a powerful contemporary example of the practice of Buddhism. From 1975 to 1978, the Khmer Rouge killed approximately one and a half million Cambodians, including thousands of Buddhist monks and nuns, to achieve "ethnic purity." But survivors remained reconcilers, working to reintegrate former Khmer Rouge soldiers and offering them forgiveness.

SIKHISM

Sikhism originated in the Punjab region of northwest India in the late sixteenth century and drew from Hinduism, Buddhism, and Jainism. Guru Nanak and the four gurus who followed him compiled the Sikh scripture, the Adi Granth, the authoritative teachings of Sikhism. Swaran Sandhu writes that the early Gurus "were clearly humanitarian and peace-loving" (Singh 2011). Sikhism commends forgiveness: "Forgiveness is as necessary to life as the food we eat and the air we breathe. Where there is forgiveness, there is God." The Adi Granth describes the noble warrior:

He alone is a *kshatriya* who is brave in good deeds. He yokes himself in charity and almsgiving. Within the field bounded by the protective fence of justice he sows seeds which benefit everyone. (Cole and Sambhi 1978, p. 140)

Guru Gobind Singh taught that maintaining the "protective fence of justice" at times excused violence: "When all efforts to restore peace prove useless and no words avail, lawful is the flash of steel; it is right to draw the sword" (Cole and Sambhi 1978, p. 140). Sikhs were attacked by the Moguls in the seventeenth century and 1820 by British forces. They raised an army and held the Punjab until they were defeated in 1849.[2]

Yet throughout their history, Sikhs have attempted to live in peace with their Hindu and Muslim neighbors. When India was partitioned in 1947, Sikhs were oppressed by both Pakistanis and Indians. Since the 1980s, Sikhs in India's Punjab have agitated for an independent state. In 1984, the worst attacks on Sikhs occurred throughout India, including the Indian Army's destruction of the most important Sikh temple in India, the Golden Temple. Over 3,000 Sikhs were killed. In retaliation, India's Prime Minister Indira Gandhi was assassinated by her Sikh bodyguards.[3]

Yet, forgiveness for their victimization goes to the heart of modern Sikh-ism. Forgiveness is reflected in a massacre a Sikh community suffered in 2012. On a Sunday morning, a white supremacist entered their Temple in Oak Creek, Wisconsin, and killed the president of the Temple and five others and wounded four others before taking his own life. The Sikh community offered to pay the funeral expenses for him as well as their own. The son of the late president of the Temple was later contacted by a white supremacist who had undergone a change of heart. Together they have worked against white supremacy ideology. A book of their dialogues is entitled *Our Wounds Are Our Gift* (Kaleka and Michaelis 2018). The quote is from the Chandi Kala, a Sikh text on compassion, self-suffering, and forgiveness.

JUDAISM

At the heart of Jewish teaching are the "law and the prophets." The Torah (In Hebrew, "law") is comprised of the first five books of the Hebrew Bible.[4] The first book, Genesis, contains the narrative of Yahweh's creation of the world, the human fall, and Yahweh's promise to Abraham that his people will become a great nation, under his patronage: "You will be my people and I will be your God" (Exodus 6:7). The Hebrews were to obey several commandments revealed by Moses (Exodus 20:2–17 and Deuteronomy 5:6–17). The first three commandments are prohibitions against idol worship; the following seven forbid acts harming others.

The Israelites' story is one of enslavement in Egypt, their rescue by Yahweh, and the Israelites finally reaching Canaan, the promised land. As the story goes, they routed out the occupants of Canaan by means of their military strength. Contemporary biblical scholars provide a more likely explanation of how the Israelites came to possess Canaan: they gradually trickled in, were taught farming by the Canaanites, and gradually outnumbered them. There was no military conquest. Biblical texts remind the Israelites of their total dependence on Yahweh. While the stories of the Israelites' military victories were comforting, Israel was in fact never powerful, certainly not like the armies of the empires that periodically swept through Israel. The Babylonians destroyed the temple in Jerusalem and sent its leaders into exile. The Assyrians conquered Israel, and the Romans occupied it. It was Yahweh alone who rescued Israel.

A story of Roman occupation was that Caesar commanded that a statue of a Roman deity—including himself by that time in the history of the empire—be installed in the great temple in Jerusalem. The Jews protested, baring their necks, ready to be slain rather than have the Temple desecrated. Such was their nonviolent response to the Empire. The statue was not installed.

A dominant command of Yahweh is that the Israelites extend compassion and care for the vulnerable: widows, orphans, and strangers. "Do not oppress an alien, for you were once aliens yourselves in the land of Egypt" (Exodus 22:20). "Before the Lord, you and the alien are alike" (Numbers 15). "Do as Yahweh did for you" (Deuteronomy 24). "Love the foreigner residing among you" (Psalm 91). A second theme, found especially in the Prophets, is the condemnation of the rich for exploiting the poor. The prophet Amos speaks for Yahweh, who wants the worship of the Israelites only if they "let justice roll down like a never-ending stream" (Amos 5:24). Isaiah speaks God's command: "Learn to do good, seek justice, correct oppression, bring justice to the fatherless, and plead the widow's cause" (Isaiah 1:17). The demand for social justice is frequent. The book of Leviticus calls for the Israelites to remove injustices by releasing slaves and prisoners, canceling debts, and returning lands lost by the poor on the Jubilee (fiftieth) year (25:8–55). These actions rebalance the scales of justice.

Since the birth of Christianity, the Jews have been targets of persecution down the centuries. Throughout their history, Jews have been the victims and not victimizers. They have had no military capability; they did not make war but suffered anti-Semitism that led to the Holocaust. All they desired was to be accepted and free to practice their faith.

Historically, Judaism had no need for a Just War teaching, at least not until the creation of the state of Israel in 1948, a homeland to be defended against hostile surrounding Arab nations and then from the Palestinians. Israel now has a very robust military defense force. Israelis remain divided on the issue of how Israelis can co-habit Palestine with the Palestinians.

In the book of the prophet Isaiah, a curious figure is described. He is not a messiah of worldly power whom some were hoping would liberate Israel from the Romans. Instead, he will

> give his life as an offering for sin, he shall see his descendants in a long life, and the will of the Lord shall be accomplished through him. Because he surrendered himself to death and was counted among the wicked, he shall take away the sins of many. (Isaiah 53:10, 12)

CHRISTIANITY

Christians have seen this prophecy as describing the coming of Jesus, their messiah. At the beginning of his ministry, Jesus spoke the words of Isaiah:

> The spirit of the Lord is upon me; therefore he has anointed me. He has sent me to bring good news to the poor, liberty to captives . . . to announce a year of favor from the Lord. (Isaiah 61:1–2; in Luke 4:18)

In many New Testament stories, Jesus is merciful especially to the poor, misfits, lepers, and the blind, teaching that their afflictions were not caused by their sinfulness or their parent's sinfulness. Like Gandhi's embrace of the untouchables, Jesus denied that they were impure

Jesus' Sermon on the Mount is his embrace of nonviolence: "Do not seek revenge" (Mt 5:10) but "Bless those who persecute you, bless and do not curse them" (Mt 5:45). "Blessed are the peacemakers they shall be called the children of God." (Mt. 5:9). In three parables, Jesus describes the practices of revolutionary nonviolence. A slave who "turns the other cheek" to his master was not cowering but stood his ground as best he could. A man whose cloak is taken by a creditor in court gives him all of his clothes, his nakedness reflecting badly on the creditor. A centurion presses a farmer into carrying his pack for a mile, but the farmer refuses to put it down at the end of the mile, as the military rule required, putting the soldier at his mercy. The point of the stories is that the powerful were embarrassed by powerful actions of subordinates but not with retaliatory violence. Jesus also admonished his disciples to put down their swords, for "he who habitually draws the sword will die by the sword." (Mt. 26:52).

Andre Trocmé describes Jesus as a nonviolent revolutionary preaching the time of the jubilee, in which justice would be restored by eliminating the great disparities of wealth and power (Trocmé 1973). When attacked by the powerful, Jesus did not retaliate with violence. Trocmé describes what he called Jesus' "third way," neither calling for armed resistance nor turning away from injustices toward the poor.

> Nonviolence is less a matter of "not killing" and more a matter of showing compassion, of saving and redeeming, of being a healing community. One must choose between doing good to the person placed in one's path, or the evil which one might be doing by mere abstention. (Trocmé 1973, p. 159)

While admiring Jesus, Gandhi was not keen on Christianity, calling it a religion of kings. Indeed, throughout their history, Christians have behaved terribly—and some still do—especially toward the people of their parent religion, the Jews. This is among the greatest sins for which Christians must continue to repent.

Terrence Rynne describes the impact that Jesus's crucifixion had on Gandhi: "Gandhi understood Jesus's crucifixion as the fate of persons living an aggressive nonviolence in an atmosphere of violence" (Rynne 2008, p. 33). Other prominent theologians write about the strong theme of pacifism in Christianity, including C. F. Andrews, an Anglican who spent many years with Gandhi, Mennonite John Howard, Methodist Stanley Hauerwas, and Catholic Fr. Bernard Häring. John Howard Yoder's landmark study is *The Politics of Jesus*, which examines the liberating nonviolence in the Hebrew Scriptures. In *The Peaceable Kingdom*, Hauerwas argues that Christian communities are to be witnesses of the nonviolent Good News that Jesus proclaimed. Fr. Häring's final book, which he referred to as his most important, is *The Healing Power of Peace and Nonviolence*. To this list must be added the work of James Douglass, including *The Nonviolent Cross*. All of these theologians are reshaping the moral teaching of Christianity and—if slowly—Christian communities.

Jews and Christians are exhorted to practice social justice. They are warned against idolatry, the source false security as inflated nationalism and militarism are today. Karen Armstrong says that Amos a prophet of ancient Israel "wanted to puncture the national ego." (Armstrong 2006, p. 89).

ISLAM

In the first years of Islam, Muhammad and his followers were attacked by Meccans and fled to Medina, and there defended themselves with force. For Muslims, self-defense remains justified. However, the weight of the Qur'an affirms living nonviolently and at peace:

> If only we had [Allah's] extensive vision and could see beyond our small self. There would be fewer antagonisms and less desire to demand revenge. Harsh judgments would be pulled back and our meager mercy greatly expanded. For you [Allah] observe the deepest part of us, our silent motivations and expectations. You focus on what unites, not divides. You see how we are more alike than different. (Qur'an, Kabir 2)

In Islam, as in Hinduism and Buddhism, peace is achieved by inner discipline and struggle. Ramadan and fasting are meant for developing self-discipline. Many Westerners misunderstand the concept of jihad (struggle), equating it with violence, a dangerous distortion of Islam. Jihad means two different things. "Greater jihad" is disciplining the self, similar to how Gandhi interpreted the teaching of the Gita, while "lesser jihad" is the use of force to defend Muslim communities.

Irfan Omar examined the Qur'an and found 600 verses in the Qur'an praising "greater jihad" and only forty verses call for "lesser jihad," defensive war. Omar writes that far "more numerous are [verses] that deal with peace, patience, and eternal life" (Omar 2015, p. 34). The terrorism of a few Muslims violates both greater jihad and lesser jihad. Omar argues that for most contemporary Muslims war is not justified. He notes that Islam condemns harm to civilians, the very logic of terrorism. In addition, suicide is forbidden in the Qur'an, thus condemning suicide bombing. Omar argues that although nonviolence is not directly addressed in the Qur'an, virtues that support nonviolence permeate the sacred text.

Muslims work to counter the Western propaganda that Islam is inherently violent. But Muslim terrorists believe that they are defending Islam against Western terrorism; sadly, one man's terrorist is another man's freedom fighter. Imams around the world condemn those who engage in terrorism in the name of Islam as heretics and not faithful Muslims.

NATIVE AMERICAN SPIRITUALITIES

The spiritualities of indigenous peoples are the most ancient of all. They are addressed last because of their contrasts with both Eastern and Western religions. For indigenous peoples, some violence is unavoidable, such as taking the lives of animals for food. The North American Plains Indians killed buffalos for food and other necessities, but such killing of animals required thanking them for sacrificing their lives. Taking life wantonly was wrong. In sharp contrast, European Americans slaughtered the buffalo almost to extinction, to starve Indians, and often for little more than sport.

The worldview of indigenous peoples emphasizes harmony with all creatures and with the earth itself. Land is sacred and alive and must be cared for because all life depends on it. Indigenous religion is place-specific. *This* place, *this* land is where the Great Spirit is experienced and where the ancestors reside. Chapter 5 noted the "recovery of the center" which the First Nations of North America Native seek.

George Tinker, a member of the Osage Nation and professor of religion, critiques a violence-nonviolence dichotomy (Tinker 2015).[5] Sometimes killing other human beings in self-defense is necessary. But the wanton killing of any sort is wrong. The Conquests inflicted violence on such a scale that the earth and its people shuddered. Minimizing violence at all levels is the basis of right relationships. At one time or another in their histories, most religious communities have behaved violently, particularly when they held political power. For example, when the Christian Church in the fourth century became the chief political force of the Roman Empire, Bishops began to dispatch troops to defend its borders and eliminate so-called heretics. Hence, religion has been used to fuel the domination of other peoples. But today, religious authorities urge nonviolence as the better way.

All religions at their core teach the obligations of compassion, forgiveness, repentance, and reconciliation. Two modern developments offer hope that nonviolence is assuming a central role in contemporary religious communities. First, in the West, the just war tradition has been rejected as unfaithful to the message of Christianity. Pope John Paul II asserted that "a peace obtained by arms could only prepare new acts of violence" (John Paul II 1991). His successor Pope Francis, in his World Day of Peace message on January 1,

2017, titled "Nonviolence: A Style of Politics for Peace," referenced Gandhi, Khan Abdul Gaffar Khan, Martin Luther King, Jr, and Leymah Gbowee and the thousands of Liberian women as peacemakers. Were Christians—certainly in the United States—to become nonviolent witnesses, they could be influential around the world

Gandhi lived a seamless religious and moral life. His striving to experience *sat*—the transcendent—was at one with his struggle to create just and loving societies and people. He actively embraced the wisdom of other religions. Increasingly, all world religious leaders commend the practice of nonviolence.

A second development is "Peace Fellowships" that have arisen across the religious spectrum, reminding their faithful of the centrality of nonviolence and crossing religious lines to collaborate in working for peace. Religious communities are of strategic importance because their membership number in the millions. This is not to suggest that religious folks are "better" than nonreligious people at practicing altruism, repentance, forgiveness, and reconciliation.[6] But they are called to fidelity to their traditions, which do stress the importance of these virtues.

Can we have the fullness of Gandhi's nonviolence without the religious foundations? Gene Sharp, deeply influenced by Gandhi, eventually argued that pragmatic nonviolence is as effective as principled nonviolence. Thomas Weber says that Sharp

> now champions a "technique approach" to nonviolent action, arguing that it should be used for pragmatic rather than for religious or ethical reasons. Depending on how one looks at it, Sharp either has gone beyond Gandhi, making nonviolence a more practically available method of struggle, or has ditched key elements of Gandhi's philosophy in action in a way that diminishes nonviolence. (Weber 2003, n.p.)

Some secular nonviolent activists may be striving to live by the virtues of nonviolence without a religious underpinning. Weber writes: "Perhaps rather than debating the merits of [a religious or secular] approach, they can be seen as indicating alternative paths to the traveler who does not want to use violence."

Virtues and Nonviolence

Philip Hallie's book *Lest Innocent Blood Be Shed* telling the story of the rescue of Jews in Le Chambon and the surrounding villages and farms is subtitled "The story of the village of Le Chambon and how goodness

happened there." *Goodness happened there* because the people possessed
virtues, notably empathy, altruism, courage, and prudence.

Altruism

Empathy is acknowledging other people's pain. Altruism takes concern for
others to a higher level, insisting that others must be cared for, their essential
needs be met, even before one's own. The Chambonnais surely put the needs
of the fleeing Jews ahead of their own. Altruism is welcoming, not fearing,
the stranger. By the end of the 1930s, 175,000 German and Eastern European
Jews had fled to France looking for safety. But after France fell in 1940, many
French people regarded Jews, particularly foreign-born Jews, as a danger. But
Jews and other refugees were regarded as kin to the people of Le Chambon
and the plateau.

Magda Trocmé spoke at a conference in India in 1948. She recalled the
factors that lead to war, saying

> We have contempt for other countries, for people of other races and religions,
> for people who speak other languages, especially when they challenge us in the
> name of other ideals. The sincere and truthful people among us must open their
> eyes to their own behavior and see it as it is, without excuses, without hiding it
> in a religious or moral shell. (Unsworth 2012, p. 243)

Maggie Paxson came to Le Chambon to learn about Daniel Trocmé,
André's second cousin, who in 1942 came to Le Chambon to care for a house
of Jewish boys. In the midst of the great danger in which he had put himself,
he wrote home that he had come to care for the boys, so different from him,
and regarded them as family, feeding, clothing, and schooling them. Paxson
discovered that sixty years later the Chambonnaise had taken in new refugees.
The "Center for Those Seeking Asylum" (CADA) had been established in the
town. CADA is a private organization established in France in 1973, initially
to assist Chileans seeking political asylum during dictator August Pinochet's
reign of terror. By the 1990s, asylum seekers from Eastern Europe, the repub-
lics of the former Soviet Union, from Asia, and from Africa had also made
their way to CADA centers in France to be cared for as they filled out applications for political asylum with the help of volunteer lawyers.[7] Since 2000,
Le Chambon has been a CADA center, with an estimated fifty to a hundred
refugees living there at any given time. Some succeeded in being granted
political asylum; others did not but remained with local families while they
considered what to do next.

As Paxson sipped tea with a refugee family, one day she reflected: "I feel
oddly at ease here in their house, among the strangers—or rather I, the
stranger, among them. Which is it? "We are all 'strangers' just as others are.
But we are also kin" (Paxson 2019, p. 112). Her experience with CADA

had shown her that Armenians, Kazakhstanis, and so on. were not strangers. She perceived them as fellow human beings. Paxson warns what happens when that does not occur:

> if you are a society that fears outsiders, all kinds of other things can get wrapped up in that fear: your ideas about other people (other nations, other races); your religious orientations (does it get you to heaven to hate other people, or rather to love them?); your economies (slavery, colonialism, capitalism); your habits of power (caste systems of a million different flavors). It all gets knotted up together. Within that knot, everything seems solid, oak-like, eternal. (Paxson 2019, p. 211)

How is this knot untied? Nonviolence begins with avoiding the trap of judging others negatively. Tragically, "others" easily come to be regarded as inferiors and sometimes as dangerous strangers. It begins with an us-versus-them attitude. They are different in color, religion, language, culture; they are backward and used to behaving violently. We are advanced, they are ignorant, we are trustworthy, they are deceitful. Our religion is the right path, theirs is based on wrong and dangerous beliefs. As prejudice progresses, they may come to be regarded as subhuman. "Strangers" are not only foreigners. Racism in the United States is treating people of color as inferiors. Ariella Tilson calls racism "the great othering."[8] Murthy observes that we don't know people as fellow human beings because they don't look like us, and that "makes it easy to dismiss them for their beliefs and attachments" (Murthy 2020, p. 134).

In wartime, soldiers are conditioned to kill the "other," the "enemy," without hesitation. An American Vietnam War veteran described what happened after he killed a North Vietnamese soldier (O'Brien 1990). He approached the body of the dead man, and he found a photo of his family and realized that he was a man with a family who would be devastated by their loss, just as his own would be. Had the dead man been forced to go to war? Was he any different from me? Was he really an enemy? No.

But when others are recognized as like us, we are more likely to empathize and to help them. The moral challenge is to care for those who seem unlike us. Activists contending with others cannot lose sight of the fact that their opponents are like them in many ways. Martin Luther King, Jr. urged those committed to a just cause to fight evils but not evildoers. Gandhi taught that killing adversaries prevents them from undergoing transformation.

Treating Women as Negative Others or Cherishing Them

Besides the "great othering" of people of color is the "great othering" of women. In most, though not all world religions, men have formulated religious doctrine and monopolized leadership positions. Women have been treated as inferior and made subservient. They are often denied participation in public life. They are subjected to sexual abuse and domestic violence, until recently this violence has not been condemned by religious authorities.

Men seldom admit treating women as the "other" whom they must control. Gandhi's satyagrahis were male, with women playing auxiliary roles. In the early years of the U.S. civil rights movement, the Southern Christian Leadership Conference led the way but was made up of only all-male pastors. Although King at first objected to the prominent role of women in SNCC, he came to admire them. Patriarchy once characterized women as weak and gentle, unable to stand their ground (Yuval-Davis 2004, p. 185).

In Poland's Solidarity movement, women factory workers in the Danzig shipyard were at the bargaining table. Dolores Huerta co-organized LaCausa with César Chávez. Serbia's Otpor included women. The liberation of Liberia occurred almost solely because of the activism of women. Native American societies are not as hierarchical, and women have played as powerful roles as men in protesting the treatment of Indians and working for their dignity.

Women bring special strengths and commitments to nonviolent struggles. The first and obvious one is that because women are the principal caregivers of children and the elderly, they are most likely to oppose violence. Their priority is the defense of the vulnerable. Where men call for war, women seek to avoid or end war. Women form relationships more readily to multiply their power and to reach out to negotiate. Swanee Hunt quotes the President of Bosnia Herzegovina after the Balkan wars: "If we'd had women around the table, there would have been no war, because women think hard and long before they send their children out to kill other people's children" (Children and Eliatamby 2011, p. 115).

Saira Yamin describes how women in Pakistan created the Women's Action Forum (WAF) in 1981 during the drive of Islamic fundamentalists to punish and exclude women. She writes:

> WAF has inspired the formation of a vast network of women's rights organizations across the country working on such issues as service delivery, government social and development programs, rights-based advocacy, lobbying, capacity building, and research. (Yamin 2011, p. 252)

Working for justice is equally women's and men's work. When women's equality and inclusion are part of the struggle, there is greater hope of justice. The "women's movement" needs to also be the "men's movement," in which men respect women and do not permit violence against them.[9]

Repenting

Repentance begins with the humility and courage to admit fault. Gandhi called humility "turning the spotlight inward." One admits fault, accepts blame and accountability, and makes amends. Gandhi came to recognize and repent for his violence toward his wife Kasturbai early in their marriage. At the political level, guilt is often denied because it appears weak.

The United States has a long history of intervention in other countries, often contributing to the overthrow of governments viewed as uncooperative in maintaining U.S. interests. Rarely has the United States admitted its role in deaths and destruction when civil wars break out. One exception was an instance when President Bill Clinton apologized to the Guatemalan people. The *Los Angeles Times* reported:

> Reflecting on the break in Central America's cycle of repression and revolution, President Clinton apologized Wednesday. He also promised "to do everything I possibly can" to eliminate discriminatory provisions in U.S. immigration laws that favor refugees from Cuba and Nicaragua over those who fled to the United States to escape right-wing governments in Guatemala and El Salvador that were supported by Washington. (Gerstenzang and Darling 1999)

Some in the press mocked him as the "sorry president." But Clinton's apology fell short. He offered no reparations, only pledging that Guatemalan refugees would be able to enter the United States more easily. But these were the people who had to flee a lawless and impoverished state, for which the United States was partially responsible.

The Vietnamese narrator in Viet Thanh Nguyen's novel, *The Sympathizer*, says

> You know how Americans deal with [innocence and guilt]? They pretend they are eternally innocent no matter how many times they have lost their innocence. The problem is that those who insist on their innocence believe anything they do is just. At least we who believe in our own guilt know what dark things we can do. (Nguyen 2015, p. 190)

But American veterans, however, often experience guilt for what they did or saw in the war. Part of their recovery from PTSD is offering an apology. After the Vietnam War, some U.S. veterans had the opportunity to return to Vietnam to meet with Vietnamese veterans to apologize. To their surprise, Vietnamese veterans were not hostile but welcoming. By apologizing and feeling forgiven the weight of guilt was lifted.

Camilo Mejía served in Iraq in 2003. He refused orders to deploy for a second tour of duty and was court-martialed, sent to prison, received a dishonorable discharge, and was denied veterans' benefits. Mejía offered an apology to the Iraqi people, "I say I am sorry for the curfews, for the raids, for the killings. May they find it in their hearts to forgive me" (Wright and Dixon 2008, p. 144). Another Iraq War veteran agonized over an Iraqi woman he had killed. He said he wanted to apologize but lamented that there was no one to whom he could.

Other countries have done better than the United States in accepting responsibility for the harm that they caused and by offering a public apology. In 1985, forty years after the Holocaust, Richard von Weizsäcker, president of the Federal Republic of Germany, stood before the German Bundestag and acknowledged in great detail what he said every German must recognize the "unprecedented crime" of genocide, the Holocaust. He provided an extraordinarily detailed account of the ways in which the Germans had committed heinous acts against the Jews. He expressed repentance in the name of the German people but said they could not ask forgiveness from the Jewish people. In fact, von Weizsäcker said: "it would be presumptuous to expect forgiveness even after repentance" (Shriver 1995, p. 108). The German government offered reparations to Jewish families, a gesture that von Weizsäcker knew was little consolation.

In 1997, the bishops of France gathered at the train station in Paris where deportations of Jews had begun. The bishops acknowledged their sin of omission for not doing what the Catholic Church could have done to save the Jews. They wrote: "We confess this sin. We beg God's forgiveness and ask the Jewish people to hear our words of repentance" (Roman Catholic Bishops of France 1997). In the early 2000s, the government of Canada acknowledged the harm it had done to Canada's Indigenous peoples and offered reparation. (See chapter 5.)

Forgiving

Robert Enright is a therapist who has worked in Northern Ireland and other conflict zones. He sees forgiveness as beginning with self-reflection? (Enright 2001). How is my anger hurting me? How can forgiving change me and hopefully the person whom I forgive? What gift might I give to that person to bring more good into his or her life? Forgiving is risky. If I forgive others, are they getting off too easy, not suffering enough? What if they refuse to accept blame or are unrepentant? Extending forgiveness ought not to be contingent on whether it is gratefully received. Forgiveness is a personal journey and a choice. Forgiveness is also a gift to the victimizer, allowing him or her to express remorse when acknowledging the pain inflicted. Robert Brault observes that life gets easier when we forgive even if an apology was never given.

Reconciling

What does reconciliation require? Victims have every reason to feel anger; perpetrators may be living without guilt or regret. But if victims and perpetrators are willing to meet, healing on both sides can begin. It may go even further, with both coming to care for one another. As miraculous as it may seem, it is liberating when it happens. Victims come to see victimizers as fellow human beings.[10]

One of the first acts of the Mandela government was to create the Truth and Reconciliation Commission (TRC) in 1994. Its mandate was to address politically motivated crimes committed under Apartheid between 1960 and 1994. Several sites for the Commission to hear testimonies were set up around the country. Victims and those who committed crimes were encouraged to come forward. If the latter described their crimes in full, they would be granted amnesty. If they did not tell the whole truth, they would not be granted amnesty but still not prosecuted. either. Decisions by the Commission were published in newspapers almost daily. Archbishop Desmond Tutu, chair of the TRC, explained why the Commission did not seek prosecutions. Offering amnesty, he said, would encourage perpetrators to come forward while the slow process of criminal trials would drag on for years and would require resources needed to assist the recovery of black South Africans. For South Africa to move forward, acknowledgment of crimes was the best that could be done.[11] The outcomes of the TRC hearings were mixed. Many survivors came forward to tell horrific stories. Few South African police, intelligence service operatives, and soldiers were willing to participate, fearing the consequences if their identities were known. For some of those who told the truth about their crimes, the burden of their past was lifted. Yet for victims, there was some relief to be able to express their pain and learn the truth about the fate of their loved ones.[12]

Other truth commissions were established after peace accords ended civil wars in El Salvador and Guatemala. In 1995, the Guatemalan Catholic Church organized the "Recovery of Historical Memory" (REHMI) process, dispatching 700 clergy, religious, and lay people throughout the country to take testimonies from survivors of the genocide. Its findings were published in 1998 in four volumes, containing the names of 55,000 Guatemalan victims, mostly indigenous Mayas, their ages, villages, and how they had been killed. REHMI was only able to hear the testimonies of one-quarter of the victims. It did not identify perpetrators by name, but it did accuse the Guatemalan military and the intellectual authors of the genocide but without naming them. They did not need to; everyone knew who they were. Bishop Juan Gerardi oversaw the REHMI process. He was assassinated two days after the report was made public. Truth commissions such as the TRC and REHMI are permanent records that make truth available to future generations so that they may know what happened in their country and ensure that victims will not be forgotten.

Nonviolent struggles for justice happen from inside out. When "negative othering" grips persons and communities, they may be trapped in fear, alienation, distrust, prejudice, and hate. The struggle for "positive othering" requires courageously repenting, forgiving, repairing, and sharing (retributive, social, and reparative justice). Only then comes reconciliation. The task of nonviolent activists is to mirror to the wider society these struggles for justice.

FOR DISCUSSION

1. Negative "otherness" can be contagious as more people believe what they hear or read. Lies seem easily believed while correcting them is difficult. Why is that? What are the best ways to teach positive regard for others?
2. Membership in peace fellowships is admittedly small. How can they grow?
3. One hears calls to "teach tolerance." Is that a good enough prescription for overcoming negative "otherness"? what more may be required?
4. Explain how Buddhist and Native American visions of good morality and how they challenge societies today.

Afterword

REAFFIRMING THE POWER OF NONVIOLENCE

When Gandhi and his family returned to India in 1914, he found Indians yearning for freedom from British rule. How could India win independence nonviolently rather than by a violent rebellion against the British occupiers, he pondered? Meanwhile, next door to Britain, the Irish were also intent on freedom. While Indians won their freedom without resorting to violence, the Easter Rising in 1916 marked the beginning of almost a century of Irish-British armed conflict. India secured its freedom with almost no bloodshed. Ireland's came with the spilling of much blood.

IRELAND'S VIOLENT JOURNEY TO PEACE

The day after Easter in April 1916 3,500 Irish rebels stormed Dublin's government buildings. The Easter Rising lasted a little more than a week until the rebels ran out of ammunition (the German ship bringing more weapons failed to rendezvous at the place expected), and British troops arrived and engaged them in gun battles that killed 485 and wounded 2,200. A total of 141 buildings were destroyed or damaged. The rebels hoped that other Dubliners would join them. But most Dubliners did not support armed rebellion, placing their hopes on negotiating independence after the war.

The leaders of the rebellion believed fervently that God ordained their freedom. The swift executions of sixteen leaders of the rebellion put them in the pantheon of Irish martyrs. But none were innocent; all had been involved in the killing of British soldiers. The "justness" of their rebellion overshadowed other concerns they ought to have had. Were they any match for the well-armed British Army? If the chance of victory was slim, would their deaths only symbolize the desire for freedom but not achieve it? Were the deaths and destruction be justified?

In Ireland, the 2016 commemoration of the Easter Rising was remembered as a glorious event in which patriots had given their lives. But some registered the more somber judgment that the rebellion did not further the cause of Ireland's self-rule. In *The Irish Times*, Dennis Kennedy urged the country to resist revisionary history. He described the Easter Rising as

> an act of armed rebellion by an extremist group outside the mainstream of nationalist politics, and with no electoral mandate. . . . The rebels no doubt showed bravery in openly, and in uniform, confronting the authority of the state. . . . But they were still ideologues with no electoral support, prepared to kill and destroy in pursuit of their political aims at a time when unprecedented progress, albeit stalled by the war, had been made by democratic processes towards the goal of an independent Ireland. Should, a hundred years on, a modern parliamentary democracy, committed to the rule of law and peaceful settlement of all disputes, celebrate as the seminal event in its history an armed insurrection by a small minority with no mandate? Should a state with a long history of sporadic armed challenge to its authority be celebrating such an event? Should it do so when there are still organizations and individuals who believe their political aspirations are such that they entitle them to kill and destroy in pursuit of them? . . . The long shadow of the gunmen of 1916 has helped inspire IRA [Republican paramilitary] campaigns in practically every decade since 1922 and still does so today. (Kennedy 2016)[1]

The violence sown in 1916 reaped violence for eighty more years. British troops waged war against Irish rebels from 1921 to 1923. When a treaty with Britain was finally signed, anti-treaty rebels assassinated pro-treaty Irish politicians. When the Irish achieved full status as the Republic of Ireland in 1939, the violence moved North; the six northern most counties were determined to keep their status as a British province and became a battleground where British troops and pro-British paramilitaries fought pro-Republican paramilitaries. Beginning in 1970, violence reigned for 30 years, with 3,000 deaths and atrocities in a deeply divided society. In *Getting to Yes*, two conflict resolution theorists described what Unionists (pro-British and Protestant) and pro-Republicans (Catholics) needed:

> Protestant leaders tend to ignore the Catholics' need for both belonging and recognition of being accepted and treated as equals. In turn Catholic leaders often appear to give too little weight to the Protestants' need to feel secure. (Fischer and Ury 1991, pp. 49–50)

In 1998 after fifteen years of negotiation, a shared government emerged in the Good Friday Agreement. Finally, there was hope that the walls would come down. Those who for decades denounced each other agreed to work together, and most of the paramilitaries agreed to disarm.

High walls of hatred and resolve to settle scores blocked the channels for the sides to meet and negotiate. The lesson of Ireland's modern history is that violence did not advance freedom but delayed it. A democratic mandate, an electoral process, and respectful dialogue were surer ways to justice and peace.

The violence in tribal Ireland bears resemblance to another country in violent turmoil, Somalia, where tribes have made endless war on one another. Ayaan Hirsi Ali was among the thousands of Somalis who fled their country; Ali had been subjected to female genital mutilation, the breakup of her family when her father went into hiding for opposing the government, and forced marriage. Ali eventually reached Holland, where she experienced a society that settled its difference in civil ways. Ali contrasts political life in Holland with that in Somalia:

> Holland was once a country that was half Catholic and half Protestant, and that was a recipe for massacres . . . but in Holland people worked it out. After a period of oppression and bloodshed they learned that you cannot win a civil war: everyone loses. . . . They learned negotiation, they learned that reason is better than force. Above all, they learned to compromise. (Ali 2007, p. 238)

Her hope is that Somalis can learn that lesson that only peaceful means of addressing differences produce peaceful societies. The modern histories of Ireland, Somalia have a lesson to teach. This book offers lessons of conflicts resolved without resorting to violence.

HOW RISKY IS NONVIOLENCE?

A skeptic's question is whether nonviolence can protect innocent people. But another question should be posed: how well does violence protect? On the home front, street violence is condemned, while "castle laws" give homeowners the right to protect themselves and their property with guns. When the United States intervenes abroad, the assumption is that it is facing fanatics who cannot be reasoned with and can only be stopped by force. Although U.S. military power is unrivaled, it is seldom able to defeat adversaries who have little military strength. Robust weapons are blunt instruments. Regardless of whether or not they hit their targets, they harden opponents' resolve.

Witness Slobodan Milosevic who survived several weeks of the bombing of Belgrade, boasting that he had stared down NATO. The bombings united Serbs behind him. When the United States becomes frustrated, it doubles down with more force, with more destructive results but not victory. The more desperate it becomes the more destructive are the results. Gandhi observed that bruised egos produce ruthless behavior.

In all of the cases described in this book, people choosing nonviolent methods became a force that could not be defeated. The key was that the growing popular support did not become mobs but disciplined nonviolent movements. Governments that unleashed military force on their people quickly lost legitimacy. The United States should learn that lesson when it goes abroad, supporting violent regimes.

Violence erects walls behind which are dangerous and demonized "others." Nonviolence finds openings through which to encounter people on the other side. King, Gandhi, Walesa, John Lewis, and many more saw opponents as people with whom to negotiate. Respect made living together possible.

Two final examples illustrate the power of nonviolence to create trust. The first is a micro-story that involved Theodore Roosevelt, who in 1913 organized an expedition in Brazil to explore an uncharted tributary of the Amazon River (Millard 2005). His expedition's co-leader was Brazilian colonel Candido Rondon. As the expedition moved down the river, they caught a glimpse of tribal people watching them. Rondon himself was partly indigenous but had never encountered this group. The tribesmen announced their presence by killing Rondon's dog with a poison arrow. That night, the worried expedition set up camp on a riverbank. Rondon ventured into the jungle looking for a village. Returning to the camp, he gathered gifts and left them at the edge of the village. That goodwill gesture was enough for the tribesmen to trust these strangers and allow the expedition to continue. There is no knowing what Roosevelt would have done had he not been too sick with malaria to do anything. He might have used the expedition's few weapons to defend it, probably at the cost of the lives of the entire expedition.

A macro example of effective nonviolence is the growing number of organizations that are providing "unarmed civilian protection" (UCP) in many conflict zones. Their mission is to build trust by remaining neutral, encouraging openings between warring factions. As their name indicates, they are also present to protect civilians in harm's way but do so unarmed.

Consider in contrast, the armed UN Peacekeeping Force, comprising 90,000 soldiers drawn from member states, periodically dispatched to conflict zones to impose ceasefires. Though its mission is to quell conflict, it is nonetheless a foreign armed force, often perceived as allied to one side or the other. Ceasefires that the UN may impose often burst into flame when its armed forces leave because they are not grounded in local peacemaking processes.

Rachel Julian writes that the peacekeeping model of unarmed civilian protection organizations "works from the inside and has been proven to save lives, empower communities and can secure strong and lasting peace in areas plagued by violent conflict" (Julian 2018, n.p.).

One UCP organization is the Nonviolent Peaceforce (NP), currently employing 255 personnel from 32 countries working in the Philippines, Myanmar, Iraq, and South Sudan. They are paired with host country personnel who speak local languages. Mel Duncan, the co-founder of NP, describes its goals as

- building enduring relationships at the grassroots while remaining neutral in order not to be perceived as working with "the enemy"
- addressing small conflicts before they spread
- supporting women to actively engage in all levels of the peace process
- protecting marginalized people including LGBT individuals, who are among the most vulnerable
- working to prevent violence surrounding elections and
- working to understand cultures and the roots of conflict (Duncan 2018).

NP personnel learn skills for defusing hostility. They also identify local peacekeeping resources and enable local peacemakers. Here is a story of an NP action.

Andres Gutierrez from Mexico and Derek Oakley from Great Britain were stationed in a region of South Sudan when they were alerted that a heavily armed militia was heading toward a small village. Gutierrez and Oakley made it to the village before the militia, where they found five women and four children panicking. The militia arrived and confronted Gutierrez and Oakley, who showed them their identification cards and told them they had no weapons. The militia leaders twice ordered them to leave, but they refused. Then the militia left without firing a shot. Recalling the confrontation, Gutierrez said that he and Oakley would have been killed had they been armed. In its eighteen years of work in conflict zone, none of the NP personnel have been harmed. Annie Hewitt writes that NP succeeds because

nonviolent peacekeeping allows people to see humanity visibly manifested; unarmed peacekeepers must be decent and kind, they must listen actively and make all parties to a conflict feel as though they matter. In doing so, humanity is revealed to be not the property of one side or another, nor something that must be imported from outside. (Hewitt 2018)

Since the end of World War II, Stéphane Hessel has been a powerful voice for nonviolent struggle. When France was occupied by German forces in 1940, Hessel joined what was left of the French army. He was captured by the Germans but escaped and fought with de Gaulle's resistance government. After the war, Hessel joined the French diplomatic corps and in 1948 helped author the United Nations' Universal Declaration of Human Rights. Hessel became a prolific writer, urging the French people to work for social and economic justice in a world of great poverty and to protect immigrants and minorities. In 2011, Stéphane Hessel published *Time for Outrage* in which he wrote: "I am concerned that the future [must belong] to nonviolence, to the reconciliation of different cultures. It is along this path that humanity will clear its next hurdle" (Hessel 2011, p. 32). Hessel prescribes nonviolence as the "surer way" to stop violence, writing:

> We must realize that violence turns its back on hope. We have to choose hope over violence—choose the hope of non-violence. [Mandela's and King's] message is one of hope and faith in modern societies' ability to move beyond conflict with mutual understanding and a vigilant patience. (Hessel 2011, p. 34)

His passionate hope and call for nonviolence have never been more critical than now, in a time of violent interventionism, intra-communal killing, and deadly fear of the "other."

Americans have challenges and opportunities to transform their violence. Nonviolence succeeds because it respects others, even the violent, and believes that communication is always possible. Recall Gandhi's "rules of engagement" that makes it possible for that to happen.

1. Do not delay action until perfect conditions exist; act even without perfect knowledge.
2. Refuse to cooperate with evil customs and structures.
3. Seek to eradicate evil, not those who commit it.
4. Seek to understand an opponent's stance and to empathize.
5. Choose means that are least likely to escalate the conflict.
6. Do not provoke or humiliate adversaries.
7. Remain in contact and conversation with adversaries.
8. Do not assume that opponents cannot change; instead, assume their inherent goodness which will require time to be manifested. Mutual transformation is the goal.
9. Be willing to compromise on nonessentials. They must recognize their own fallibility.
10. Be willing to change even if one is accused of weakness.
11. Be more self-critical than critical of opponents.
12. Attitudes of respect promote nonviolent action that in turn is the pathway to justice and peace.

Appendix 1

Two Unsuccessful Nonviolent Struggles for Justice: Egypt's Arab Spring and the Israel-Palestine Conflict

Chenoweth and Stephan found that nonviolent campaigns were more than twice as likely to succeed as violent ones. But though the "Arab Spring" succeeded in Tunisia, it failed in Syria, Libya, Yemen, and Egypt. The Arab Spring in Egypt aroused hope that dictatorships could be overthrown through citizen pressure. But that hope was disappointed. Elsewhere in the Middle East, the long-standing conflict between Israel and Palestine continues, despite years of both diplomatic efforts, citizen-dialogues between Israelis and Palestinians who have suffered great losses over the years, and the nonviolent strategies employed in the Occupied Territories to achieve statehood. What lessons can be learned from these failed attempts to resolve conflicts nonviolently? Below are suggestions for continuing to work to overcome the struggles for a just society in Egypt and an end to violence in Israel-Palestine.

EGYPT'S ARAB SPRING

Fifty-two percent of Egyptians are under twenty-five. A similar demographic appears across the Middle East (Haas and Lesch 2012, p. 3). Many Egyptians are unemployed, despite being well educated. The Arab Spring in Egypt arose after the murder of Khaled Saeed in Alexandria by state security police in June 2010. In late January 2011, a young woman posted on her Facebook page, "We are all Khaled Saeed," urging people to come to Cairo's Tahrir Square on January 25. Another Egyptian, Wael Ghonim, a Google executive living in Dubai, made a similar plea. The Revolutionary Youth Coalition had initiated the protest that saw an unprecedented event in Egypt occur when a massive crowd poured into the Square demanding the removal of President

Hosni Mubarak who had ruled Egypt since 1981.[1] The protest lasted eighteen days and Mubarak lost the confidence of the Supreme Council of the Armed Forces (SCAF) and resigned. Ghonim had returned from Dubai and was arrested, interrogated, and tortured.[2] A protestor described his own transformation in Tahrir Square:

> I ran with a group of others, trying to scramble away from the carnage and escape the riot police . . . suddenly a man next to me stops and shouts: "Do not run! Egyptians, when will you stop running away? Turn around and let's face them once and for all!"
>
> **Another protestor wrote:** "we fought for our freedom and dignity in a peaceful and peerless revolution that will go down in history. (Ghafar 2015, p. 55)

Another protester was Mohammed el-Beltagy, a physician who worked in a Cairo slum, a member of the Egyptian Parliament, and the Muslim Brotherhood (MB).[3] El-Beltagy came to Tahrir Square to demand an end to military rule. "Stay strong in our demands; do not make a bargain with the military," he told the protestors. A positive development was that several anti-corruption and anti-military rule opponents of the government joined the protest, including members of the Muslim Brotherhood (MB) as well as religious conservative Salafis (who usually were not politically active), and Gamaa Islamiyya (farther right Islamists).[4] But the ominous shadow cast over Tahrir Square was the strong Security Central (whose officers had killed Khaled Saeed). They were capable of dousing any revolutionary flames.

The cohesion of these groups was soon challenged. In the November 2011 parliamentary election, the Muslim Brotherhood won a plurality, and the Salafis garnered 25 percent of the parliamentary seats. But the Salafis were intent on Egypt as a Muslim state, which the MB blocked. But the MB won a ban preventing participation of women in public life, leaving only one woman in the 400-member parliament. In the 2012 presidential election, Muhammad Morsi, another strongman, defeated Mubarak. The following year, retired general Abdelfattah Al-Sisi, another strongman, was installed by the SCAF. The MB organized a protest against the Al Sisi regime and the SCAF fired on the protestors, killing 600 and wounding a thousand. The Supreme [military] Court sentenced hundreds of the MB members to death and banned the Brotherhood as a terrorist organization.

The Egyptian Arab Spring failed for several reasons. Military rule remained unassailable. The Ministry of the Interior was still filled with upward of half a million security and police personnel, many holdovers from the Mubarak era. Al-Sisi has the support of the military that extended his presidential term to 2030. Egypt's legal system did not work; no one was ever prosecuted for the deaths and torture of Egyptians. There was no consensus whether Egypt should be a secular rather than a religious state. A critical weakness was that rural and poor Egyptians did not share the revolutionary aspiration of Cairo's youthful protestors. Their long held strategy was not to call attention to themselves. One activist, recognizing the weakness of mostly urban support for change, said, "We need to realize that in order to have real change, society has to change, and this means that every person's behavior has to change." Finally, no international support for reform arose. Hope remains that action for change will arise another day.

PALESTINE/ISRAEL

In 1947 the newly established State of Israel was immediately attacked by several Arab nations, fending off the Egyptian, Syrian, Lebanese, and Jordanian military forces. In 1967, in the "Six Day War" Israel destroyed Egypt's, Jordan's, and Syria's air forces. The Israel Defense Forces (IDF) also took control of the Gaza strip and West Bank. In 1973, Egypt, Jordan, and Syria again attacked Israel to recover territories lost in 1967. Again, Israel prevailed, continuing to control Gaza and the West Bank. Soon after it signed a peace treaty with Egypt—the first with an Arab nation.

Thousands of Palestinians had fled Israel in 1948, claiming that 700,000 were driven out by the Israeli army. Israel's occupation was to war with Palestinians effectively in what was referred to as "Occupied Territories." The Palestinian Authority was eventually allowed civil governance, but the IDF was the ultimate enforcer of several hundred laws imposed by Israel to control Palestinian life.[5] Thomas Friedman describes the Palestinians' loss of identity:

> Under the Jordanian occupation, Palestinians were never quite sure what their identity was. Their passports were issued by Jordan, and they were represented in the Jordanian Parliament; but although some thought of themselves as Jordanian nationals and assimilated into Jordanian society, many others viewed themselves as Palestinians and resented the Jordanian attempts to play down their separate identity. But under the Israeli occupation, this Palestinian political identity is not allowed to find expression in political parties, political assembly, or self-rule. (Friedman 1987, n.p.)

Friedman found that as the years passed, Palestinian youth were as militantly opposed to their imprisonment as their grandparents had been. In 1973, Israel began to build Jewish settlements in the West Bank on land confiscated from Palestinians. Since 1973, Israel has encroached on land owned by Palestinians in the West Bank, establishing Jewish towns as the first step in annexing the territory Despite condemnation from the UN, the number has increased to more than 130.

What can resolve this standoff? Palestinians demand autonomy in the form of statehood. Israelis need security. A nonviolent initiative to achieve Palestinian autonomy began in 1983. Arab Christian Mubarak Awad, born in Jerusalem and living in the United States, founded the Palestinian Centre for the Study of Nonviolence in the West Bank, together with Gene Sharp and others. Awad traveled to 300 towns and villages in the West Bank encouraging nonviolent means of resisting Israel's occupation. He published articles describing a hundred nonviolent actions that would make it impossible for the IDF to hold the West Bank. Among Awad's suggestions were boycotting Israeli products, resigning from working for Israel's civil administrations in the occupied territories, refusing to fill out any form printed in Hebrew, refusing to pay taxes and carry identity cards, demonstrating wearing yellow armbands, and interrupting traffic. Nonviolent actions could then escalate to blocking roads to Jewish settlements and cutting power and telephone lines to them (Awad 1983/1984, pp. 23–36).

But Awad always urged Palestinians to remain nonviolent. As Gandhi and King knew, that would require accepting arrest and imprisonment, soon creating a major problem for Israel, an overwhelmed criminal justice system. Echoing Gandhi and King, Awad writes:

> Bravely and steadfastly to accept persecution for one's beliefs brings one very close to the power of nonviolence. Palestinians who can liberate themselves from fear and will boldly accept suffering and persecution without fear and striking back have managed to achieve the greatest victory. They have conquered themselves, and all the rest will be much easier to accomplish. (Awad 1983/1984, p. 36)

He also encouraged Palestinians to construct "alternative infrastructures" providing independent educational institutions, Palestinian-owned factories, Arabic newspapers, electronic media, and medical centers. These and other systems would lessen Israeli control of Palestinian life and prepare Palestinians for full autonomy.

A largely nonviolent protest broke out in 1987, referred to as the *intifada* ("shaking") that challenged Israel's control of the West Bank. Many Palestinians were arrested. Checkpoints at crossing points into Israel were carefully monitored, slowing Palestinians who worked in Israel from entering Israel. Israel also closed Palestinian schools, leaving 300,000 students on the streets to throw stones at the IDF and drawing IDF fire in return. However, Chenoweth and Stephan note that a report by the Israeli Defense Forces found that 97 percent of the Palestinian resistance was nonviolent.[6] Yet the face of resistance seen around the world were two violent paramilitaries, Hamas and Hezbollah, both demanding Israel's destruction.

A hopeful peace plan was laid out in the Oslo Accords (1993) with the signing of a "Declaration of Principle" by Israeli Prime Minister Yitzhak Rabin and Palestine Liberation Organization (PLO) President Yasser Arafat. The PLO pledged to maintain security in the Occupied Territories and Israel pledged to begin with drawing its military forces from the Occupied Territories; within seventeen months, the details for the creation of a Palestinian state and the status of Jerusalem were to be negotiated. But that failed to materialize. In September 2000, Ariel Sharon and members of his hawkish party ascended the Temple Mount in Jerusalem, a site sacred to both Jews and Muslims, and the site of the Al Aqsa mosque, which Jews had long avoided to prevent conflict with Muslims. A second *intifada* broke out, this time very violent. In the next decade, an estimated thousand Israelis and five thousand Palestinians were killed. The Palestinian Authority controlled the West Bank, but Hamas controlled Gaza, and eventually began to fire rockets at towns in southern Israel, though doing little damage. However, in 2014, a Hamas missile struck an Israeli village and killed six civilians. In retaliation, the Israeli Air Force bombarded Gaza relentlessly for seven weeks to destroy the Hamas leadership. Israel claimed it had killed a thousand members of Hamas but according to the UN, the death toll was 1,500, half of them civilians. Large urban areas of Gaza were destroyed or damaged. Since then, even peaceful protests by Palestinians within Gaza have been suppressed by the IDF.

The Israeli-Palestinian conflict has suffered setback after setback. Conflict theorist Johan Galtung met with Palestinians and Israelis. He urged Palestinians to construct a "great chain of nonviolent resistance" to win freedom(Galtung 1989, p. 13f). He identified three "links." Since military service is mandatory for both male and female Israelis, they represent all strata of Israeli society. First, he addressed them, urging them to refuse deployment or redeployment to the West Bank because the human rights of Palestinians were being violated. The soldiers who refuse the so-called refuseniks became very vocal in describing what they saw and did in the Occupied Territories. A tank driver who served in the West Bank wrote:

> Our commander told us that the entry was going to be "disproportionate." That was the word he used. We were to cleanse—and that word made me ill—the neighborhoods and buildings. Every house gets a shell. (Chacham 2003, p. 28)[7]

Rami Kaplan expressed regret: "I could have stopped the beatings, but I didn't do a thing. I had already lost my soul . . . I was witness to deeds that I am ashamed to remember to this day" (Chacham 2003, p. 43). "Combatants for Peace" was established in 2005 by Israeli soldiers and former Palestinian guerrilla fighters who laid down arms and advocated for nonviolent processes to bring peace.[8] The Israeli government prefers to ignore refuseniks, hoping that they will not gain a larger hearing.[9]

Galtung's second link is a dialogue between Israelis and Palestinians who have lost loved ones in the conflict, united by mutual loss. Their mutual suffering often forges a strong bond and makes them advocates for stopping the conflict. The third link Galtung describes and encourages is the potential activism of the Palestinian diaspora. Palestinians living outside of Palestine can keep the plight of those in the Occupied Territories in the consciousness of the wider world and can celebrate the distinctive Palestinian culture. All three groups—former combatants, victims' families, and the Palestinian diaspora—are part of a grassroots initiative.

None of this has yet altered the determination of Israeli political leaders who want complete control and in the future, annexation of the West Bank. Nor has it lessened the determination of Hamas to destroy Israel. Resentment and fear run deep as setback after setback continue. As helpful as the resources of nonviolence might be, they have not worked because the narratives of injustice are deeply embedded in the psyches of Israelis and Palestinians. What has yet to occur is what Galtung calls a "change of brain" (Galtung 1989, p. 14). He is not insulting Israelis and Palestinians who are living in insecurity and must revaluate what each needs to be secure.

In *The Lemon Tree*, Sandy Tolan chronicles the radical differences in the psyches of an Israeli, Dalia Eshkenazi, and a Palestinian, Bashir Kahairi, who had many painful conversations about the conflict and how it could be overcome. In June of 1967, the garden gate bell rang at the Eshkenazi's home. Dalia Eshkenazi, a student at Tel Aviv University, opened the gate to find three young men dressed in suits. Bashir introduced himself and his two cousins. He was twenty-five and a Palestinian lawyer. He had come by bus from the West Bank to see the house that his father had built in 1936 and lost in 1948 when his family fled to the West Bank in fear of the IDF. Dalia had been raised with a different story of why Palestinians left Israel: they preferred to live with a majority of Palestinians.

For the next twenty years, they continued to talk. Bashir insisted that the Palestinians had the "right of return" (why could Jews across the world be easily granted citizenship in Israel while Palestinians were forbidden to return?). Dalia saw Israelis as entitled to a secure home. She inherited her family's house and made a goodwill offer to return it to Bashir's family or at least pay reparation. She had come to acknowledge that it had been confiscated unjustly. He refused her offer; it fell far short of the rights due to his people. They finally agreed to convert the house into a kindergarten for Jews and Arab children in Israel.

Dalia was deeply sorry for what had happened to the Palestinians. She recognized their suffering. But for her, reconciliation was possible only if

Palestinians acknowledged the right of the Jewish people to a homeland. She appealed to Bashir: "If I knew or if we knew that you could make space for the state of Israel, first of all in your heart, then we could find a solution on the ground. How much less threatened my people would be. I don't have a right to ask you for this. I'm just asking. That is my plea" (Tolan 2006, p. 259). She urged Bashir to move beyond the injustice of the past and work to find a way to co-create a future. "Our enemy," she recognized, "is the only partner we have" (Tolan 2006, p. 262).

But for Bashir, reconciliation required the "right of return" for Palestinians to reclaim what was theirs. Israel could then become one state for both Jews and Palestinians. His solution was "one state, and all the people who live in this one state are equal, without any consideration of religion, nationality, culture, language . . . [with] the right to vote and choose [their] own leadership" (Tolan 2006, p. 259). Dalia had visited Bashir's family several times, moving into and out of the West Bank with ease, while Palestinians waited for hours at checkpoints to enter Israel for work. In 1969, hope for a continued relationship was dashed when Bashir was implicated in the bombing of a store near her house. He never admitted to the crime but was found guilty and sentenced to fifteen years in prison. Dalia cut off contact with his family. She lamented that "if national interest comes before our common humanity there is no hope for transformation, no hope for *anything*" (Tolan 2006, p. 176). For Bashir, recognition of common humanity meant meeting his people's essential needs, a place to be recognized as citizens with equal rights. Dalia reestablished contact with Bashir while he was living in exile in Cyprus. She wrote an open letter to him published in the *Jerusalem Post*. In it, she appealed to him to "demonstrate the kind of leadership that uses nonviolent means to struggle for your rights" (Tolan 2006, p. 203). She expressed hope that both sides would recognize that violence would not resolve but deepen the conflict. Both peoples will be liberated, she said, or neither would. Several months later, a letter arrived from Bashir, still in exile. He asked that "you and me struggle together with other peace-loving people for the establishment of a democratic popular state . . . and to struggle with me for my return to my old mother, to my wife and my children, and to my homeland" (Tolan 2006, p. 203). Bashir then revealed something he had never told Dalia over the many years of their friendship. When he was five years old, an Israeli soldier had booby-trapped a toy. When Bashir picked it up, it exploded and he lost four fingers and the palm of his left hand. The story of two peoples' pain is typified in Bashir and Dalia. What they have suffered, how they remember the past, and what peace and justice require are questions that go to the heart of resolving their conflict.

The cases of Egypt and Israel-Palestine involve different violent dynamics. In Egypt, different Islamic religious groups vie for control. In Israel, different political parties see the Israeli-Palestinian conflict differently. But both nations maintain control by military means. Injustices remain rife.

FOR DISCUSSION

1. How can the nonviolent movement for democracy in Egypt that began in 2011 be supported internationally?
2. How do different groups understand reform in Egypt? If not compatible, how can they nonetheless create a just society? How have different Egyptians' understandings of Islam impacted reform?
3. What forces prevented democracy from taking root?
4. Years of trying have not brought a resolution to the Israeli and Palestinian conflict. Conflict mediators distinguish between an adversary's *needs* that must be acknowledged and met and an adversary's *wants* that are negotiable. Can you identify the needs and wants of Israelis and Palestinians and then consider how to move forward?
5. What leverage could the international community have?
6. Why has the peace plan proposed recently by the United States been rejected by Palestinians?

Appendix 2

A Thought Experiment: Could Emancipation Have Been Achieved without the Civil War?

Violence against African Americans, all freed by the Thirteenth Amendment in 1865, has continued for 155 years since the Civil War ended. The destructiveness of the war, especially in the South, has left a legacy of bitterness. Were there nonviolent means of ending American slavery?

In *Emancipating Slaves, Enslaving Free Men: A History of the Civil War*, Civil War historian Jeffrey Rogers Hummel writes:

> Northerners clearly had available other good prospects for bringing down the South's peculiar institution if that had been their primary goal. . . . No one denies that it was the war that brought emancipation. Yet if history is to be more than just a factual rendition of past events . . . then why foreclose any consideration and study of untried alternatives to the carnage and destruction of war? (Hummel 1996, p. xx)

The first opponents of slavery were Quakers in the eighteenth century who eventually succeeded in banning from their meeting houses, Quakers who refused to free their slaves. In the nineteenth century, William Lloyd Garrison (1805–1879) was a tireless organizer of abolitionists in the North although some Northerners were hostile to the movement. Frederick Douglass (1818–1895) was born a slave in Maryland, and at the age of twenty, he escaped to Philadelphia and eventually made his way to Canada to escape capture. Douglass knew that emancipation would be utterly opposed in the South. From his own experience, he described the most pernicious form of slavery, "chattel slavery." Like other properties, chattel slaves were legally owned, branded like cattle, tortured, and killed at the whim of their masters, and bred like animals to ensure future generations of slaves.

Northerners too owned slaves, far fewer, and treated them less inhumanely. The Constitution was silent on the matter of slavery. Ten of the first twelve presidents owned slaves, including George Washington and Thomas Jefferson. Some slaveholders made provisions that after their death, their slaves were to be freed, but most passed slaves on to their children.

CONGRESSIONAL ACCOMMODATION

In 1807, Congress passed the act "Prohibiting Importation of Slaves." It did not threaten slavery insofar as the supply of slaves was assured by breeding them. For the next fifty years, Northern and Southern congressmen contended over the slave issue. The political strategy was not to abolish slavery but to maintain a balance of slave states and free states. At first it worked. The Missouri Compromise (1820) admitted Missouri as a slave state and Maine as a free state. But acrimony grew in Congress over permitting slavery as more states sought entry into the Union. When the Louisiana Purchase and the territory annexed from Mexico were carved into states, some of them intended to be admitted to the Union as free states, others as slave states but it was a divided Congress that was to decide. In 1846, the Wilmot Proviso proposed that Kansas and Nebraska be admitted as free states. The proposal was defeated by Southern members of Congress, and Kansas was made a slave state. In 1854, the Missouri Compromise was repealed, and Missouri was made a free state. In 1850, slavery was made legal in the District of Columbia while California was admitted as a free state. For Northerners, the most odious slave law passed that same year was the Fugitive Slave Law, requiring that runaway slaves be apprehended and returned to their masters and made assisting runaways a crime. In the *Dred Scott* decision in 1857, the Supreme Court held that slaves were legal property, not citizens of the United States, and that Congress had no right to regulate the spread of slavery.

In Lincoln's campaign for the presidency, he argued that slavery would spread if not abolished. Some Northern politicians even proposed that the Southern states be dissolved and a federal reservation be created banning slavery. The final straw for Southerners was the election of Lincoln in 1860, who warned that freeing the slaves might require "military emancipation." When seven states seceded and formed the Confederate States of America, Lincoln declared war. Six more Southern states joined the Confederacy.

There is a canny resemblance between the lead-up to World War I and the Civil War. Hubris prevented aristocratic leaders from negotiating. Both sides believed that a war could be won quickly. Both wars lasted five years. The union was preserved at a great cost. The Civil War took an estimated 700,000–800,000 lives: 600,000 soldiers, 50,000 civilians, and 56,000 soldiers in prisoner of war camps. In 1865, the Thirteenth Amendment abolished slavery everywhere in the United States, freeing four million slaves. A few months later, the war ended. Wide swaths of the South lay in ruin, and Southerners starved after crops were destroyed.

Jim Powell, a Civil War historian, shares the opinion of other contemporary historians that the war was avoidable. Abolishing slavery without war, he writes:

> did not mean wait[ing] for Southern slaveholders to decide when, if ever, they might emancipate their slaves. The alternative was to recognize that slavery was a gigantic beast, and no single strategy was likely to bring it down [but that] multiple strategies, including buying off slaveholders, had to be pursued—patiently, persistently, relentlessly. (Powell 2017, n.p.)

However, he does not suggest what the "multiple strategies" might have been, except for the federal government to buy slaves' freedom from slaveholders, a strategy rejected by slaveholders. The question remains: what strategies might have borne fruit? What could have been proposed and accepted in the South?

HOW MIGHT SLAVE OWNERS HAVE BEEN PERSUADED TO FREE THEIR SLAVES?

The Southern economy depended almost solely on cotton, which depleted minerals from the soil and was becoming less productive; by the mid-nineteenth century, planters in the border states were moving deeper south to find more fertile land. Powell notes that in contrast to the agrarian economy of the South,

> The principal centers of American finance, manufacturing and commerce were in the North. With each passing decade, the North became more prosperous than the South, and this must be counted among the significant, long-term factors working against peace. (Powell 2017, n.p.)

Until the invention of the cotton gin, cotton was a labor-intensive crop. How dependable was slave labor, given increasing rebelliousness of slaves? The first slave rebellion was led by Nat Turner and sixteen other slaves in Virginia in 1831, taking the lives of fifty-five whites. The underground railroad was growing. In 1856, John Brown (1800–1859) and his small anti-slavery band led a raid into Kansas, killing several pro-slavery supporters. Brown's boldest act was the attack on a federal armory in Harpers Ferry, Virginia, in 1859 to obtain arms and train slaves to revolt. Southerners were alarmed and armed themselves.

The greatest pressures for ending slavery were economic, principally boycotting the sale and purchase of cotton. To whom could planters sell their cotton if northern textile mills refused to buy it? What if northern consumers refused to buy cloth made of southern cotton? What if European markets stopped purchasing southern cotton? In addition, what if embargoes on products made in northern factories prohibited selling them in the south?

Boycotts and embargoes might bring slaveholders to the bargaining table. What was being asked of them had to be economically palatable. How could they free their slaves without economic ruin? Planters needed workers. What if conditions were created making it attractive for freed slaves to remain on plantations as paid laborers if they chose? Where wages would come from would have to be determined. Freed slaves would now be paid workers, free to leave if working conditions were oppressive. Owners must now treat their work force humanely or would lose them.

For freed slaves who chose to strike out on their own what most essential was land for farming. The federal government could buy small tracts of land from plantation owners and compensate them. As the war was ending in 1865, Union general William Sherman had ordered that plantations be expropriated and divided into forty acre allotments (and an army mule) and given to freed slaves. But plantation owners quickly reclaimed their land, driving the freedmen off. Black farms were burned.

Wages for field workers and compensation for land lost by plantation owners had to be negotiated if cotton production and small farming were to be viable. Would wages be paid by planters? By the government? Planters were among the richest Americans, in fact, the country's first millionaires. Those in the highest income ranges might have been required to pay full labor costs. Government subsidies might have been for specified time limits. Whoever bore the cost of labor, that cost would pale in comparison with the cost of war. Another benefit of a wage economy would be for freed slaves to be able to participate in the economy with their new buying power. What they earned would be spent in the local community, contributing to the prosperity of businesses. In terms of the need for economic diversity, what if producers in the north agreed to establish factories in the south? All of these initiatives had the potential to expand wealth in the South.

All of these suggestions are hypothetical. Other might have been developed, all to avoid the war. As it was, no negotiations ever happened. The resulting consequence of their emancipation was that freed slaves roamed the countryside destitute. Recognizing that something needed to be done, in 1865 the federal government established the Bureau of Refugees, Freedmen, and Abandoned Lands in order to offer

> provisions, clothing, and fuel . . . for the immediate and temporary shelter and supply of destitute and suffering refugees and freedmen and their wives and children [with] tracts of land within the insurrectionary states to be parceled into 40-acre plots for refugees and freedmen.

Congress funded the Bureau for one year and then extended funding until 1872. It encouraged the rebuilding of plantations on which white owners and ex-slaves would work together, but without any compensation for freed slave. Southerns had had no part in establishing the Bureau, contending that states' rights were again being violated. The Bureau had very limited success. In 1875, Frederick Douglass painted a bleak picture of his people's condition:

> The world has never seen as many people turned loose to such destitution as were the four million slaves of the South. . . . They were turned out without roofs to cover them, or bread to eat, or land to cultivate, and as a consequence died in such numbers as to awaken the hope in their enemies that they would soon disappear. (Darrity 2020, p. 1)

The swath of destruction in the South and the loss of slave labor fueled a swath of bitterness toward the North and the avenging of freed slaves, regarded as the material cause of the War. Asserting states' rights after the War, the Southern states passed the Black Codes, laws aimed solely at prosecuting former slaves and subjecting them to brutal punishments and leasing black prisoners to work on plantations. Decades of lynching and the Jim Crow era followed. The Ku Klux Klan was organized in 1866, and with other white supremacist organizations, roamed the South attacking blacks. Powell writes that

> the military strategy for emancipation backfired badly. Massive destruction and loss of life embittered Southerners, giving them powerful incentives to avenge their losses whenever they had the chance. Pro-slavery Southerners were bad before the war and worse afterwards. (Powell 2017, n.p.)

The hundred years from the end of the war to the civil rights movement was a continuation of white supremacy, the control of black Americans by law, custom, and violent enforcement of the "rules." Only in the civil rights movement of the 1960s did black Americans win legal protections. Yet, fifty years on, racism remains entrenched in the United States. The Civil War left deep wounds. The very people it freed continue to be oppressed. Historians of the Civil War urge us not to see war as a fore gone conclusion but to tirelessly imagine alternatives.

FOR REFLECTION

1. Describe other economic strategies that you think might have persuaded Southern slaveholders to free their slaves.

Notes

INTRODUCTION

1. See Eric Baum, "War and Peace" *The Guardian* (Feb 2002). https://www.theguard
ian.com/education/2002/feb/23/artsandhumanities.highereducation#:~:text=The%20
total%20number%20of%20deaths,without%20organised%20armed%20conflict%20
somewhere. Accessed 6 May 2020.

1. A HUNDRED YEARS OF HORRIFIC WAR-MAKING

1. Today the International Criminal Court is located at The Hague in the Netherlands.

2. The seventeenth century moralist Hugo Grotius wrote the claims of all parties in international disputes were simultaneous both just and unjust. Justice is not black or white, though one side may have the stronger justice claim of.

3. Balkan war.

4. Williams went on to a successful political career. When she was seventy she served as Leader of the Liberal Democrats in the House of Lords. Later she was Adviser on Nuclear Proliferation to Prime Minister Gordon Brown. She also taught politics at the John F. Kennedy School of Government at Harvard University. Shirley Williams was the daughter of Vera Brittain.

5. Haunting literature appeared after the war. Two very powerful novels are *All Quiet on the Western Front* by Erich Maria Remarque and *Johnny Got His Gun* by Dalton Trumbo.

6. Peter Arnett insisted that the quote was accurate, though some said he got the correct meaning but not the soldier's exact words. It would seem to be a moot point.

7. Crawford is quoting from the U.S. Air Force, "Targeting Air Force Doctrine Document," 2–1.99 (U.S. Air Force, 8 June 2006), p. 113.

8. Shrapnel from a 2,000-pound bomb can travel a radius of 4,000 feet from the point of its target. That is about the length of 103 football fields laid end to end. Pilots try to avoid dropping such bombs when U.S. ground forces are within that range; accidental killings of soldiers within that radius have occurred.

9. The International Conflict Group was established in 1995 with the mission to "prevent, mitigate and end deadly conflict." Its seventy-five foreign policy experts travel to conflict zones "listening, engaging, and persuading" opposing sides.

10. See Caroline Goerzig, *Talking to Terrorists: Concessions and the Renunciation of Violence* (London: Routledge, 2010). Goerzig's research challenges the notion that making concessions only encourages other terrorists. She describes how concessions stopped the violence being done by the Egyptian Jihad-a-Qaeda and the Turkish Hezbollah. French journalist Nicolas Hénin was kidnapped by ISIS in Syria and held with others for ten months. He was released after the French government negotiated with ISIS. The other foreign captives, including four Americans, were executed. Their governments had refused to negotiate.

11. Cheney had large financial interests in U.S. defense contracts in Iraq.

12. She is quoted in *The Common Truth*, a documentary about the Iraq War's impact on U.S. veterans.

13. *Associated Press*, August 16, 2012.

14. U.S. diplomats and state department officials who occupy country desks should be consulted.

15. He said that one day he had "forty-five." around Baghdad. Asked if he meant a Colt 45, he responded "No, I mean forty-five thousand dollars."

16. The next chapter describes the decisive pacifism of the Protestant Huguenots in southern France during World War II.

17. Zahn makes three especially noteworthy points. First, in his research on the U.S. camps for COs during the war he found that the men performed eight million hours of unpaid labor. Second, the U.S. government had a punitive or at least negligent stance toward the camps: food shortages and lack of health care were continuous for the six years the camps existed. So bad were conditions that some COs petitioned to serve in the military. Third, COs in the camps only rarely found support from local bishops and surrounding townspeople, and harsh living conditions. But as will be noted in the final chapter, a sea change in the Catholic attitude toward war occurred in the 1960s and 1970s. The witness of COs and the Catholic Worker Movement that had tried to provide much needed funds to upgrade Camp Simon, helped to move the Catholic Church away from a pro-American war making stance. Zahn also spent WW II in such a camp.

18. Technically, Franz Jäggerstätter, Howard Levy, Ehren Watada, Camilo Mejiá, and Pablo Paredes were *selective* conscientious objectors, because their dissent was to a particular war, not to all wars. Thus, they were not claiming to be pacifists. One note about pacifists is that their refusal to serve may sometimes be individualistic and not given to social activism. But other have engaged in peace advocacy, e.g., organizing the Vietnam Veterans Against the War and the Iraq Veterans Against the War.

19. Organizations supporting individuals' efforts to receive CO status include the GI Network, the National Lawyers Guild Military Task Force, and the Center for Conscience and War.

Notes

2. MOHANDAS GANDHI, THE FATHER
OF MODERN NONVIOLENCE

1. Rynne's study of Gandhian principles and Gandhi's influence on Christian theologians is one of the most thorough available.

2. The philosopher is unknown. But he or she put a sharp point about the relationship between means and ends.

3. A very thorough analysis of Gandhian campaigns in India is Joan V. Bondurant's *Conquest of Violence: The Gandhian Philosophy of Conflict* (Berkeley: University of California Press, 1967).

4. Unfortunately, Brahmin attitudes remained unchanged. Eventually a by-pass road was constructed to which neither Dalits nor Brahmins objected. Gandhi and the satyagrahis had actively opposed India's great inequality and human rights violation, the treatment of untouchables. But to this day, almost a century later, untouchability remains India's most serious and intractable form of discrimination. Unlike Gandhian campaigns against the injustices of British occupation, the Vykom campaign hit a high wall of religious and cultural taboos. The campaign did not change Brahmin attitudes, but it did change the status quo. In retrospect, the failure to change Brahmin's attitudes at Vykom was the failure to include Harijans in the protests. Their participation might have demonstrated their activist determination to oppose discrimination and elevated respect for them.

5. I have chosen this phrase to underscore its contrast to the Department of Defense use of the phrase in reference to military operations on the battlefield.

6. Charles Boycott was a British landlord agent in Ireland who in 1880 was shunned by tenant farmers for his part in enforcing land laws impoverishing small farmers. They also refused to shop in all stores with which he had connections.

7. Tragically, it was because of his openness to other religious teachings that Gandhi was assassinated by a fundamentalist Hindu.

8. Terrence Rynne provides a masterful study of Gandhi and his influence on Christianity in *Gandhi and Jesus: The Saving Power of Nonviolence* (Maryknoll, NY: Orbis Books, 2008).

9. Niemoeller wrote this self-reflection 1946. In the early 1930s, he had believed that National Socialism was good for Germany. He also held the view that Jews were responsible for the death of Christ. As a leading Lutheran pastor in Germany, he once had an audience with Hitler. Hitler assured Niemoeller that he had no intention of harming the Jews. As Nazism became more brutal, he renounced the regime and was imprisoned in a concentration camp from 1937 to 1946. The poem was part of his expression of repentance for his anti-Semitism and sins of omission.

10. Only once were saboteurs caught. Several young Danes were caught and were among the very few Danes to be executed.

11. John Steinbeck, *The Moon Is Down* (New York: Viking Press, 1942). Steinbeck had learned about the experiences of the occupations from war refugees. *The Moon Is Down* describes a fictitious town that is invaded by foreign forces. The objective of the occupation is the town's coal; the soldiers' task is to force the miners to produce it. The resistance is at first passive. The soldiers are shunned and eventually become paranoid. What are the townspeople plotting? The soldiers are homesick and

depressed. In their fear they accidently shoot two innocent civilians. The conquerors had come to fear the conquered. The story suggests how resistance succeeds as soldiers can no longer perform their task. The commandant wants to remain civilized and yet must accomplish what he has been sent to do. He gives the mayor an ultimatum: force the townspeople to cooperate or be executed. The town doctor tells the commandant that execution of the mayor will have no effect, for "we are a free people: we have as many heads as we have people, and in a time of need leaders pop up among us like mushrooms." *The Moon Is Down* was a morale booster in occupied Europe. It was translated into the languages of every occupied nation in Europe, and went through ninety-two printings. The Nazis made possession of the book a crime.

12. In the seventeenth and eighteenth centuries, Huguenots had been hunted down as heretics in Catholic France, their men killed or enslaved on ships and their women imprisoned.

13. André Trocmé was born into a wealthy family in northern France. World War I had a profound effect on the Trocmé family. One of his brothers was killed on the front. Their home was occupied, and André witnessed scores of soldiers breathing their last. He also met a German soldier who was a pacifist and realized that some Germans refused to kill. The Trocmé family was forced to flee to Belgium. After the war, André studied in Paris and then in New York City. There he met his future wife, Magda Ingrilli, who was from Florence.

14. Those who helped rescue Jews were spread throughout and beyond the plateau. A secret underground rescue network developed. Jewish children whose parents had been or were about to be deported from French internment camps were gotten out of the camps by several groups of relief organizations. Help came from the International Fellowship of Reconciliation and the Cimade, a group of Protestant Students, who were able to lead children across the mountains into neutral Switzerland. Homes for children in Le Chambon were supported with help from American Quakers. Patrick Henry offers a fuller discussion of the groups who worked to rescue Jewish children, including a Jewish organization and a Swiss Protestant network. As for the French Catholic Church, only a few bishops condemned anti-Semitism and urged assisting the Jews.

15. After the liberation of France, the Trocmé moved to Versailles where André and Magda became co-secretaries of the European chapter of the International Fellowship of Reconciliation (IFOR). In 1960, they relocated in Geneva, where André became pastor of the largest Protestant Reform church.

3. SUCCESSFUL NONVIOLENT REVOLUTIONS

1. The United States granted Marcos and his family asylum, and they took up residence in Hawaii. One may wonder why the United States granted asylum to Marcos, a corrupt dictator who had violated the rights of Filipinos for so long. Marcos was a longtime ally who had supported the U.S.' large military presence in the Philippines, including its naval base at Subic Bay.

2. The government claimed that there were only a few casualties, but others estimate 300 deaths among the protestors. The government had hastily buried many.

3. An excellent study of the nonviolent revolution in East German is Jorg Swoboda's *The Revolution of the Candles* (Wuppertal und Kassel: Onken Verlag, 1990).

4. The story of Russia's collapse is equally dramatic, though it is not told here. In that nonviolent movement, the Orthodox church and massive crowds played key roles.

5. These quotes are from the documentary "Bringing Down a Dictator" produced by York Zimmerman, Inc in 2001.

6. What came to be called the "Arab Spring" occurred in Tunisia, Egypt, Iraq, Libya, Syria, Yemen, and Bahrain. The Tunisian revolution is examined here. Tragically, the hope for freedom from military and autocratic ruled that succeeded in Tunisia failed in all of these other nations. See Marwah Bishara, *The Invisible Arab: The Promise and Peril of the Arab Revolutions* (New York: Nation Books, 2012).

7. Those whom the regimes killed are referred to as the martyrs of the Arab Spring.

8. Similarly, the use of social media by young activists in Egypt was critical.

9. Ninety-five percent of Liberians are tribal peoples; only 5 percent are Americo-Liberians.

10. In 2006, Firestone was sued for its labor practices by the International Labor Rights Fund.

11. An excellent documentary on many women who brought peace to Liberia is "Pray the Devil Back to Hell," by Abigail E. Disney and Gini Reticker (Roco Films Educational, 2008).

12. Sharp came of age during the Korean War and spent nine months in prison for protesting the draft. He studied Gandhi's and A. J. Muste's theories and practices of nonviolence and went on to earn a doctorate in political theory at Oxford University. He worked for *Peace News* in London, continuing his peace research in Europe before returning to the United States. Sharp taught at several universities and in 1983 established the Albert Einstein Institution to study and promote nonviolent action.

4. SYSTEMIC RACISM FROM THE CIVIL RIGHTS STRUGGLE TO THE BLACK LIVES MATTER MOVEMENT

1. Gandhi also stressed liberation of all (*moksha*).

2. For its many bombings of black institutions, including the Sixteenth Street Baptist Church where four young girls were killed, Birmingham earned the name "bombingham."

3. Speech in Charlotte, North Carolina.

4. But that is not the end of Seller's story. He went on to finish college at Howard University. He earned an MA from Harvard and an EdD from the University of North Carolina. Sellers directed the African American Studies program at the University of South Carolina for many years and served as president of Voorhees College from 2008 to 2015. Cleveland Sellers never lost his abiding hope in racial justice. Bakari Sellers, his son, at age 22, became the youngest South Carolina state representative.

5. Malcolm once sent a note to Coretta King to explain why he was present at one of her husband's rallies, telling her he was there to remind segregationists that if they did not negotiate with nonviolent activists like King they would have to answer to much more disruptive forces.

6. We are focusing on the BPPSD rather than only on Huey Newton. However, we should note that his conviction for manslaughter was overturned. Newton continued the struggle after his release from prison in 1971. However, he battled alcohol and drug addiction in the 1980s and was killed by a young drug dealer in 1989. See a biography of Newton by David Hilliard, a BPP leader and close associate, *Huey: Spirit of the Panther* (New York: Thunder Mouth's Press, 2006).

7. iPhones, cameras, and mandatory police cam recorders have brought to light what has always been known: the killing of black men by law enforcement agents under questionable circumstances. Fifty years after the BPPSD was established, the Black Lives Matter was formed, again in Oakland and again for the same reason.

5. NONVIOLENT STRUGGLES U.S. FARM LABORERS, NATIVE AMERICANS, AND BLACK SOUTH AFRICANS

1. Americans growing up in the 1960s will remember being taught that green table grapes were "forbidden fruit."

2. For a full account of what happened at Wounded Knee, see Dee Brown, *Bury My Heart at Wounded Knee* (New York: Henry Holt and Co., 2011).

3. Native American studies programs had recently been established in some California universities. Another effort was the "White Roots of Peace," a mobile school that began traveling to reservations and urban areas.

4. Afrikaans, derived from the Dutch, is the language spoken by Afrikaners.

5. King's successes in the United States were well-known. A South Africa government official vowed that what King had done in America would never be allowed to happen in South Africa.

6. Fischer was treated brutally by guards. After breaking a leg, he languished for thirteen days before being taken to a hospital. He died of cancer, only given humanitarian release one day before he died.

7. The Pan African Congress (PAC) advocated black rule. Its leader, Robert Sobukwe, was also convicted and imprisoned.

8. The woman was interviewed in "South Africa: Freedom in Our Lifetime." *Force More Powerful*, Peter Ackerman and Jack Duvall.

9. Security forces attempted to assassinate Chikane by lacing his suitcase with poison at the Johannesburg airport as he was leaving for a speaking tour in the United States.

10. It must be acknowledged that while Nelson Mandela opposed violent options, he insisted that individuals could use violence in self-defense.

6. VIOLENT AMERICA

1. Anonymous source.

2. It must also be noted that in addition to the defense budgets are the budgets of the spy agencies and the Veterans Administration which in FY 2020 are $86 billion

dollars and $220 billion dollars, respectively. As U.S. wars continue, veteran needs will require more spending.

3. The Aerospace Industries Association provides these numbers for 2018.

4. The top five weapons makers are Boeing, Lockheed Martin, Raytheon, BAE (British), and Northrop Grumman.

5. Foster continues: "This new age of U.S. imperialism will generate its own contradictions, amongst them attempts by other major powers to assert their influence, resorting to similar belligerent means, and all sorts of strategies by weaker states and non-state actors to engage in "asymmetric" forms of warfare. Rather than generating a new 'Pax Americana' the United States may be paving the way to new global holocausts."

6. Saad's data is based on the Gallup Poll's report for 2016–2018.

7. All of these quotes are from Patrick Blanchfield's interview on National Public Radio, August 7, 2019, in the wake of mass shootings in El Paso, Texas, and Dayton, Ohio. Blanchfield is a faculty member at the Brooklyn Institute for Social Research.

7. NONVIOLENT CITIZEN MOVEMENTS FOR JUSTICE

1. Alison Gopnik is director of a cognitive development and early learning lab and teaches psychology and philosophy at the University of California at Berkeley. https://onbeing.org/programs/alison-gopnik-the-evolutionary-power-of-children-and-teenagers/.

2. Menakem is also emphatic in applying this need for settling to police, whose training does not address the essential need to settle body and nervous system.

3. It should be noted that the U.S. government strains to care for its own damaged veterans.

4. Cost overruns frequently occur. Lack of oversight invites corruption. Here is an example of what happened after a security firm won a contract to protect a military base in Afghanistan. The firm found two Afghanis whom it hired to recruit other Afghans. The two turned out to be connected to warlords. One group of warlords used the weapons with which they were supplied to attack a village in which rivals were believed to be. Over several hours, about forty civilians were massacred. The excuse given by the security company was that these employees were looking for a particular terrorist, who did not turn out to be there. The subcontractor was not disciplined.

5. Thomas Sheesgreen, August 12, 2020 "Report: Risks to civilians overlooked in arms sale." *USA Today*.

6. "This [court] ruling is a blow to the government and to the British arms industry. More than 40% of UK arms exports are destined for Saudi Arabia. Last year alone the largest UK defense company, BAE Systems, made £2.6bn [$3.4 billion dollars) worth of sales to the Gulf state." Accessed 20 June 2019 (https://www.bbc.com/news/uk-48704596).

7. https://www.aljazeera.com/news/2020/02/landmine-policy-reverses-global-progress.

8. There is precedent for the United States recognizing the miscarriage of justice and making monetary reparations. Soon after Japan attacked Pearl Harbor

in December 1941, the U.S. government began an internment program removing Japanese-American citizens to isolated internment camps where they remained until 1945. Most lost their homes and businesses. In 1980, Japanese-American organizations pressed for reparations for 82,000 survivors of those who had been removed from their communities. In 1988, the U.S. government passed the "Civil Liberties Act" acknowledging that the rights of Japanese-Americans had been violated because of racial prejudice. Each survivor received $20,000.

9. The author has researched and conducted interviews with experts and inmates to gather this information. Inmates provided some of the most insightful observations about necessary reforms.

10. Militarism and the degrading of the environment are closely related. The carbon footprint of the U.S. military is very large; it emits more greenhouse gasses than do many small countries.

11. Sauvage posed the question in his documentary *Weapons of the Spirit* (Los Angeles: Le Chambon Foundation, 1990).

8. NONVIOLENCE, WORLD RELIGIONS, AND THE VIRTUES

1. The U.S. judicial system's goal is to determine whether laws has been violated and to punish those who have broken them. Judicial proceedings are less focused on the "making whole" of the victim. Forms of mediation often accomplish the latter more effectively.

2. The British never succeeded in fully controlling the northwest. They blamed their inability on the Sikhs' unmatched military capability, which proved to be a good ploy for later recruiting them into the British army. However, Adi Granth described Sikh warriors as possessing a totally different kind of militancy.

3. In the United States, Sikhs are often mistaken as Muslims and since 9/11 have also been targets of hate crimes. Distrust of minorities from the Middle East and South Asia continues to plague the United States, encouraged by the rhetoric of President Donald Trump. See the Southern Poverty Law Center for its research into increase in the number of hate groups in the United States.

4. The books are Genesis, Exodus, Leviticus, Numbers, and Deuteronomy.

5. Tinker is an enrolled member of the Osage tribe. For an account of murders of the Osage in the Twentieth Century, see *Killers of the Flower Moon: The Osage Murders and the Birth of the FBI* (New York: Doubleday, 2017).

6. Indeed, there was no religious litmus test for those in the Polish Solidarity movement, in Serbia's Otpor, and those in the Arab Spring. In fact, religious fundamentalism can harm movements, as was the case in Egypt when the Muslim Brotherhood compromised the democratic vision of the young secular protestors.

7. Paxson reports that those who receive legal assistance are twice as likely to be granted asylum.

8. Ariella Tilson, a psychologist, is quoted in Menakem, 68.

9. Although it is not often pointed out, reparations are also due to Native American peoples.

10. The process of restorative justice in not a substitute for determination of guilt and punishment, which has already taken place. However, it can meet a need that court room proceedings may not. In a court of law, determination is made whether laws have been broken and what punishments will be imposed. The injured "party" is the state, for its laws have been violated. Victims may feel ignored, even if they are given an opportunity to make a statement during the sentencing phase of a trial.

11. Some legal scholars object that circumventing the justice system undermines it.

12. *Satyagraha* means searching for truth by struggling for justice. Truth commissions are dedicated to finding the truth, though criminal justice may not be possible under the circumstances. The REHMI report in Guatemala could not take the authors of genocide to court in 1998 because the judiciary was not functioning.

AFTERWORD

1. I am grateful to my son John Duffey who happened to be in Dublin during the centenary and brought the paper back. He also brought a facsimile of Dublin's *Sunday Independent* published on April 30 with the headline "Dublin a City of Dead and Ruins."

APPENDIX 1. TWO UNSUCCESSFUL NONVIOLENT STRUGGLES FOR JUSTICE: EGYPT'S ARAB SPRING AND ISRAEL-PALESTINE CONFLICT

1. In 1953, the monarchy was replaced with a republic and General Gamal Nasser became its first president (1953–1970). He was succeeded by Anwar Sadat (1970–1981), who attempted peace with Israel and was assassinated. Hosni Mubarak ruled until the 2011 Arab Spring.

2. He was interviewed after his release, saying: "We have a dream, we will not lose. Our tears are from our hearts" His jailers, he said "were simple people; when they finally took the blindfold off, I greeted them and kissed them all." Ghonim's demand was that "the billions and billions of dollars be returned . . . because the people eating out of the trash, this was their money" (CBS News interview, February 13, 2011).

3. The Muslim Brotherhood (MB) was founded in 1928 with the goal of a purified Islam and Islamic unity across the Middle East. The MB had half a million members. It provided health, educational, job, and welfare assistance to the poor. While of late declaring itself committed to nonviolence, the MB made many exceptions. It assassinated one prime minister during the monarchy period and attempted to murder another.

4. Robert Worth recorded an interview of a young liberal who reported that he spent an evening in the Square with several members of the Gamaa and was shocked at the consensus and cooperative spirit he discovered. Unfortunately, it did not last. (Worth 2016)

5. The Occupied Territories are divided into three areas with varying degrees of Palestinian governance but policing by the Israeli Defense Forces (IDF).

6. Chenoweth and Stephan.

7. The commander's order was a flagrant violation of the just war teaching.

8. The organization produced a documentary shown on Israeli television in 2008.

9. It is also estimated that one-half of Israelis do not present themselves for induction or leave early.

Bibliography

Ackerman, Peter and Duval, Jack. 2000a. "South Africa: Freedom in Our Lifetime."
———. 2000b. *A Force More Powerful: A Century of Nonviolent Conflict*. New York: St. Martin's Press.
Al Saleh, Asaad. 2015. "The Death of My Cousin and the Birth of a New Tunisia." in *Voices of the Arab Spring: Personal Stories of the Arab Revolutions*. Yazidi, Ahlem, ed. New York: Columbia University Press, 25–30.
Ali, Ayaan Hirsi. 2007. *Infidel*. New York: Atria.
Armstrong, Karen. 2006. *The Great Transformation: The Beginning of Our Religious Traditions*. New York: Alfred A. Knopf.
Ateek, Stifa. 2017. *A Palestinian Theology of Liberation: The Bible, Justice, and the Palestine-Israel Conflict*. Maryknoll, NY: Orbis Books.
Awad, Mubarek. 1983/1984. "Non-violent Resistance: A Strategy for the Occupied Territories." *Journal of Palestinian Studies*, 13, 4.
Azam, Azhar. 2019. "Defense Contractors in U.S. Politics." *Express Tribune* (December 27, 2019). https://azhar-azam.blogspot.com/2019/12/defence-contractors-in-us-politics.html. Accessed January 2, 2020.
Barry-Jester, Anna Maria, Recht, Hannah, and Smith, Michelle R. 12/15/2020. "Underfunded and Under Threat: Pandemic Backlash Jeopardizes Public Health Powers, Leaders." Kaiser Health Network. https://khn.org/news/article/pandemic-backlash-jeopardizes-public-health-powers-leaders/.
Bell, Inge Powell. 1968. *CORE and the Strategy of Nonviolence*. New York: Random House.
Bellah, et al. 1983. *Habits of the Heart: Individualism and Commitment in American Life*. Berkeley: University of California Press, 1983.
Berman, Morris. 2006. *Dark Ages America: The Final Phase of Empire*. New York: W. W. Norton and Company.
Bishara, Marwan. 2012. *Invisible Arab: The Promise and Peril of the Arab Revolutions*. New York: Nation Books.

Blanchfield, Patrick. August 7, 2019. Interview on National Public Radio.

Blansett, Kent. 2018. *The Journey to Freedom: Richard Oakes, Alcatraz, and the Red Power Movement*. New Haven, CT: Yale University Press.

Blue Cloud, Peter 1999. "Resistance at Oka" in *Nabokov*, 433–437.

Bondurant, Joan. 1967. *The Conquest of Violence: The Gandhian Philosophy of Conflict*. Berkeley: University of California Press.

Bratt, Peter. 2017. *Dolores*. Independent Lens.

Brian, Bernard. 2016. *Blessed Jerzy Popieluszko: Truth Versus Totalitarianism*. San Francisco: Ignatius Press.

Brittain, Vera. 1923. *Testament of Youth*. London: Edmundsbury Press.

Bstan-'dzin-rgya-mtsho, Dalai Lama XIV. 1982. *The Path to Enlightenment*. Ithaca, NY: Snow Lion Publications.

Cambanis, Thanassis. 2015. *Once Upon a Revolution: An Egyptian Story*. New York: Simon & Schuster.

Camus, Albert. 1947. *The Plague*. Gilbert, Stuart, trans. New York: Alfred A. Knopf.

Carson, Clayborn. 1981. *In Struggle: SNCC and the Black Awakening of the 1960s*. Cambridge, MA: Harvard University Press.

Centre for the Study of War, State and Society. "The Bombing of Germany 1940–1945." United Kingdom: University of Exeter Press. https://humanities.exeter.ac.uk/history/research/centres/warstateandsociety/projects/bombing/germany/. Accessed November 12, 2020.

Chacham, Ronit. 2003. *Breaking Ranks: Refusing to Serve in the West Bank and Gaza*. Assaf Oron. New York: Other Press.

Chávez, Cesar. 1969. "Creative Nonviolence." New York: The Catholic Worker.

Chávez, César. 2008. *César Chávez: An Organizer's Tale*. New York: Penguin Classics.

Chenoweth, Erica and Stephan, Maria. 2011. *Why Civil Resistance Works: The Strategic Logic of Nonviolent Conflict*. New York: Columbia University Press.

Civlitá Cattolica. 1991. 1991. Vatican City Press.

Clancy-Smith, Julia. 2013. "From Sidi Bou Zid to Sidi Bou Said: A *Longue Duree*, The Tunisian Revolutions." In *The Arab Spring: Change and Resistance in the Middle East*. Haas, Mark L. and Lesch, David W., eds. Boulder, CO: Westview Press.

Cleaver, Kathleen, ed. 2001. *Liberation, Imagination, and the Black Panther Party*. New York: Routledge.

Coates, Ta-Nehisi. 2015. *Between the World and Me*. Melbourne, Australia: The Text Publishing Co.

Cohn, Marjorie and Gilberd, Kathleen. 2009. *Rules of Disengagement: The Politics and Honor of Military Dissent*. Sausalito, CA: PoliPointPress, LLC.

Cole, W. Owen and Sambhi, Piara Singh. 1978. *The Sikhs: Their Religious Beliefs and Practice*. London: Routledge & Kegan Paul.

Collier, Peter and Horowitz, David, eds. 1997. *The Race Card*. Rocklin, CA: Prima Pub.

Craig, Mary. 1987. *Lech Walesa and His Poland*. New York: Continuum.

Crawford, Neta C. 2013. *Accountability for Killing: Moral Responsibility for Collateral Damage in America's Post-9/11 Wars*. New York: Oxford University Press.

Dalton, Frederick John. 2003 *The Moral Vision of Cesar Chávez*. Maryknoll, NY: Orbis Books.

Deloria, Jr., Vine. 1988. *Custer Died for Your Sins: An Indian Manifesto*. New York: Macmillan, 1969; Norman: University of Oklahoma Press.

Douglass, Frederick. 1845. *Narrative of the Life of Frederick Douglass, An American Slave*. http://utc.iath.virginia.edu/abolitn/dougnarrhp.html.

———. 1875. "Celebrating the Past, Anticipating the Future." https://cornellpress. manifoldapp.org/read/in-the-words-of-frederick-douglass/section/896091cc-2ddc-47e5-ae2f-4ced94e59924.

Duffey, Michael K. 1995. *Peacemaking Christians: The Future of Just Wars, Pacifism, and Nonviolent Resistance*. Kansas City, MO: Sheed and Ward.

Duncan, Mel. 2019. www://nonviolentpeaceforce.org/unarmed-civilian-protection. Accessed September 3, 2020.

Easwaran, Eknath. 1972. *Gandhi the Man: The Story of His Transformation*. Tomales, CA: Nilgiri Press.

———. 1989. *Nonviolent Soldier of Islam: Badshah Khan, A Man to Match His Mountains*. Tomales, CA: Nilgiri Press.

Einstein, Albert. www.openculture.com. Accessed September 5, 2020.

Enright, Robert. 2001. *Forgiveness Is a Choice: A Step by Step Process for Resolving Anger and Restoring Hope*. Washington, D.C.: American Psychological Society.

Etheridge, Eric. 2008. *Breach of Peace: Portraits of the 1961 Mississippi Freedom Riders*. New York: W. W. Norton and Company.

Fischer, Louis. 1954. *Gandhi: His Life and Message for the World*. New York: New American Library.

Fisher, Roger, Ury, William, and Patton, Bruce. 1991. *Getting to Yes: Negotiating Agreement without Giving In* (2nd edition). Boston: Houghton Mifflin.

Fleming, Maria. 2001. *A Place at the Table: Struggles for Equality in America*. New York: Oxford University Press.

Foster, John Bellamy. 2003. "The New Age of Imperialism." *Monthly Review:* July 2003, 55, 3.

Frankel, Glenn. 1999. *Rivonia's Children*. New York: Farrar, Straus, Giroux.

French, Marilyn. 1992. *The War Against Women*. New York: Summit Books.

———. 1987. "Palestinians Under Israel: Bitter Politics." *New York Times*. https://www.pulitzer.org/winners/thomas-l-friedman.

Friedman, Thomas L. 2003. "Because We Could." *New York Times:* June 4, 2003.

Gallen, David. 1992. *Malcolm X: As They Knew Him*. New York: Carroll and Graf.

Galtung, Johan and Weber, Charles, eds. 2007. *Handbook of Peace and Conflict Studies*. London: Routledge.

Galtung, Johan. 1989. *Nonviolence and Israel/Palestine*. Honolulu: University of Hawaii Institute for Peace.

———. 1992a. *The Way Is the Goal*. Ahmedabad, India: Vinoa Revashankar Tripathi.

———. 1992b. *The Way Is the Goal: Gandhi Today*. Ahmedabad, India: Gujarat Vidyapith Peace Research Centre.

———. 1996. *Peace by Peaceful Means*. Oslo: International Peace Research Institute.

Geissler, Christian, "Auschwitz, Hiroshima und die Hoffnungen des Menschen." *Werkhefte* 15 (July 1961): 229–235.

Gerstenzang, James and Darling, Juanita. March 11, 1999. "Clinton Gives Apology for U.S. Role in Guatemala." *Los Angeles Times*.

Ghafar, Adel Abdel. 2015. "The Moment the Barrier of Fear Broke Down." In *Voices of the Arab Spring*. Al-Saleh, Asaad, ed. New York: Columbia University Press.

Giles, Wenona and Hyndman, Jennifer, eds. 2004. *Sites of Violence: Gender and Conflict Zones*. Berkeley: University of California Press.

Goldman, Peter. 1979. *The Death and Life of Malcolm X*. Urbana: University of Illinois Press.

Goldstein, Joshua S. 2011. *Winning the War on War*. New York: Dutton.

Gwynne, S. C. 2010. *Empire of the Summer Moon: The Rise and Fall of the Comanches, the Most Powerful Tribe in American History*. New York: Scribner.

Haas, Mark L. and Lesch, David W., eds. 2012. *The Arab Spring: Change and Resistance in the Middle East*. Boulder, CO: Westview Press.

Hallie, Philip. 1979. *Less Innocent Blood Be Shed*. New York: Harper Torchbooks.

Hallward, Maia and Norman, Julie M., eds. 2015. *Understanding Nonviolence: Contours and Contexts*. Cambridge, UK: Polity Press.

Harding, Vincent. 1996. *Martin Luther King, Jr.: The Inconvenient Hero*. Maryknoll, NY: Orbis Books.

Henderson, Michael. 1996. *The Forgiveness Factor: Stories of Hope in a World of Conflict*. London: Grosvenor Books.

Henry, Patrick. 2007. *We Only Know Men: The Rescue of Jews in France During the Holocaust*. Washington, D.C.: The Catholic University of America Press.

Hénin, Nicolas. 2015. *Jihad Academy*. London: Bloomsbury.

Hessel, Stéphane. 2011. *Time for Outrage!* London: Quartet Books.

Hewitt, Annie. 2018. "Why Unarmed Civilian Protection Is the Best Path to Peace." WagingNonviolence.org.

Hickman, Renee. 2021. "Experts on both sides work against polarization." Wausau, WI: Wausau Daily Herald.

Huddleston, Trevor. 1956. *Naught for Your Comfort*. London: Collins.

Hummel, Jeffrey Roger. 1996. *Emancipating Slaves, Enslaving Free Men: A History of the Civil War*. Chicago: Open Court.

Hunt, Swanee. 2011. "Building a Peace Network." In *Women Waging War and Peace: International Perspectives of Women's Roles in Conflict and Post-Conflict Reconstruction*. Children, Sandra I. and Eliatamby, Maneshke, eds. London: Continuum International Publishing Group.

International Crisis Group. 2016. "Exploiting Disorder: al-Qaeda and the Islamic State." Brussels: International Crisis Group.

Jahanbegloo, Ramin. 2014. *Introduction to Nonviolence*. New York: Palgrave.

Jensen, Derrick. 2010. *Resistance Against Empire* (ten interviews). Crescent, CA: PM Press.

Johnson, Ellen Sirleaf. 2009. *This Child Will Be Great*. New York: HarperCollins.

Johnson, James. 1984. *Can Modern War Be Just?* New Haven, CT: Yale University Press.

Johnson, Troy R. 1996. *The American Indian Occupation of Alcatraz Island: Red Power and Self-Determination*. Lincoln: University of Nebraska Press.

Julian, Rachel. 2018. "Why Unarmed Civilian Protection Is the Best Path to Peace." www.WagingNonviolence.org. Hewitt, Annie, ed.

Kaleka, Pardeep Singh and Michaelis, Arno (with Robin Gaby Fisher). 2018. *The Gift of Our Wounds: A Sikh and a Former White Supremacist Find Forgiveness after Hate.* New York: St. Martin's Press.

Karnad, Raghu. 2015. *Farthest Field.* New York: W. W. Norton and Company.

Kashmiri, Kesav. n.d. "Is Bhagavad Gita a Poem Which Triggers War?" www.quora.com/Is-Bhagavad-Gita-a-poem-which-triggers-war. Accessed 3 December 2017.

Kelsay, John. 2007. *Arguing the Just War in Islam.* Cambridge, MA: Harvard University Press.

Kennedy, Dennis. January 14, 2016. "The Centenary Is a Time for Reflection Not a Time for Celebration." *The Irish Times.*

Kerner Commission. 1968. *Report of the National Advisory Commission on Civil Disorder.* Washington, D.C.: Government Printing Office (1968).

King, Martin Luther, Jr. 1958. *Stride Toward Freedom.* New York: Harper and Row.

———. 1963. *Strength to Love."* Minneapolis, MN: Fortress Press.

———. 1964. ACOA PAPERS, Part 11, Reel 7, Frame 00545.

Kramer, Naomi, ed. 2007. *Civil Courage: A Response to Contemporary Conflict and Prejudice.* New York: Peter Lang Publishing.

Kristol, William. 1997. *The New American Century.* www://newamericancentury.org. Accessed August 8, 2016.

Krous, Susan Applegate. 2003. "What Came Out of the Takeovers: Women's Activism and the Indian Community School in Milwaukee." *American Indian Quarterly* 27, 3–4 (Summer/Fall): 533–547.

Kurlansky, Mark. 2004. *Nonviolence: Twenty-five Lessons from the History of a Dangerous Idea.* New York: The Modern Library.

Lader, Lawrence, 1979. *Power on the Left.* New York: W. W. Norton.

Lewis, Claude. 1992. "Getting it in the record." Interview (December, 1964). See *Malcolm X as They Knew Him,* Gallen, David, ed.

Lewis, John. 1998. *Walking with the Wind.* New York: Simon & Schuster.

Marlantes, Carl. 2010. *What It Is Like to Go to War.* Berkeley, CA: Atlantic Monthly Press.

Marsden, Peter. 2009. *Afghanistan: Aid, Armies, and Empire.* London: I. B. Tauris.

Martel, Gordon. 1987. *The Origins of the First World War.* London: Longman.

Mayotte, Judy A. 1992. *Disposable People? The Plight of Refugees.* Maryknoll, NY: Orbis Books.

Mayton, Daniel M. II. 2009. *Nonviolence and Peace Psychology: Intrapersonal, Interpersonal, Societal, and World Peace.* New York: Springer.

Merton, Thomas. 1968. *Faith and Violence: Christian Teaching and Christian Practice.* Notre Dame, IN: University of Notre Dame Press.

Metcalf, Stephen. March 23, 2020. "Albert Camus's *The Plague* and Our Own Great Reset." *Los Angeles Times.*

Millard, Candice. 2005. *The River of Doubt: Theodore Roosevelt's Darkest Journey.* New York: Doubleday.

Miller, Walter, trans. 1913. De officiis (On Moral Duties) transl.; Loeb Classical Edition; Latin/English parallel text. Cambridge, MA: Harvard University Press.

Murthy, Vivek H. 2020. *Together: The Healing Power of Human Connection in a Sometimes Lonely World.* New York: HarperCollins.

Musynske, Gavin. 2009. "Danish Citizens Resist the Nazis, 1940–1945." https://nvdata base.swarthmore.edu/content/danish-citizens-resist-nazis-1940-1945. Accessed October 5, 2020.

Nabokov, Peter. 1999. *Native American Testimony: A Chronicle of Indian-White Relation from Prophecy to the Present*. New York: Penguin Classics.

National Conference of Catholic Bishops. 1986. *Economic Justice for All*. Washington, D.C.

Newton, Huey. 1968. "Jail Interview." www.youtube.com/watch?v=cGI9MjeOTc0. Accessed 5 July 2014.

Ngcokoane, Cecil Mzingisi. *Apartheid in South Africa: Challenge to Christian Churches*. New York: Vantage Press.

Nguyen, Viet Thanh. 2015. *The Sympathizer*. New York: Grove Press.

———. 2016. *Nothing Ever Dies: Vietnam and the Memories of War*. Cambridge, MA: Harvard University Press.

Niemoeller, Martin. "First They Came for the Socialists. . . ." en.wikiquote.org/wiki/ Martin_Niemoeller. Accessed January 3, 2019.

———. "When the Nazis Came for the Communists . . ." en.wikipedia.org › wiki › First_they_came. Accessed October 10, 2018.

Nojeim, Michael. 2004. *Gandhi and King: The Power of Nonviolent Resistance*. Westport, CT: Praeger Publishers.

O'Brien, Tim. 1990. *The Things They Carried*. Boston: Houghton Mifflin.

O'Connor, Brendan. 2016. "Our Rebel Hearts." *Irish Independent*. 111, 2, March 27, 2016.

Oakes, Richard. 1969. "Proclamation." https://www.youtube.com/watch?v=7QNfUE 7hBUc. Accessed March 2, 2019.

Omar, Irfan. 2015. "Jihad and Nonviolence in the Islamic Tradition." In *Peacemaking and the Challenge of Violence in World Religions*. Omar, Irfan and Duffey, Michael, eds. New York: Wiley Blackwell.

Packer, George. 2005. *The Assassins' Gate: America in Iraq*. New York: Farrar, Straus, and Giroux.

Paxson, Maggie. 2019. *The Plateau*. New York: Riverside Books.

Pew Research Center. 2014. "Political Polarization in the American Public: How Increasing Ideological Uniformity and Partisan Antipathy Affect Politics, Compromise and Everyday Life."

Pope John Paul II. 1991. "Annual Address to the Vatican Diplomatic Corps." *Origins* January 12, 1991. Vatican Press (Vol. 20).

Popovic, Srdja, Milivojevic, Andrej, and Djinovic, Slobodan. 2007. *Nonviolent Struggle: 50 Crucial Points*. Belgrade: Center for Applied Non-Violent Action and Strategies.

Postman, Neil. 1985. *Amusing Ourselves to Death: Public Discourse in the Age of Show Business*. New York: Viking Penguin.

Powell, Jim. 2008. "Was the Civil War a Terrible Mistake?" *Historical News Network*. 2/13/2008. http://historynewsnetwork.org/articles/46037.html. Accessed May 10, 2018.

Rauhula, Emily. 2017a. "'False Prophet': The Catholic Church and the Fight for the Soul of the Philippines." *The Washington Post*. March 4, 2017. https://www.wash ingtonpost.com/world/asia_pacific/. Accessed May 5, 2017.

————. 2017b. "Thousands March Against Duterte's War on Drugs." *The Washington Post.* https://www.aljazeera.com/news/2017/02/thousands-march-duterte-war-drugs. Accessed May 5, 2017.

Rieff, David. 2016. *In Praise of Forgetting: Historical Memories and Its Ironies.* New Haven, CT: Yale University Press.

Risen, James. 2014. *Pay Any Price: Greed, Power, and Endless War.* Boston: Houghton, Mifflin, Harcourt.

Roman Catholic Bishops of France. September 30, 1997. *Declaration of Repentance.*

Rosch, Eleanor. 2015. "'Peace Is the Strongest Force in the World': Buddhist Paths to Peacemaking and Nonviolence." *Peacemaking and the Challenge of Violence in World Religions.* Omar, Irfan and Duffey, Michael, eds. New York: Wiley Blackwell.

Roy, Arundhati. 2004a. *Public Power in the Age of Empire.* New York: Seven Stories Press.

————. 2004b. *An Ordinary Person's Guide to Empire.* Cambridge, MA: South End Press.

Ruskin, John. 1907. *Unto This Last and Other Essays.* London: J. M. Dent and Sons, Inc.

Rynne, Terrence J. 2008. *Gandhi and Jesus: The Saving Power of Nonviolence.* Maryknoll, NY: Orbis Books.

————. 2014. *Jesus Christ Peacemaker: A New Theology of Peace.* Maryknoll, NY: Orbis Books.

Saad, Lydia. 2019. "What Percentage of Americans Own Guns." Gallup: The Short Answer. August 14, 2019. https://www.google.com/search?q=Saad%2C+Lydia.+2019+%E2%80%9CWhat+Percentage+of+Americans+Own+Guns%E2%80%9D+Gallup%3A+The+Short+Answer&rlz=1C1CHBF_enUS878US887&oq=Saad%2C+Lydia.+2019+%E2%80%9CWhat+Percentage+of+Americans+Own+Guns%E2%80%9D++Gallup%3A+The+Short+Answer&aqs=chrome..69i57.7125j0j15&sourceid=chrome&ie=UTF-8. Accessed January 15, 2020.

Salam, Reihaan. January 4, 2020. "Democrats Are Wrong about Defense Spending." *The Atlantic.* https://www.google.com/search?q=Salam%2C+Reihaan.+2020.+%E2%80%9CDemocrats+are+Wrong+about+Defense+Spending%2C%E2%80%9D+The+Atlantic+(January+4%2C+2020).&rlz=1C1CHBF_enUS878US887&oq=Salam. Accessed January 4, 2020.

Sale, Kirkpatrick. 1990. *The Conquest of Paradise: Christopher Columbus and the Columbian Legacy.* New York: Knopf.

Sandhu, Swaran S. 2011. "Nonviolence in Indian Religious Thought and Political Action." In *Sikhism in Global Context.* Singh, Pashaura, eds. New Delhi: Oxford University Press.

Santana, Carlos. 2018. *Dolores.* San Diego: Independent Lens.

Sassaman, Nathan. 2006. "It Looked Weird and Felt Wrong." Washington, D.C.: *The Washington Post* (July 24, 2006).

Sauvage, Pierre. 1987. "Weapons of the Spirit" (a documentary).

Schock, Kurt. 2005. *Unarmed Insurrections: People Power Movements in Non-Democracies.* Minneapolis: University of Minnesota Press.

Seale, Bobby. 1970. *Seize the Time: The Story of the Black Panther Party and Huey Newton.* New York: Random House.

Sellers, Cleveland. 1973. *The River of No Return: The Autobiography of a Black Militant and the Life and Death of SNCC.* New York: William Morrow and Company, Inc.

Sharp, Gene. 1990. *Civilian-Based Defense: A Post-Military Defense System.* Princeton, NJ: Princeton University Press.

———. 2010a (fourth edition). *From Dictatorship to Democracy: A Conceptual Framework for Liberation.* East Boston, MA: The Albert Einstein Institution.

———. 2010b. *From Dictatorship to Democracy.* Boston: Albert Einstein Institution.

Shriver, Donald. 1995. *An Ethic for Enemies: Forgiveness in Politics.* New York: Oxford University Press.

Smith, Tony, 2007. *A Pact with the Devil.* New York: Routledge.

Solomon, Norman. 2005. *War Made Easy.* Hoboken, NJ: John Wiley and Sons, Inc.

Stassen, Glen H., ed. 2008. *Just Peacemaking: The New Paradigm for the Ethics of Peace and War.* Cleveland, OH: The Pilgrim Press.

Stavans, Ilan, ed. 2010. *Cesar Chávez an Organizers Tale.* New York: Penguin.

Steinbeck, John. 1939. *The Grapes of Wrath.* New York: Viking Press.

Stephan, Maria J., ed. 2009. *Civilian Jihad: Nonviolent Struggle, Democratization, and Governance in the Middle East.* New York: Palgrave Macmillan.

Styron, William. 1967. *The Confessions of Nat Turner.* New York: Random House.

Swarthmore College Peace Collection. 2007. https://www.swarthmore.edu/library/peace/conscientiousobjection/co%20website/pages/OtherResourcesNew.htm. Accessed 2 April 2012.

Teachout, Terry. 2017. "When Music Could Not Transcend Evil." *Commentary* (July/August). https://www.commentarymagazine.com/articles/terry-teachout/orchestras-and-nazis. Accessed August 13, 2018.

Tinker, George. 2015a. "The Irrelevance of Euro-Christian Dichotomies for Indigenous Peoples" (206–225). In *Peacemaking and the Challenge of Violence in World Religions.* Omar, Irfan and Duffey, Michael, eds. New York: Wiley Blackwell.

Tirman, John P. 1997. *Spoils of War: The Human Cost of America's Arms Trade.* New York: The Free Press.

Tocqueville, Alexis de. 1835 and 1840. *Democracy in America.* Lawrence, George, trans., Mayer, J. P., eds. New York: Doubleday, Anchor Books, 1969.

Tolan, Sandy. 2006. *The Lemon Tree.* New York: Bloomsbury, 2006.

Trocmé, Andre. 1973. *Jesus and the Nonviolent Revolution.* Scottdale, PA: Herald Press.

Turshen, Meredeth and Twagiramariya, Clotilde, eds. 1998. *What Women Do in Wartime: Gender and Conflict in Africa.* New York: Zed Books, Ltd.

Unsworth, Richard P. 2012. *A Portrait of Pacifists: Le Chambon, the Holocaust, and André and Magda Trocmé.* New York: Syracuse University Press.

Villegas, Socrates. 2020. "A Twenty-one Day Fast for National Healing." https://www.vaticannews.va/en/church/news/2020-0. Accessed July 5, 2019.

Vizenor, Gerald. 1999. "Confrontation or Negotiation," in *Nabokov.*

Volf, Miroslav. 1996. *Exclusion and Embrace.* Nashville: Abingdon Press.

Walton, Neva and Wolf, Linda. 2001. *Global Uprising: Confronting the Tyrannies of the Twenty-first Century.* Gabriola, Canada: New Society Publishers.

Walzer, Michael. 2001. "Excusing Terror: The Politics of Ideological Apology." American Prospect.

Washington, James Melvin, ed. 1992. *I Have a Dream: Writings and Speeches that Changed the World: Martin Luther King, Jr.* San Francisco: Harper San Francisco.

Weber, Thomas. 2003. "Nonviolence Is Who? Gene Sharp and Gandhi." *Peace and Change: A Journal of Peace Research.* https://onlinelibrary.wiley.com/doi/abs/10.1111/1468-0130.00261. Accessed January 19, 2021.

Weigand, Krista E. 2010. *Bombs and Ballots: Governance by Islamic Terrorist and Guerrilla Groups.* Surrey, England: Ashgate Publishing Limited.

West, Cornell. 2015. *The Radical King.* Boston: Beacon Press.

Wilkerson, Isabel. 2020. *Caste: The Origins of Our Discontents.* New York: Random House.

Williamson, Marianne. 1997. *The Healing of America.* New York: Simon & Schuster.

Winbush, Raymond A., ed. 2003. *Should America Pay? The Raging Debate on Reparations.* New York: HarperCollins.

Wink, Walter. 1986. *Violence and Nonviolence in South Africa: Jesus' Third Way.* Philadelphia: New Society Publishers.

World Council of Churches. 1985. *Kairos Document: Challenge to the Church: A Theological Comment on the Political Crisis in South Africa.* Geneva: Commission on the Programme to Combat Racism.

Worth, Robert F. 2016. *A Rage for Order: The Middle East in Turmoil from Tahrir Square to ISIS.* New York: Farrar, Straus, and Giroux.

Wright, Ann and Dixon, Susan. 2008. "Camilo Mejía's Statement." In *Dissent: Voices of Conscience.* Kihei, HI: Koa Books.

www.MessageOfTheTruth.com. "Jerzy Popieluszko: Messenger of the Truth" (documentary, nd).

Yamin, Saira. 2011. "Challenging Patriarchy: Pakistan, Egypt, and Turkey." In *Women Waging War and Peace.* Cheldelin, Sandra I. and Maneshka, Eliatambi, eds. New York: Continuum Publishing Group.

York, Steve. 2001. "Bringing Down a Dictator." (documentary). Washington, D.C.: York Zimmerman Inc.

Young, Justin. 2005 "Andre Trocmé and Le Chambon: The Preciousness of Human Life." http://marcuse.faculty.history.ucsb.edu/classes/33d/projects/church/ChurchLeChambonJustin.htm. Accessed January 3, 2016.

Yuval-Davis, Nira. 2004. "Nationalist Imagination, War, and Peace." In *Sites of Violence: Gender and Conflict Zones.* Giles, Wenona and Hyndman, Jennifer, eds. Berkeley: University of California Press. 235–258.

Zahn, Gordon. 1962. *German Catholics and Hitler's War: A Study in Social Control.* New York: Sheed and Ward. (Notre Dame, IN: University of Notre Dame Press, 1989).

———. 1977. *In Solitary Witness. The Life and Death of Franz Jäggerstätter.* Collegeville, MN: Liturgical Press.

———. 1979. *Another Part of the War: The Camp Simon Story.* Amherst: University of Massachusetts Press.

———. 1989 c1962. *German Catholics and Hitler's War: A Study in Social Control.* Notre Dame, IN: University of Notre Dame Press.

Index

172 *Index*

Center for Those Seeking Asylum (CADA), 124
chattel slavery, 145
Chávez, César, 128
Cheney, Dick, 17
Chenoweth, Erica and Stephan, Maria, 39, 137, 140
Christianity: Jesus, 119; Sermon on the Mount, 120
churches' activism, 40–41, 50
Cicero, 6, 23
citizen activism, 93
civilian war casualties, 6; as "collateral damage," 8–9, 14; in Gulf War, 12; in Korean and Vietnam wars, 11–12, 79; in World Wars, 9–10
Coates, Ta-Nehisi, 66–67
Coles, Robert, 60
common good, 97–98
Confederate States of America, 146
Confessing Church in WWII Germany, 33
Congress of Racial Equality (CORE), 53
conscientious objection, 21
CORE. *See* Congress of Racial Equality (CORE)
Croatia, 44
Czechoslovakia, 9, 32

Danish resistance in WWII, 34
De Gaulle, Charles, 36
de Klerk, F. W., 84
Delgado, Aidan, 15
Dixon, Susan, 20
Doe, Samuel, 47
Douglass, Frederick, 145, 149
Douglass, James, 121
Du Bois, W. E. B., 53
Duncan, Mel and Nonviolence Peaceforce, 135
Duterte, Rodrigo, 50–51

East German Communist Party, 44
East German Lutheran Church, Ten Days of Peace and Day of Repentance, 12, 43

East Germany and Soviet Union, 43
East Germany nuclear war, 43
Egypt: Mubarak, Hosni, 138; Muslim Brotherhood, 138; Revolutionary Youth Council, 137; Saeed, Khaled, 137; Salafis, 138; Sisi, Abdelfattah, 138; Supreme Council of the Armed Forces (SCAF), 138; Tahrir Square, 137
Einstein, Albert, 3, 38
El-Beltagy, Mohammad, 138
electronic media and critical thinking, 94
empire, 88
Enright, Robert, 128
entertainment, 94
environment degradation and protection, 19
Eshkenazi, Dalia and Kahairi, Bashir (*The Lemon Tree*), 141–43

Fellowship of Reconciliation, 56, 102
Filipino Catholic Church, 40, 50
Fischer, Bram, 80–81
Floyd, George, 53, 66, 98
forty acres and a mule, 148
Foster, John Bellamy, 90–91
Freedom Rides and Freedom Summer, 58–60

Galtung, Johan, Gandhian principles, strategies, and tactics, 30–31, 141–42
Gandhi, Mohandas K.: campaigns: Bihar, Rowlatt, Vykom, Salt March, Dharsana Works, 28–30; on ego, 26; letter to Hitler, 32; on means and ends, 26; principles: satyagraha, ahimsa, tapasya, moksha, 2, 27; South Africa campaigns, 25–26; tapasya, 54; views on war, 32; village uplift, 28; wife Kasurbai, 25
Garrison, William Lloyd, 101, 145
Gaza, 141
Geneva Conventions, 21, 24
German Aryan women's nonviolent protest against roundup of their Jewish husbands, 33–34

Mejia, Camilo, 128; Nguyen, Viet
Thanh, 127; US veterans, 127
Roman Empire, 6
Rondon, Candido, 134
Roosevelt, Theodore, 134
Roosevelt Corollary, 88
Rosch, Eleanor, 116
Rumsfeld, Donald, 17
Russia, 10
Rynne, Terrence J., 27, 120

SASO. *See* South Africa Student
Association (SASO)
Sassaman, Nathan, 13
Saudi Arabia, 20
Schwarzkopf, Norman, 13
SCLC. *See* Southern Christian
Leadership Conference (SCLC)
Seale, Bobby, 63
Sejr, Arne, 34
Sellers, Cleveland, 60, 63
Serbia: Balkan War casualties and
rape, 44; Kosovars, 44; Muslims,
44; NATO bombing of Belgrade, 45;
Otpor, 44–46; voter fraud and
mass protests, 45; Yugoslavia
Federation, 44
Sharon, Ariel, 141
Sharp, Gene, 49–50, 123
Sikh Gurus Nanak and Adi Granth, 117
Sikh Temple massacre, Oak Creek,
Wisconsin, 118
Sin, Cardinal Jaime, 40
Singh, Kaleka, 117–18
Smiley, Glen, 56
SNCC. *See* Student Nonviolent
Coordinating Committee (SNCC)
Sobrino, Jon, 73
Somalia, 133; and Holland, 133
South Africa Council of Churches, 82
South African struggle: apartheid
and repressive apartheid laws,
77–79; Boers (Dutch: "farmers")
and Boer War, 77; Communist
Party, 80–81; Dutch Reformed
Church, 78; Freedom Charter, 78;
Kairos Document, 78; Truth and

Reconciliation Commission, 129;
Umkhonto we Sizwe ("Spear of the
Nation"), 78; United Democratic
Front, 84
South Africa Student Association
(SASO), 81
South Carolina State University
massacre, 60
Southern Christian Leadership
Conference (SCLC), 55
southern cotton boycott/embargo,
147–48
South Sudan, 135
Soviet Union, 10, 88
Stephan, Maria J., 39
Student Nonviolent Coordinating
Committee (SNCC), 53, 56–60
surrogate wars, 10
Syria, 16

Taliban, 14–15, 91
Taylor, Maxwell, 12
Teachout, Terry, 33
terrorism, 15
Theis, Edoward and Mildred, 36
Third Reich, 2, 9, 21, 32–33
Thoreau, Henry David, 101
Till, Emmet, 53
Tocqueville, Alexis de, *Democracy
in America*, individualism and
competitiveness, 97
Trocme, Andre, 36–37, 120
Trocmé, Daniel, 124
Trocme, Magda, 36, 124
Trump, Donald, 96
truth commissions, 129
Tunisia, 46
Turner, Nat, 147
Tutu, Desmond, 83

UCP. *See* Unarmed Civilian Protection
(UCP)
Unarmed Civilian Protection (UCP), 134
United Nations Universal Declaration of
Human Rights, 55, 135
United States: abolition of slavery,
145; Act Prohibiting the Importation

of Slaves (1807); boycott and embargo of southern cotton, 53, 147; Bureau of Refugees, Freedmen, and Abandon Lands, 148; civic activism, Chapters 6 and 7; Civil Rights Act (1963), 66; Civil War, Appendix Two; COVID-19 and U.S. deaths, safety mandates, health care workers, public health officials, unemployment, U.S economy, racial disparity in deaths, 95–97; defense contracts, 90; Dred Scott decision, 146; empire *vs.* superpower, 88; environment, 113; freed slaves, 148; gun violence and control, 9, 112–13; incarceration, 112; incivility and dialogue, 99; intelligence agencies (CIA, etc.), 88–89; law enforcement, 97; Louisiana Purchase, 146; Manifest Destiny, 2; Mexican-American War, 88; military contracting, 89–90; Missouri Compromise (1820), 146; paramilitaries, hate groups, 98; partisan politics, 99; potential of embargos of goods to Confederacy, 148; "Prohibiting Importation of Slaves" (1807), 146; reparations for slavery, 111; restorative justice after war, 116–20; social alienation, disconnection, 99; social polarization, 97–99; Spanish-American War, 88; systemic racism, 53–67, 93, 96, 109–11; Thirteenth Amendment, 147; Veterans Administration, 90;

Voting Rights Act (1965), 66; war in Afghanistan, 12; war on crime, drugs, poverty, and terror, 91–93; War Powers Act (1973), 90; war reparations, 107; wars in Iraq (1991 and 2003), 12, 15; wars in Korea and Vietnam, 10–12; Weapons of Mass Destruction, 15

UN Peacekeeping Force, 134

upward mobility, 93

virtues of altruism/empathy, apology, forgiveness, and reconciliation, 124–30

Von Weizsäcker, Richard, 127–28

Wael Ghonim, 137

Walesa, Lech, 41–43

Walzer, Michael, 7

Watada, Ehren, 22

West, Cornel, 56

white supremacy, 77, 109–11

Williams, Shirley, 9

Wilmot Proviso, 164

Wink, Walter, 84

women: caregivers, demand for equality and inclusion, networking, nonviolence, peacemaking skills, violence toward, war and, 125–26

World Wars, 8–10

Wright, Ann, 20

Yamin, Saira, 126

Zahn, Gordon: conscientious objection, 22; German Catholic Bishops, 33